The

TAO

of
Personal
Leadership

ALSO BY DIANE DREHER

The Fourfold Pilgrimage
Domination and Defiance
The Tao of Inner Peace

The
TAO
of
Personal
Leadership

DIANE DREHER

HarperBusiness
A Division of HarperCollins*Publishers*

HarperCollins books may be purchased for educational, business, or sales promotional use. For information please write: Special Markets Department, HarperCollins Publishers, Inc., 10 East 53rd Street, New York, NY 10022.

FIRST EDITION

Designed by Alma Hochhauser Orenstein

Library of Congress Cataloging-in-Publication Data
Dreher, Diane, 1946–
    The Tao of personal leadership / by Diane Dreher. — 1st ed.
        p.   cm.
    Includes index.
    ISBN 0-88730-792-2
    1. Leadership. 2. Tao. I. Lao-tzu. Tao te ching. English. Selections. 1996. II. Title.
HM141.D74 1996
303.3'4—dc20   95-38547

96 97 98 99 00 ❖/HC 10 9 8 7 6 5 4 3 2 1

To President Jimmy Carter,
whose vision, courage, and integrity
have transformed problems into possibilities,
and conflict into cooperation

CONTENTS

ILLUSTRATIONS

ACKNOWLEDGMENTS

I would like to acknowledge the many leaders, past and present, who have held out a new, more democratic vision of leadership. This vision creates dynamic partnerships, combining the best of what we are collectively while empowering us as individuals. Among those from whom I've learned the most are Eleanor Roosevelt, Norman Cousins, Jimmy Carter, Carl Rogers, John Vasconcellos, Gay Swenson-Barfield, Mitch Saunders, Dudley Weeks, Frances Moore Lappé, Jerry Lynch, Robert Numan, and Sunny Merik. I am also grateful to my friends and colleagues in the English department at Santa Clara University, who continue to teach me about leadership and to affirm my faith in democracy.

I would like to thank my agent, Sandra Dijkstra, for her belief in this project, as well as her enduring wisdom and encouragement. My aikido sensei, Sunny Skys and Miki Yoneda-Skys, have taught me the *aiki* way of transforming conflict into cooperation, affirming more in the way of courage, compassion, and community than I can verbalize. Sunny is also responsible for the beautiful calligraphy in this book. I am grateful to John Diamond for his valuable legal advice and to Harry Stephens and Stephen Moore, who helped critique working drafts of the manuscript. Finally, I would like to thank Stephanie Gunning, my first editor at HarperCollins, for her encouragement during the early stages of the project, along with executive editor Hugh

Van Dusen, associate editors Jennifer Griffin and Kate Ekrem, and copy editor Wendy Almeleh, for helping me see the book through to completion.

The *Tao Te Ching* teaches that nothing exists in isolation, that we are all part of an intricate, all-inclusive pattern. I am grateful to the individuals just mentioned, as well as to many others—my friends, family, and companions on the journey. As my gift in return, a portion of the royalties from this book will support ongoing work for conflict resolution to help create a more peaceful future for all on this beautiful planet we call home.

Introduction

With the best of leaders,
When the work is done,
The project completed,
The people all say
"We did it ourselves."

(Tao, 17)

For over two thousand years, people have drawn inspiration from the ancient Chinese classic, the *Tao Te Ching*. Written by the venerable sage, Lao-tzu, as he crossed the boundaries of civilization into the Western Paradise, this small volume of eighty-one poems has been translated more than any book but the Bible.[1] It has inspired leaders in fields as diverse as philosophy, politics, the martial arts, and humanistic psychology. Georg Wilhelm Hegel lectured on Chinese philosophy at Heidelberg University in the early 1800s, and his dialectic reflects the spiraling energies of the Tao. Nearly two centuries later, the influence of Taoism has only increased. Dag Hammarskjöld's journal, *Markings*, resonates with the Taoist balance of compassion and detachment. Morihei Ueshiba, the founder of aikido, based his nonviolent martial art on the Taoist principles of centering and blending, redirecting energy to overcome aggression without harming the aggressor. Carl Rogers, who practiced the *Tao's* philosophy of empowerment in his therapy and work for peace, carried in his wallet the quote that begins this chapter.

Composed during the warring-states period in ancient China, the *Tao Te Ching* was drawn from Lao-tzu's close observations of nature. It has endured because its principles are as real today as they were twenty-five centuries ago. The *Tao* reveals the wisdom of living systems, describing the patterns of energy within and around us. The Chinese call this vital energy *Qi,* and the Japanese call it *Ki*. It is life itself, which flows in dynamic patterns throughout all existence. The ebb and flow of the tides, the phases of the moon, the changes of the seasons, all are variations on the cycles that occur not only in the natural world, but in individuals, families, relationships, institutions, and nations. Designed as a handbook for leaders, the *Tao Te Ching* can help us make wiser choices by being mindful of these patterns.

Much has been written in recent years about the difference between managers and leaders. Managers handle the day-to-day operations of business. Supervising workers, they make sure that people perform as expected: providing services, manufacturing goods, filling orders, or making deliveries. Managers handle budgets, keep offices running, and generally maintain the status quo, whereas leaders are men and women of vision, who see how the daily details fit into larger patterns of significance. Good leaders plan ahead, facilitate change, and develop their people and their institutions. Great leaders inspire us with a vision of further possibilities. They share their vision and challenge us to develop our own, joining with us to fulfill our highest human potential. Great leaders have always had the vision of living systems, the wisdom of Tao.

Research on leadership has been informed in this century by general systems theory, which originated in the 1940s and 1950s, when researchers in engineering, mathematics, and physics observed that an organism or mechanism functions as a unified whole. A change in one part results in a corresponding change in the whole system as it adjusts to regain balance, or homeostasis. Systems theory became part of psychology in the 1950s, when therapists Murray Bowen and Virginia Satir noticed that families, too, function as systems: A change in one family member precipitates a change in the entire group. More recently, organizational psychologists have recognized that people who work together take on the dynamics of families, and often dysfunctional families at that.[2]

But the lesson of living systems was known long ago by societies that lived close to nature. The teachings of Taoism and Buddhism, as well as of Native American religions, affirm that we are all part of a larger whole. With classic precision and grace, the *Tao Te Ching* describes the essential principles of systems theory in nature and human society.

Throughout human history, people have been fascinated by leaders, describing their strengths and weaknesses in classical epics, popular dramas, histories, and biographies, as well as handbooks for self-conduct, the precursors of modern self-help books. In the Renaissance, people learned about famous leaders of the past from epics, chronicles, and Shakespeare's history plays, but access to leadership strategies and principles was limited. Handbooks for leaders were written for only a privileged few. Desiderius Erasmus, Sir Thomas More, Baldassare Castiglione, and Niccolò Machiavelli wrote for kings; aspiring princes; and, at most, a small group of royal advisers. As we approach the twenty-first century, the complex challenges of our times compel us *all* to be leaders, men and women of vision, regardless of our professions or stages in life.

In the past few decades, people and institutions have been progressively unsettled by the rapid pace of social and technological change. In earlier eras, the world around us seemed more stable, and major changes in values, institutions, and technology occurred more slowly. It took centuries for the Middle Ages to become the Renaissance, yet many of us have experienced major technological revolutions in one lifetime. My father grew up riding a mule on a Kentucky farm that had no electricity or modern conveniences. In his youth he went barnstorming in biplanes and later became an air force colonel, flying jet airplanes and watching astronauts walk on the moon. What science made possible in his adult world would have been dismissed as the wildest science fiction when he was a child.

The ancient philosophers from Lao-tzu to Boethius were right about one thing: The world around us is constantly changing. And with the fast-forward pace of our technology, success in life no longer comes from externals: from mastering a single skill or even a single profession. By the time you or I master it, the field could well be obsolete.

In this fast-paced postmodern world, the most relevant lessons are, ironically, some of the oldest. Successful leaders in any field see their work in terms of systems, informed by principles as old as the *Tao Te Ching* and as new as quality circles, Japanese management, archetypes, empowerment, and shared governance. Today's leader is not someone who knows all the answers because in this world that is impossible. He or she is not someone who makes decisions and gives orders in the old military model of leadership. Rather, the new leader is someone who can assess a situation, bring people together, build consensus, and discover solutions, drawing on the talents of everyone involved. The new leader is a facilitator, a communicator, a team builder, who realizes that our greatest natural resources are our minds and hearts, together with those of the people around us.

Drawing on natural principles as old as time, the new leader brings the wisdom of Tao into daily life. He or she constantly faces the unknown, standing on the edge of previous knowledge and ability. Yet, empowered by the principles of Tao, these new leaders blend with the energies around them, realizing that they can redefine and reform situations by their own responses. They work to create community, transcending conflict with cooperation, transforming problems into solutions. Tao leaders do not shrink from the unknown in fear, but embrace change with a consummate faith in the deepest principles of existence. Living on the edge, leading from the edge, they respond to uncertainty by joyously seeking their balance in dynamic interaction with the challenges of life.

The Tao of Personal Leadership shows how we can all become leaders, courageous and resourceful individuals who make leadership an art, creating new harmonies from the experiences around us. Each chapter sets forth the leadership principles of the Tao with quotes from the *Tao Te Ching* and lessons from

Taoism, Buddhism, and the martial arts. The book is divided into two sections. Part 1, The Yin of Inner Leadership, concentrates on the more personal elements of leadership. Part 2, The Yang of Leadership in Action, focuses on the leader's relationships and responsibilities.

The book's two parts imply a linear progression from personal wisdom to pragmatic action, but like the *Tao Te Ching* itself, the book's structure is cyclical, repeating the various principles of Tao—which are at once internal and external—in different contexts. Like the ocean waves continually casting themselves to shore, the Taoist principles recur in patterns at once familiar and new.

In different ways throughout this book, you will discover the principles of oneness and dynamic growth. We see how everything is connected, forever evolving in cycles of change, blending the complementary opposites, *yin* and *yang*, into new forms of creation. The more we study the Tao, the more we recognize these patterns and can blend with them, finding our own balance in the process. Learning the lesson of timing, we understand the interdependence of action and contemplation in all that we do. We discover how to cultivate spaces for contemplation within the busy landscape of our lives. In so doing, we develop greater respect for ourselves and others, greater joy on the path. More and more, we perceive life as a journey, a continuing education. External challenges become opportunities for self-realization and creative new solutions as we learn to work with the energies within and around us: leading with the Tao.

The principles in each chapter are reinforced by questions, personal exercises, and examples of innovative leadership. All the examples are taken from real life. Some are historical and others are current. Some are famous people, and others you've never met. Some cases are composites, and some names have been changed to respect people's privacy. Others you may recognize as people on the news or your own neighbors, for Tao leaders are emerging everywhere—from around the globe to around the corner. Tao leaders are found in politics, small businesses, large corporations, educational institutions, and community groups. They are corporate CEOs, legislators, medical researchers, scientists, artists, publishers, teachers, and parents. With the wisdom of Tao, each of us can be a leader in our field, and together, we can lead our world into new cycles of harmony and cooperation.

PART I

The
Yin
of
Inner
Leadership

CHAPTER 1

Zanshin

The Tao is an empty vessel,
Infinitely useful,
The source of ten thousand things.

It blunts all sharpness,
Unties all knots,
Softens the light,
And blends with the earth.

Deeper than the oceans,
Its scope is infinite,
Its power eternal.

(Tao, 4)

We are in the midst of what some have called "a major turning point in history."[1] As we face recurrent waves of technological, social, and political change, many of us are searching for a new source of hope to guide us through these tumultuous times.

Twenty-five centuries ago in ancient China, during another period of change and upheaval, two contrasting philosophies arose. During the warring-states period, after the breakdown of the Chou Dynasty, Confucius constructed a philosophy of moral order, emphasizing duty, manners, ceremony, and respect for family and authority. An elaborate tapestry of social interactions, Confucianism was his answer to the disorder he witnessed around him.

It is not surprising that Confucianism was adopted by China's feudal lords, who appreciated its strong emphasis on duty and obedience. For Confucius and his followers, all society was bound together by *li,* a complex set of rules and rituals. Even the emperor, or *Tian Zi* ("son of heaven"), had to perform regular rituals to maintain the cosmic order. At imperial shrines, such as *Tian Tan,* the Temple of Heaven in Beijing, the emperor would stand on a large stone disk on a triple-tiered platform to offer public prayers. Echoing up from the stone, his voice would supposedly reverberate to the heavens. Clad in heavy robes of embroidered silk, bearing heavy responsibilities, the Confucian leader was the ultimate agent of control, responsible for holding the fabric of society together.

In contrast to Confucius's elaborate rituals and rigid social order, his contemporary Lao-tzu upheld the dynamic philosophy of Taoism. Walking through the woods and observing the lessons in a mountain stream, a grove of bamboo, or the changing seasons, Lao-tzu drew inspiration from the world around him. Watching the natural cycles, he realized that nature cannot be forced or controlled and that nothing in the universe stands still. His philosophy embraces change as the very essence of life.

These two contrasting views, evolving through time in a succession of philosophies, have been known by dozens of different names. Today, some people call these views traditional and progressive. While more traditional "Confucian" leaders find their security in the social hierarchy around them, "Taoist" leaders find their security within them, affirming strength of character as they navigate life's shifting currents.

In contrast to modern books on leadership that focus on power plays, one-minute solutions, clever strategies, and game plans, the *Tao Te Ching* affirms *personal leadership,* the enduring power of character. It tells us:

> *The ancient leaders who followed the Tao*
> *Did not give people elaborate strategies*
> *But held to simple practice.*
>
> *It is hard to lead*
> *When we try to be too clever.*
> *Too much cleverness undermines group harmony.*
> *Those who lead without such strategies*
> *Bring blessing to all.*
> *To know these principles*
> *Is to follow Tao.*

> **(Tao, 65)**

Lao-tzu knew that clever strategies or power plays may work in the short run. But in the long run, people realize they are being manipulated and resent it. Not too long ago, I met George, who had an impressive résumé for someone in his thirties. He had held a variety of management jobs and started three companies, but he never stayed in one place for long. George began a new computer service business. A few months later, after sowing discord among his business partners and exhausting the start-up money, he moved out of state, probably making another addition to his lengthy résumé. George has intelligence and good ideas, but he uses them to control people. His manipulative strategies undermine his basis of support. "Too much cleverness undermines group harmony." The *Tao Te Ching* teaches that without trust, there can be no enduring power.

Te: *The Power of Character*

The eighty-one verses of the *Tao Te Ching* emphasize strength of character. The Chinese symbol *Te,* the second word in the book's title, has been variously translated as "virtue," "goodness," "power," and "morality," but it is actually made up of three separate symbols: "to go," "straight" and "the heart." Thus, *Te* means integrity or character: living "straight from the heart." With the power of character, we continuously influence and transform the world around us. The *Tao Te Ching* tells us:

> *All actions flow from the Tao.*
> *Character* (Te) *shapes them.*
> *Circumstances complete them.*
>
> *The ten thousand things*
> *Honor Tao*
> *And revere* Te
> *Not by custom or law,*
> *But by their own nature.*
> *Therefore the Tao creates*
> *And* Te *cultivates,*
> *Nurtures and protects,*

Promotes, but does not possess,
Empowers, but does not take credit,
Leads without dominating.

This is the power of character.
(Tao, 51)

Studying the *Tao Te Ching* develops our strength of character, along with our awareness of the principles of nature. This combination gives us the power to face any challenge with courage, effectiveness, and grace.

Leadership Skills for a Changing World

Adapting to change is an essential survival skill in today's world. Many jobs will change as soon as we master them. College career centers, once known as "placement offices," now emphasize career development. Instead of helping students find the right jobs, career counselors help them develop the skills they'll need to chart their own career paths. Counselors teach students everything from résumé writing and interviewing techniques to personal assessment, networking, and long-range planning. Carolyn Hennings, Santa Clara University's director of career services, says, "Instead of focusing on a product—'get me the right job,' we focus on the process, working to empower students to make their own choices."[2]

As we move into the twenty-first century, this greater emphasis on process will be required of all of us. As sociologists Charles Powers and Jerald Hage wrote in *Post-Industrial Lives*, we'll need radically different skills as we move from an industrial to a postindustrial world. Increased automation will take care of the routine repetitive work, and specialization in a given field will be superseded by the ability to adapt to a changing world. "Work tasks will be defined in terms of information gathering, problem solving, the production of creative ideas, and the ability to respond flexibly to new situations or adjust flexibly when interacting with others."[3]

To succeed in any field, we must develop those skills that make us fully human: the ability to learn continuously through-out life, to communicate with others, to come up with creative new solutions, and to deepen our understanding, looking to the larger patterns within and around us.

The dynamic postindustrial world calls us to turn from a static Confucian concept of security to the dynamic world of the Tao, expanding our vision from specific *rules* and situations to enduring *principles* that recur throughout nature. Instead of conforming to preconceived *roles,* we will focus on developing *relationships*—with ourselves, one another, and the world around us. A bright affirmation of hope as we face the great unknown of our collective future, the Tao calls us to exchange rules for principles and roles for relationships, discarding the static to embrace the dynamic.

This book describes the dynamic principles of Tao, showing us how to lead—and live—more effectively. This chapter focuses on *zanshin,* learning to recognize the energy cycles that inform all existence. Recognizing these cycles, we are empowered. Consciously responding to our world with the wisdom of living systems, we become Tao leaders, no longer reacting to the world unconsciously, but participating in its ongoing creation.

Flowing with Change: Zanshin

Many passages in the *Tao Te Ching* speak of the energy of the universe: in Chinese, *qi;* in Japanese, *ki.* It is the energy that informs all creation. The *Tao Te Ching* explains:

> *The great Tao is everywhere,*
> *Flowing left and right.*

The ten thousand things flow from it.
Yet it never dominates,
But achieves its purpose
Without taking credit.
Seen with detachment,
It appears infinitely small,
The energy that flows
Through all creation.

(Tao, 34)

This energy flows through "the ten thousand things," *wan wu,* the Chinese symbol for all creation. It is circulated and developed in the martial arts of tai chi and aikido, which literally mean "great energy" and "the way of harmonizing energy." Traditional Chinese medicine treats the circulation of energy through the body, stimulating it with acupuncture and herbal tonics. As Fritjof Capra explained in *The Tao of Physics,* the *ki* or *qi* of Eastern philosophy finds its modern expression in quantum mechanics, which posits that these all-pervasive and "infinitely small" units of energy are the particle/waves of modern physics.

To recognize the flow of energy between ourselves and another person or event is the wisdom known in Japanese as *zanshin.* In aikido, *zanshin* is the ability to extend our energy outward, to blend with the energies around us to create harmony.[4]

Flowing with Change

In the context of modern life, *zanshin* is the ability to recognize and flow with change. Tao leaders welcome change because they perceive the world dynamically. In the early 1980s, researchers S. R. Maddi and S. C. Kobasa conducted a longitudinal study of how hundreds of executives responded to stress. They published their results in *The Hardy Executive,* explaining that leaders who believe a static condition is normal feel unsettled and victimized by change, regarding it as an abnormal stressor. These people get sick far more often than "hardy executives," who see change as a normal part of life.[5]

Tao leaders not only greet life's changing panorama with the wisdom of *zanshin*. They also subtly communicate *zanshin* to their group, so the organization develops a spirit of flexibility and openness. Such groups develop an attitude of confidence. Combining their energies to achieve a common goal, they welcome change as part of the process of mutual discovery, making adjustments when new challenges arise.

Detachment and Zanshin

Tao leaders flow with change by developing *Te,* or strength of character. One essential character strength is detachment, described as one of the "three treasures" in Chapter 67 of the *Tao Te Ching.* Detachment clears our vision; instead of emotionally overreacting to circumstance, we remain centered. Detachment helps us develop greater *zanshin.* We make wiser choices when we perceive the energy cycles within and around us.

The key to detachment is a vital balance of opposites. Eastern philosophies, from the code of the samurai to the peaceful path of Buddhism, have affirmed the combination of courage and compassion. In the Western world, epics, from *Beowulf* to *The Song of Roland,* praised heroes for *sapientia* and *fortitudo,* wisdom and strength. In the East or West, the important principle is balance: courage and compassion, wisdom and strength, *yin* and *yang.* While one polarity alone would produce brutality or weakness, together they constitute what the *Tao Te Ching* calls *Te,* the ability to care deeply while detaching from specific events long enough to see the larger patterns, the ability to act strategically while maintaining a reverence for life. This is the way of virtuous action, the path taken by men and women of character.

"Who do I know (in my experience or in history) who combines courage and compassion?"
"How did this person develop and express these qualities?"
"What can I do to develop greater courage and/or compassion myself?"

Tao Exercise

Read a biography of someone you admire. Learn some important lessons from this person's example. Role models are powerful motivators. Both the samurai classics and the leadership manuals of the Renaissance drew on compelling examples from history.

Stretching Ourselves: Flowing with Zanshin

Asian calligraphy emphasizes another aspect of *zanshin:* fluid movement. Instead of seeking perfection, limiting themselves with inhibition, master calligraphers have always valued fluid strokes, spontaneity, and natural grace. *Hagakure,* the book of the samurai, applies this lesson of calligraphy to all life, explaining that each day should be lived with power and grace.[6] There are no rigid strokes, no stilted movements, in the art of Tao.

Flowing with *zanshin,* we become part of the process. We no longer listen to the inner judge that tells us we're "not good enough," replays our past, and chokes us up with inhibitions. One with the moment, we blend with the experience itself, detaching from judgment. Transcending the limits of ego, our lives become works of art. We improvise, combining different energies, reaching out courageously to produce new harmonies. The act of creation requires us to take chances, to risk making mistakes. Not to risk means staying within preordained bounds of what has been, never daring to discover what might be.

Harmonizing the Unexpected:
The Music of Zanshin

With *zanshin* we become so fully present that we move gracefully through life, dealing effectively with unforeseen challenges. We can blend even "mistakes" or mischance into a virtuoso performance. Years ago, while on sabbatical in England, I attended a performance of *The Four Seasons* by the English Chamber Orchestra. Vivaldi's masterpiece swept the audience up into exquisite harmonies, when suddenly the unthinkable happened. During a particularly demanding solo, the concert master's violin string broke with a loud twang. The audience gasped. He paused for a second, shrugged his shoulders and smiled, exchanging instruments with the second violinist. In less than a minute, the concert recommenced, and Vivaldi's spell continued. The liquid sounds mounted in dramatic crescendos, and the concert ended with a standing ovation.

While a lesser individual would have been devastated by the broken string, the soloist's concern was not his ego, but the present moment of performance. His personification of *zanshin* remains with me still, and his smooth recovery made a perfect concert all the more impressive.

What separates the professionals from the amateurs is not that they don't have problems. Everyone has problems, challenges, moments of discord. It's how soon we return to the music, how well we recover, that marks a true professional.

Like a violin virtuoso, Tao leaders never surrender to adversity; they rise above it. Transcending ego, maintaining inner harmony, they keep time with the music that governs all our lives.

Zanshin *and the Courage to Reach Out*

Becoming a Tao leader means daring to take risks. It means making mistakes and then returning to the music. It is the courage to live with integrity, to be honest, to live what we believe—in the dozens of small choices we make every day.

Becoming Tao leaders means daring to be ourselves in the fullest sense, not surrendering to external pressures, not being afraid of who we are. Sometimes it means reaching out to do something new as a spiritual exercise.

One Sunday I went horseback riding with a friend in the Los Gatos mountains. Since I had not really ridden a horse since I was twelve, I was somewhat uneasy. I had to trust myself, my friend, and the beautiful copper-colored horse named Cali. But my anxiety gave way to delight as I rode through the mountains, responding to the serenity of nature after a gentle rain. Immersed in the wonder of early spring, I found the experience truly magical, an equestrian meditation.

Whenever we reach out to new adventures, we learn valuable lessons. I found out something else about *zanshin* as I realized that this magnificent animal followed my lead with the same amount of focus I expressed.

Animals are incredibly honest. A tentative or confused signal to Cali invariably produced a confused response. She would either ignore my halfhearted command or stop in midstride, tossing her head quizzically as if to ask what I meant.

How often do our fears and doubts get in the way, short-circuiting our communications to the people in our lives, who may not understand us either? When we want to communicate clearly, we need to say what we mean. Sometimes saying what we mean involves admitting our anxieties, clearing the emotional clouds that block our desired expression.

TAO QUESTION

Is there something you'd like to do that you've been putting off?

To develop your leadership qualities, it need not be work related. In the Tao, *everything* is related.

Does this activity make sense? (I'm not encouraging foolhardiness or self-destructive behavior.)

If so, make a commitment to yourself to do it and take the first step.

Afterward, take some time to record what you learned about yourself and the energy of *zanshin*.

Facing Your Fears

Any truly courageous person will tell you that courage is not the absence of fear. Like everything else in life, the important thing is not fear, but our response to it. Denying fear is not courage but foolhardiness. Surrendering to fear only paralyzes us. The *Tao Te Ching* shows us another way: to become aware of what these energies may mean, to listen and to learn.

Fear gives us the opportunity to face danger, assess the risks, and take action. Psychologist Jerry Lynch, who counsels Olympic athletes, said, "Fear is a natural part of life. [It is] a friend that you must acknowledge and embrace. If you feel endangered or fearful, ask yourself why you're feeling that way."

TAO QUESTIONS
The next time you experience fear about some new experience, ask yourself:

"What am I feeling?"
"What am I *really* afraid of?"

Try to determine whether your fear is a healthy alarm that is reminding you of some vital information you may have overlooked. Are you well prepared? Have you done everything you need to? Take whatever action is necessary to ensure your safety.

But perhaps your fear is a phantom of your imagination, an emotional reaction to a new challenge, job, or relationship. If so, what is your reaction telling you? What are you *really* afraid of? What could happen—and can you handle it? Is there anything you can do now to prepare for this challenge and make yourself feel better? If so, do it.[7]

The wisdom of Tao reminds us to listen to our fears, to learn from them and make wiser choices.

Zanshin *as Flexibility:* The Strength of Bamboo

The *Tao Te Ching* tells us:

> *We begin life gentle and yielding.*
> *At death we are rigid, inflexible.*
> *The grasses that grow are green and supple.*
> *In death they are withered and sere.*
> *Therefore, the rigid and inflexible*
> *Belong to death.*
> *The gentle and yielding*
> *Are filled with life.*

(Tao, 76)

Tao leaders have the strength of bamboo. Able to bend, blend with circumstances, adjust to change, and overcome adversity, they can meet any challenge with courage and compassion.

One of my favorite leaders had an unpromising background. Today we would say he came from a "dysfunctional family." His mother died when he was young. He grew up in poverty and had to drop out of school, but taught himself to read and loved books all his life. He tried to make money hauling cargo on a Mississippi flatboat, but was unsuccessful. He ran for the state legislature, but lost the election. He opened a general store with a friend, but his partner was an alcoholic, who then died, leaving him so deeply in debt that he had to close the store and auction off all his possessions. This man was finally elected to the state legislature, but his personal life was filled with heartbreak. His friend Ann—some say she was his one true love—died at age twenty-two. He courted the sister of a friend for over a year until she rejected him. After a troubled courtship, he finally married, but his wife was subject to temper tantrums, crying fits, and episodes of mental illness. His little boy Eddie died. He himself was plagued by recurrent bouts of depression; some say he was manic-depressive. Yet he rose above his troubles, determined to develop his talents and serve his country. He educated himself and studied law, ran for Congress, lost, was elected, and then was voted out of office. He ran for the Senate, but was defeated twice in a row.[8]

Elected president of the United States in 1860, Abraham Lincoln was strengthened by adversity, educated by years of disappointments. Instead of giving up or giving in, he affirmed the wisdom of bamboo, which bends but does not break. His ability to overcome defeat and disappointment gave him the moral courage to lead our nation through one of our darkest periods in history.

Tao Exercise

Is there some failure or mistake in your past that is still haunting you?

Face that failure squarely and ask yourself what you learned from it.

What would you do differently?
What have you learned about yourself?
What will you do in the future?

Now take the next step—forward. Leave the past behind and boldly get on with your life.

Remember that any successful political leader, artist, scientist, or Olympic athlete has had many failures. What separates the leaders from the losers is that they *learn* from their difficulties, make adjustments, and go on. Like bamboo, they bend, but do not break. Persevering, they stay the course to reach the finish line.

Facing the Unknown

One of the most unsettling things about something that we've never done before is simply that we've never done it before. Whether this unknown is a new job, a new project, a new environment, or a new love in our life, we are in unknown territory without a map. What do we do now?

Training Through Your Doubts

Everyone has moments of self-doubt when facing the Great Unknown, whatever that may be for you. As Tao leaders, we are always charting new paths. Moving through unknown territory tests our resolve, our courage, and our faith. Can we stay centered and keep moving forward?

Any truly creative person realizes this fundamental lesson of Tao: that life is a process much larger than we are. Momentary challenges and setbacks will occur, but the Tao leader is a pathfinder, a long-distance runner who won't let these things throw him or her off course.

Moving with *zanshin* means not becoming fixated on mistakes or doubts, not letting them break our connection to the here and now.

When I reached an impasse in my aikido training, I asked a wise black belt what to do. "Keep training," he said. His words were so simple that they annoyed me. Surely, there had to be something else—some technique I could try, some book I could read—but there are no shortcuts, no easy answers, in aikido and no *Cliffs Notes* in the course of life. I kept training and realized he was right. Now his words echo in my mind whenever I face the Great Unknown. "Train through your doubts, train through your fears. Train from your heart and stay with the process." Surrendering to worry and doubt only splits our consciousness, breaks our flow. Transcend ego, move forward with *zanshin,* and dare to follow your heart into the Great Unknown. This is the courage of Tao.

Aware of the process, we can flow with *zanshin* from the known to the unknown, from self to other, creating harmony from uncertainty. The poet John Keats called this quality "negative capability," which is essential for any artist. And at their best, leadership and life are works of art. As Keats realized, we demonstrate negative capability when we are "capable of being in uncertainties, mysteries, doubts, without any irritable reaching after fact and reason."[9] With *zanshin* we can overcome doubt and impatience, facing the Great Unknown with an essential faith in ourselves and the universe.

The *Tao Te Ching* tells us that all nature follows this process of *zanshin,* moving from conception to creation one step at a time:

> *A tree that grows beyond your reach*
> *Springs from a tiny seed.*
> *A building more than nine stories high*
> *Begins with a small mound of earth.*
> *A journey of a thousand miles*
> *Begins with a single step.*

(Tao, 64)

When I was in China in March 1993, I saw a vivid example of this lesson. All over Shanghai and Beijing, massive construction projects were going up. My companions on the journey were astounded to see the Chinese using bamboo scaffolding to build these towering skyscrapers. Bamboo seems so light and fragile, yet the Chinese have relied on it for thousands of years. I smiled and thought of the strength of bamboo, the ability to build on what we know, the courage to reach beyond what we know to achieve what was once thought impossible.

As we develop greater strength of character, we're able to face the unknown, to create new possibilities for ourselves and our world. We develop the wisdom of detachment, the skill of *zanshin,* the ability to recognize and blend with the patterns evolving within and around us. The *Tao Te Ching* tells us:

> *With strength of character,*
> *Nothing is impossible.*
> *When our hearts expand*
> *To embrace the impossible,*
> *We are able to lead with Tao.*

(Tao, 59)

CHAPTER 2

Centering, Presence, and Process

Analyzing others is knowledge.
Knowing yourself is wisdom.
Managing others requires skill.
Mastering yourself takes inner strength.

Knowing when enough is enough
Is wealth of spirit.
Be present, observe the process,
Stay centered, and prevail.

(Tao, 33)

For centuries, Eastern philosophy has taught the lesson of self-mastery. The *Tao Te Ching* tells us "to stay centered and prevail." Wise leaders maintain their inner balance. They are not reactive:

> *However events may whirl around them,*
> *They remain centered and calm.*
>
> **(Tao, 26)**

Maintaining emotional control in a crisis is an essential leadership skill. Yet how often have we let situations throw us off balance, reacting in anger, fear, desire, or frustration? The *Tao Te Ching* upholds a vital paradox: We remain centered in a crisis not by turning away but by being present. Becoming more aware of the storms around us and the energy patterns they represent helps us deal with them more effectively.

Tao leaders don't make excuses, denying what is or has been. They don't resort to pretense, trying to be something they're not. Because they remain calm in the whirlwind of challenge and change, no situation can throw them off balance. The following pages draw on examples from management to the martial arts to help us become more centered in leadership and in life.

Centering and Aikido

Like many Eastern disciplines, the martial art of aikido teaches the lesson of centering. While giving demonstrations in the West during the 1950s, tenth-degree black belt Koichi Tohei amazed onlookers with his centering ability. Not only did he defeat individual challengers, but a group of seven strapping young men could not overcome him. Centered, he stood his ground, facing their multiple attack and throwing them to the mat. Many men at once could not even budge his five-feet, four-inch body when they tried to lift him. Deeply centered in the energies of earth, he prevailed against his attackers with a smile.[1]

Drawing on ancient Chinese medical philosophy, aikido teaches that the energy center of the body is in the lower abdomen, about two inches below the navel. This point is known in Chinese as the *tant'ien* and in Japanese as the *hara*. Focusing our attention on this one point brings our energies naturally back to center, making us stronger, less easily swayed by circumstance.

TAO EXERCISE: CENTERING

When aikido students defend against an attack, they become stronger by bending their knees, breathing into the *hara,* and feeling their connection with the earth. This practice works off the mat as well. The next time you feel confused or imbalanced, try it: Bend your knees slightly, breathe into your *hara*, and feel yourself rooted in the earth.

This response is the opposite of rigid armoring. It is not defensiveness, but awareness, leaving us flexible enough to deal with whatever comes our way.

The power of aikido is based not on muscle, but on energy. Like the teachings of Tao, many aikido techniques involve balancing the energies within and around us. One technique, *Tenchi-nage,* is known as "Heaven and Earth." We can throw an opponent by reaching upward with one hand and down to the earth with the other, building our energy by drawing on both powerful forces.

In our own lives, we can center ourselves by finding that

dynamic balance of earth and sky, body and mind, within us. When we're too cerebral, our minds haunted by past mistakes or worrying about what may happen next, all our energies go to our heads. Physically and emotionally off balance, we're easily thrown: by a challenge, another person, anything unexpected. Our task is to return to center, to balance body and mind. Getting back to center brings us new insights and new solutions.

Seeing New Possibilities

Centered and strong, the Tao leader transcends the past, reaching out to what may be, finding dynamic new potential in the present. Problems around us don't drag us down, but reveal their promise of something better. In their approach to life, Tao leaders ask this courageous question expressed by George Bernard Shaw and often asked by the Kennedys: Most people look at things the way they are and ask "Why?" I dream of things that never were and say "Why not?"[2]

Centered, we look more deeply into things as they are, recognizing new possibilities in the present moment. Seeing beyond what has been, we say "Why not?" to our dreams of a better life. We move beyond old patterns to forge a new future for ourselves and our world.

Creativity and the Practice of Centering

All the creative people I know have one thing in common: a regular practice of centering. Committing yourself to such a discipline unites you with artists, innovators, and spiritual seekers throughout the ages. Realizing that the material world too often takes us away from our deepest selves, men and women on the spiritual path have adopted a variety of disciplines to restore their connection: meditation, chanting, ritualistic exercise, voluntary simplicity, periods of silence and solitude. Marsha Sinetar's book, *Ordinary People as Monks and Mystics*,[3] describes how many modern individuals have based their lives on spiritual practice.

Your centering practice need not be traditionally "religious." Many people, like my friend Tina Clare, return to center by observing regular periods of silence, finding renewal and inspiration in a day alone at home without the incessant socializing that often wears us down.

Some people find their attunement in music. Cellist Pablo Casals began each day at the piano, playing Bach before breakfast. Dr. Albert Schweitzer, a concert organist, found renewal playing classical pieces on a battered old piano in his clinic in Lambaréné. Others find their practice in regular physical exercise. Norman Cousins loved a vigorous game of tennis, and Joseph Campbell was a world-class runner.

After a recent ten-kilometer race in San Jose, I heard two runners talking about their training. One man said he liked to run where he could meet other people and enjoy the scenery. The other replied, "I don't need the scenery at all." He pointed to the space between his eyes. "It's all in here," he said. The first man runs for fitness and recreation, the second for centering, for spiritual re-creation. His running is his practice, a moving meditation, like the exercises of the ancient Shaolin priests.

Many of my friends engage in regular physical practice. Bob runs, Eileen swims, Mary does tai chi, John plays racquetball, Tracey plays tennis, and I do aikido. My parents remain vital in their seventies by pursuing their own practices. My father does yoga each morning, and my mother does aquathenics, and they also take daily walks together.

As we live the path of Tao, our exercise promotes more than physical fitness. What we *do* contributes to who we *are*. It centers us, building cardiovascular health and flexibility while polishing our spirits to meet any challenge with courage and grace.

In the nineteenth century, Ralph Waldo Emerson took regular walks in the woods and wrote about the renewal he found there. One phrase of his has remained with me through the years: "All mean egotism vanishes. . . . I am nothing. I see all."[4] "All mean egotism vanishes"—and with it the thousand distractions, concerns, disappointments, and regrets that have become emotional blocks, dividing us from ourselves. Through our centering practice, we break through all those layers of dust, debris, and self-doubt that diminish us. Renewed and refreshed, we realize once more all that is possible.

TAO QUESTIONS
What is your practice?
What benefits does it bring you?

Centering and Strength of Character

The *Tao Te Ching* asks:

> *Why do many people rush about*
> *Reactively losing their balance?*
> *They give way to emotion,*
> *Impatience and haste,*
> *Thereby losing their center.*
>
> **(Tao, 26)**

When we're centered, we respond wisely to any challenge; uncentered, we're emotional and reactive. I learned this lesson while studying John Milton's *Areopagitica* in graduate school. Over three hundred years ago, Milton realized that it's not the situation that makes a hero out of one person and a coward out of another, but the person's response to it. About courage and cowardice, Milton wrote, "the matter of them both is the same."[5] Off center, we become reactive: reduced to fight or flight. Centered, we see new solutions, new possibilities. The lesson is age old yet forever new. What happens around us or what happens between us is never as important as what happens *within* us.

Life is not some predetermined pattern and we its hapless victims. It is, to a great extent, our response to a situation that determines whether we're heroes or cowards, successes or failures. As the *Tao Te Ching* forever reminds us: to stay centered is to prevail.

The Power of the Present Moment

The *Tao Te Ching* asks:

> *Who can work with natural patterns,*
> *Wait until the mud settles,*
> *Patient and flexible,*
> *In harmony with life?*

(Tao, 15)

As we become centered, we develop the power of presence, our awareness focused on the here and now. Zen Buddhism, influenced by Taoism, upholds this lesson. For centuries, Zen monasteries have combined the spiritual with the mundane, requiring all monks, even those of high rank, to chop wood, carry water, work in the garden, prepare meals, and perform all the daily duties of life with deep awareness. Thus, every task becomes part of their spiritual practice, and every moment expands into the radiance of continuous meditation.

Developing such awareness takes time and commitment. Buddhist teacher Thich Nhat Hanh gives his students affirmations to help them stay in the present moment. One of these affirmations, to be held in mind while slowly breathing in and out, is: "Present moment, wonderful moment."[6] Deepen your awareness right now by breathing in, slowly exhaling, and savoring the present moment.

Our fast-paced Western world too often splits our consciousness with overstimulation, competing demands, and days fragmented by frantic activity. As a result, many of us tune out, walking unconsciously through life. How often have you seen some driver pull out in front of you without looking? When did you last catch yourself in an unconscious action, unaware of what you were doing, your body one place, your mind another?

The Tao is now. Living the Tao brings us back to the power of the present moment, truly the only life we have. In the present moment is all the depth and transcendent beauty the poets have known. Walking on the beach one rainy day in March, I was struck once more by the ineffable beauty of the world we inhabit. The English poet William Blake put it this way:

> *To see a world in a grain of sand*
> *And a heaven in a wild flower,*
> *To hold infinity in the palm of your hand,*
> *And eternity in an hour.*[7]

It's all there—in the present moment.

Tao Affirmations

My aikido teacher, Sunny Skys, reminds his students of a Japanese expression, *Tadaima:* only now. We cannot respond well on the mat unless we leave our concerns outside and concentrate on training. Similarly, at work or at home, we cannot respond well unless we're fully present. But sometimes being fully present isn't easy. Clouds of memories, worries, and obligations float across our brains.

ONLY NOW

Whenever I find my mind wandering, I use this simple affirmation. Say to yourself:

"Only now."

"I'm here now."
Then breathe into your center and *be* here now.
Try it.

When confronted by conflict and confusion, another practice is to take a deep breath, pause and ask:
"Where is the gift in this?"
The Tao reminds us that life is a path, a journey of continuous growth, filled with lessons and unexpected gifts. Look for the gift and you will find it.

Your Daily Ritual

The ancient samurai spent all their lives preparing for the unexpected. They began each day with a precise ritual. Rising early, they would bathe, dress, and arrange their hair with perfumed oils, paying careful attention to the slightest details of grooming. Why? Because this ritual prepared them for a day that could be life's greatest blessing or greatest battle. They knew each day could be their last. Their morning ritual was a *misogi*, a cleansing of spirit, centering them for whatever lay ahead.

Twentieth-century warrior General George Patton was scrupulous about the slightest details of his uniform and his person. Even on the battlefield, his uniform was pressed, his boots polished, and his insignia gleaming. His daily *misogi* not only centered him, but inspired his troops with the vision of a leader who was composed in every detail.

How many of us rush out the door each morning without breakfast, let alone time to prepare for the day ahead? Appropriate attention to your morning ritual is not self-indulgence but a powerful centering practice.

What is your morning ritual?
What can you learn from the samurai?
What can you do for yourself to prepare for the day ahead?

Commit to one centering practice, set your alarm a little earlier, and begin—tomorrow.

The Lesson of Process

Our culture too readily confuses product with process. I saw a vivid example of this confusion recently while watching television. An ad for body-building equipment showed a muscular man and a slender, physically fit woman. The voiceover promised viewers: "You can have a body like this for only thirty-nine dollars a month." But this claim was simply not true. The *equipment* may cost thirty-nine dollars a month, but exercise is a process that takes time, effort, and discipline, not just a credit-card purchase from a TV ad.

The pervasive advertising in our culture often convinces people to seek the product, looking for instant gratification and quick fixes, when only active commitment to the process can produce the desired result. Lately even education has become infected by mercantile metaphors. Students are described as "clients" or "customers," since they (or their parents) presumably pay the tuition and get their product. But education requires more than paying tuition or buying a book. For knowledge to be transmitted from the book to the brain, a student must actively participate in the process. And education is more than merely the transfer of information. It is an ongoing process of discovery. The mercantile metaphor misleads us, portraying students as passive consumers. To turn to a naturalistic metaphor, education—and life—are more like gardening: The more we put into a garden, the more we get out.

The Tao leads us back to natural metaphors, giving us a clearer insight into energy dynamics. In his book on creativity, Roger von Oech told of an aerospace manager who began designing backyard waterfalls for himself and his friends. He realized that this hobby had made him a better manager because he was now more aware of the natural flow of energies.[8] Like the teachings of Tao, the waterfalls had revealed to him natural principles that pervade all life.

Consciously participating in the energies around us—wherever we find them—puts us more directly in touch with the principles of Tao. Years ago, while in graduate school at UCLA, I used to play my guitar and sing folk songs with my neighbors Bill and John in the laundry room of our apartment building. With its bare walls, this room was a perfect echo chamber. After a hard day of classes, exams, and studies, we would make music together.

Our voices were hardly alike. We were amateurs. Sometimes we even sang in different keys, but every so often it happened: We blended into a harmony so beautiful that it nearly took my breath away. After an hour of folk singing, we returned to our respective apartments, relaxed and renewed.

I remember my wonder at the way our voices blended into those unexpected chords, convinced that if families, friends, and neighbors would only make music together, they might discover new levels of harmony for themselves. The applications are different, but the principles are the same: respect for differences and an awareness of how these differences flow together to create deeper, more beautiful patterns than any one of us could make alone.

Years later, I learned from aikido the same principles of focus, flow, and follow-through. These three skills enable aikido masters to blend with the energies within and around them. Flowing with graceful, swirling movements, they transform conflict into harmony.

Focus

A great leader remains focused, regardless of the situation. Legendary quarterback Joe Montana would amaze onlookers by remaining cool in the tense minutes of a game. In the last three minutes of the 1989 Superbowl, with the San Francisco 49ers behind, Joe calmly looked around, smiled at someone in the stands, and then threw a long pass for the winning touchdown. Leaders who remain focused inspire confidence in their teams, helping the groups remain more focused as well.

Focus can also mean having a clear vision or goal and then moving forward to reach that goal, intimately aware of how the present moment relates to it.

TAO QUESTIONS
What is your current focus, your goal, right now?
What are you doing to reach it?

Flow

Flow, or *zanshin,* as explained in the last chapter, is our ability to participate actively and consciously in the ongoing process of life. Aware of the energies within and around us, we can blend with a situation or relationship without losing our center. This is easy to say, but less easy to do. Flow requires us to transcend our inner blocks, built up by years of hurt and disappointment, to overcome our fear of failure and the nagging self-doubts that prevent us from reaching out to life. Flow requires us to tune in to what is happening *within* us: to monitor our wandering minds and erratic emotions, bringing ourselves back to center. It also requires us to tune in to what is happening *around* us, regarding the energy patterns in each situation.

An effective leader is willing to think about what's happening and how to understand what's going on. Facilitating flow and making others more conscious of it, the leader communicates an awareness of process to the group, making them more aware of their energies and options. One important principle is to keep track of who has *not* spoken. If a group is ready to make a decision, point this out—"We haven't heard from John yet. What are your thoughts on this, John?" It's also important to notice when people do speak out but are not heard. Effective leaders practice patience, reminding themselves to wait and observe, remembering that there's always more going on in a group than we're consciously aware of.

Monica needs to learn this lesson of flow. For years she excelled in her own creative work as a highly acclaimed computer designer. She's good at taking the initiative, at solving problems alone. But when she became a manager, she continued to solve problems by herself and presented her colleagues with solutions as faits accomplis. The result was a divided department and a tremendous drop in morale. People wanted to be included, resenting what they called her elitist management style. Fortunately, Monica is beginning to turn things around, setting up leadership teams to help make important decisions. Now, people feel more respected, and the morale has already improved.

Follow-through

Sometimes people talk about "flowing with the process," to describe a passive, fatalistic approach to life. But following the *Tao Te Ching* doesn't mean being passive. Tao leaders don't abdicate personal responsibility or surrender to circumstance. Rather, they recognize and blend with situations, using their awareness of energy patterns to make wiser decisions, to take more effective action.

Many people still need to learn this lesson of follow-through. Dan is always wishing and hoping that things will change. Recently laid off, he tells his wife that he'll get another job, but spends much of his time reading the newspaper, the comics and sports section, not the classified ads. He missed out on two good job leads because he didn't return phone calls in time. When his wife, Annie, gets upset with him, he whines, "It takes time. It's a P-R-O-C-E-S-S." But this statement is a cop-out. The Tao reminds us to take a conscious part in any process, or that particular process will move along without us.

Unlike Dan, who can't seem to get started, some people initiate action but lose heart along the way. Always excited about beginning things—new projects, new diets, new jobs, new relationships—they lack staying power. Tony is a young commercial artist who initially impresses everyone with his talk about new ideas and new approaches. But none of these ideas seems to materialize. He has elaborate excuses and dramatic stories by the dozens, but no results.

After a while, we get tired of the flashy Tonys in our lives, even if they happen to be ourselves. The Tao says:

> *Those who know*
> *Do not speak.*
> *Those who speak*
> *Do not know.*

(Tao, 56)

To this we may add, "Those who speak do not do." Talk is easy. Doing takes discipline.

Tao Exercise

The lesson of follow-through takes patience and faith. We can build our endurance and follow through with conscious effort. To develop greater follow-through,

Start with a short project.
Break the task into manageable steps.
Then take the first step.

The Tao tells us:

> *The journey of a thousand miles*
> *Begins with a single step.*
>
> **(Tao, 64)**

And we get there, one step at a time.

Sometimes our eagerness to finish something makes us rush to completion. Our passion for closure can lead to impatience, making us overlook important details near the end of a project. We can become unduly rigid. Committed to finishing a project on schedule, we can ignore the concerns of others. One sad example of this tendency was the Challenger disaster in which key people were so concerned about meeting the deadline for the launch that they dismissed reports of a defective part—with dire consequences.

The Tao reminds us to avoid falling into impatience and rigidity. We need to listen to the people around us, be aware of their energies, and adjust when necessary. The patterns of nature reinforce this lesson:

> *We begin life gentle and yielding.*
> *At death we are rigid, inflexible.*
> *The grasses that grow are green and supple.*
> *In death they are withered and sere.*
> *Therefore, the rigid and inflexible*
> *Belong to death.*
> *The gentle and yielding*
> *Are filled with life.*
>
> *If your plan is inflexible,*
> *It cannot succeed.*
> *Unable to bend,*
> *The tree will break.*

Hardness and stiffness
Lead to destruction.
Flow with the process
And live to prevail.

(Tao, 76)

The Tao leader possesses the wisdom of living systems. Aware of the energy patterns in any situation, he or she knows when to move forward, when to pause, when to cooperate, and when to intervene. Mitch Saunders, director of programs for California Leadership, values four archetypal skills that correspond to the Jungian notion of four basic human capacities: initiation (establishing new directions), following (building on and appreciating what others have started), disruption (cutting across or opposing what others have begun), and reflection or penetrating insight (perceiving the structures underlying the current situation).

Gandhi's Leadership

Mitch admits that "there are mature and immature ways of activating each of these energies. Some refer to immature expressions of these skills as 'shadows.' Mahatma Gandhi, however, appeared to be well rounded in terms of these basic leadership capacities." In addition to being "a very disruptive character" who boldly confronted the injustice of British imperialism and oppression, he possessed the other three skills as well. Gandhi was a man of penetrating insight who could initiate and inspire bold new actions. He was also a follower, building a strong power base among his people by drawing on Hindu traditions. Inspired by his combination of patriotism and spiritual leadership, his followers opposed British oppression—not by fighting, but by bravely standing for truth. Their moral courage ultimately touched the hearts of their oppressors and liberated India.

Courageous, compassionate, and flexible, Gandhi transcended ego and impatience. According to Mitch, "he knew how to hold and embrace profound tensions. This capacity is at the very heart of being able to cultivate collective intelligence."[9]

Like Gandhi, Tao leaders are multifaceted individuals, able to meet any challenge with strength of character and a vast reservoir of skills. Aware of process, they blend with the situation to bring about the best results. Always learning, always growing in awareness:

> *Tao leaders*
> *Are wise as the ages.*
> *Their depth cannot be sounded,*
> *Yet we can describe their actions:*
> *Mindful, as if crossing an icy stream;*
> *Focused, as in the midst of danger;*
> *Respectful, as if an honored guest;*
> *Fluid, as melting ice;*
> *Honest, as an uncarved block of wood;*
> *Open, as a yielding valley;*
> *Blending, as if earth and water.*
>
> **(Tao, 15)**

This is the way of Tao.

CHAPTER 3

Timing

Tao leaders live close to nature.
Their actions flow from the heart.
In words, they are true;
In decisions, just;
In business, effective;
In action, aware of the timing.

(Tao, 8)

The *Tao Te Ching* provides us with vital lessons in timing. Realizing that everything in nature moves in cycles, Tao leaders know how to blend with these cycles in their lives and work. They know when to speak, when to pause, when to remain silent, when to act, and when to wait.

Prevention: The Wisdom of Small Actions

Wise leaders see how everything is related, how one thing naturally leads to another. Empowered by this vision, they anticipate and prevent problems.

Watching the cycles of Tao makes us mindful of how small actions lead to larger consequences. We see how routine maintenance on our cars or regular aerobic exercise, nutrition, and preventive health care can make a major difference in our lives. Cultivating healthy habits sets up regular, self-reinforcing positive cycles. Taken by themselves, these small actions don't seem like much, but the cumulative effect of their presence—or absence—is undeniable.

One of the hazards of our fast-paced lives is the tendency to neglect these small actions until we're in a crisis. For years, my friend Henry, a television cameraman, was "too busy" to go to the dentist. Getting his teeth cleaned and checked was a hassle, so he kept putting it off. Then one year, during a family Thanksgiving dinner, one of his front teeth fell out. Because he hadn't taken regular preventive action, he now needs extensive periodontal work.

The cycles of Tao can be ignored, but they cannot be

denied. The small actions we take today add up to major differences tomorrow.

TAO EXERCISE

What small actions should you be taking now to maintain your job? your health? your relationship? your property?

Write them down.

Now schedule one of them into your life on a regular basis. (Studies have shown that it usually takes about thirty days of consistent action to break an old habit or set up a new one.)

When this action has become a habit, and you have successfully blended it into the rhythm of your life, you can add another.

Remember the importance of small actions. They're the building blocks in the architecture of your life, the quiet victories you win for yourself each day.

The Wisdom of the Seasons

The wisdom of Tao, like the lessons of Ecclesiastes, affirms that "To every thing there is a season, and a time to every purpose under heaven."

For centuries, Asian life, art, and rituals have revolved around the seasons, which find familiar expression in the poetry and art of the Far East. When I was growing up, I admired the embroidered pictures of the four seasons hanging in my parents' house.

Each season has its own special beauty. Spring brings the delicate plum blossoms. Summer bursts forth with profusions of orchids. Autumn is graced with golden chrysanthemums, and winter brings the strength and serenity of bamboo.

The wisdom of nature, the wisdom of Tao, teaches us that every project, every week, every day, has its four seasons: a time to plant, a time to grow, a time to harvest, and a time to contemplate. It is wisdom to observe these seasons, folly to ignore them.

Recognizing these seasons in the workweek, a Tao leader realizes that Monday mornings and Friday afternoons are not the best times to call a busy office. On Monday mornings, everyone is too busy with the flurry of new beginnings, and late Friday afternoons, people are rushing to wrap up their work before the weekend. A wise person plans the week's activities with these seasons in mind.

It took me a while to apply this lesson to my current job. For over a year, I tried to have staff meetings in my department office on Monday mornings, so we could take stock and plan for the week ahead. But with the tidal wave of Monday's activities, our meetings were often canceled or postponed. It suddenly hit me that Mondays are not the best time for long-range planning. The energies are all wrong. Now I've decided to hold staff meetings near the end of the week, when things slow down. In our office, an hour after lunch on Thursday or Friday is a much better time for reflection and planning.

A Time to Plant: The Wisdom of Spring

The beginning of any cycle holds its own lessons. The first one is discernment. Before moving ahead, a wise leader looks within and asks, "Do I really *want* to begin this project?" The Tao teaches us not to be reactive—not to do something just because it needs to be done. Perhaps we have other priorities, or perhaps we are not the right ones to do it.

TAO QUESTIONS: DISCERNMENT

Before plunging into something new, take a moment to ask yourself:

"Do I really want to begin this project?"
"Why?"
"How does it relate to my long-term goals?"

"Do I have the time to do it well?"
"Am I ready to make this commitment?"

Taking time to reflect, Tao leaders live consciously, aware of what they're doing. They make their decisions by deliberation, not by default.

Not only do Tao leaders look within, they look around to determine the right time for effective action. Before planting each spring, wise farmers watch carefully for signs that the danger of frost has passed. Many of them plant by the phases of the moon, drawing on the lunar cycles to help their seeds sprout more readily.

Many disciplines teach the lesson of timing. If we were musicians in an orchestra, we would need to know when to play our parts, combining our notes with the others to produce harmony. It is the same in life.

Aikido students are taught to look for an attacker's opening or *suki,* the place where the attacker's guard is down, where he or she is not aware. In a larger sense, a *suki* is a critical moment of opportunity: a time in the midst of an action when we can move in and transform a situation.

The Tao teaches that there are *suki,* or openings, all around us. As Tao leaders, we learn to recognize and embrace these opportunities. Aware of the larger cycles, we know the right time to initiate a project.

In late summer each year the dean of our college holds an annual retreat for all the department heads. In 1993, many of us were complaining about having to write the annual fall faculty evaluations. A friend and I decided that this was the perfect time to reform the evaluation process: A natural *suki* already existed. So we proposed a policy change at our first meeting in September, and it sailed right through. We used the energies of the new academic year and the discontent with the old process to reform the system.

The next time you want to begin a project, ask yourself, "What else is happening?"

Look at the energies and larger cycles around you.

Is this the best time to propose something new?
If so, do it.
If not, when would be a better time?

Remember to look for the natural *suki* and work with them.

Knowing When the Wind Shifts

The Tao reminds us that we live in a dynamic universe; wisdom is recognizing and moving with change. Many leaders make foolish mistakes when they become fixated on the past. They use old strategies in new situations, not realizing that the wind has shifted: What *was* no longer exists.

People who go sailing respect the shifting power of the wind. They know that moving against the wind is much more difficult than is having the wind at their backs. To keep moving forward, they adjust their sails and tack, moving in zigzag patterns in the direction of their goal. In leadership and life, different conditions require different responses.

Disasters occur when leaders rely on outmoded strategies. During the Battle of Agincourt in 1415, Henry V's small band of English soldiers defeated the mighty French army, although they were outnumbered by more than five to one. The English called it a miracle, but a closer look reveals what really happened. After a series of heavy rains, the battlefield was extremely muddy. The French had equipped their soldiers in heavy medieval armor, which protected them from arrows but made it difficult for them to move. Hundreds of French soldiers were killed not by the English but by their own strategic mistake. As they marched in to do battle, they got bogged down in the mud and fell on each other. Too heavily armored to get up, they smothered in the mud. In other battles, their armor had been a lifesaver; in this situation, it proved fatal.

There is a term in neuropsychology: "to perseverate," which means to continue to perform an action even when it no longer produces the desired result. For example, some laboratory animals continue to press a lever for food even when food is no longer delivered. Stuck in an old behavioral pattern, they cannot adjust to the new situation. How often do we humans perseverate, behaving in a way that worked in a previous job or relationship but is totally out of place in this one?

Recognizing the dynamic cycles of Tao, we learn to take actions appropriate to the context, realizing that the context is continuously changing.

Filing Your Flight Plan: Goals and Directions

Before my father makes a cross-country flight, he always files a flight plan, telling air traffic control where he's heading. This is the law in aviation; otherwise, there would be chaos in the skies overhead.

Unfortunately, there's often chaos in our lives when leaders don't communicate effectively. When they initiate new projects, many leaders give orders and assignments without telling people the goal or purpose. No one knows what they're doing and where they're headed. The result is confusion and low morale, especially when major changes are involved.

Many American universities and corporations have been experiencing budget crises and downsizing. When a leader begins cutting programs and laying people off, the results can be devastating. Not only is it harder to maintain high-quality programs with all the cutbacks, but people lose heart. They become demoralized, resentful, even paranoid, and their work suffers. If they only knew what to expect, if they could see this crisis as a temporary tunnel with an end in sight, they could work together for the greater good. Even bad news is easier to take when we know what's happening.

A few years ago, William Rewak, S.J., president of Spring Hill College in Mobile, Alabama, got his faculty and staff together to confront their budget problems and to develop solutions. This open leadership resulted in an effective action plan and increased community spirit, despite the economic challenges. For progressive leaders, such results are worth the risk of admitting that they don't have all the answers. No one does. Openness and cooperation are hallmarks of the new leadership that is emerging in our midst. Today's leaders are not expected to be medieval monarchs who rule by divine right. They *are* expected to be honest about challenges and work for effective solutions.

TAO EXERCISE

The next time you initiate a project, remember to include all the people involved in your "flight plan." Have a meeting to share goals and listen to their ideas. Include them in the process. The following guidelines will help you get started.

- *Openness.* Communicate your goals clearly.
- *Listening.* Allow time to hear the other person or persons.
- *Empathy.* You don't have to agree with the other person or persons. The greatest gift we can give someone is our respect and understanding.
- *Flexibility.* Remember the wisdom of bamboo. Be ready to adjust to the needs of others and to tack whenever the wind shifts.

Choose a comfortable, nonthreatening place for your meeting. If possible, meet other people in their territory, not yours.

Begin by stating the situation and asking for input.

Don't give people a fait accompli, but include them in the planning process. A fait accompli makes people feel that they have no choice or power, that their needs and opinions don't matter.

The solution that emerges from this process will be better for two important reasons: it will be a wiser strategy, benefiting from collective perspectives and experience, and it will naturally evoke people's commitment because they've been included in the planning process.

Remember to set goals and a time line: Who will do what? By when? Make these goals manageable and remember to set a time to check back and assess how things are going.

I've found that this process works well in almost every context, even teaching. In the past, I used to walk into a class and just start lecturing. My students often wondered where we were going. Now, on the first day of class, I ask students about their goals and expectations to help me set the tone for the rest of the course. At the beginning of each class, I write the goal for the day on the board. I also hold a midquarter evaluation to assess how the class is going.

Such an approach works not only in managing classes or teams at work, but in our personal lives as well. Remember to check with the people around you about goals, expectations, and feelings as you walk a personal or professional path together. This process is alive, flexible, dynamic; the old way is rigid and static, leading to dead-end routines, confusion, and misunderstandings. In any context, the new way, the way of Tao, incorporates the energies of all the players into the process. Try it and see how inclusiveness creates new possibilities and greater understanding.

A Time to Grow: The Wisdom of Summer

The second stage of any project, the growth process, has its own lessons. The first is simple: We must allow enough room to grow. In the late spring I picked up some vegetable seedlings to set out in my small organic garden. Since I have only limited space, I must plan carefully. I asked my friend Joyce Okumura, who runs the nearby nursery, if I could put two Roma tomato plants in a five-gallon pot and get twice as many tomatoes. She laughed. "Better just take one plant," she said. "I hate to overcrowd them."

How often do we overcrowd our new projects, cramming them into the same limited space and time? Leadership involves making careful choices. The wisdom of Tao teaches that less is more.

Every project needs room to grow. As a leader, you must delegate many projects. Part of delegating is knowing which people can handle the work. But just as important is knowing how long to leave people alone to work things out. Overcontrolling, constantly looking over their shoulders, doesn't allow them room to grow.

The Lesson of *Ma-ai*

The Japanese have a word for this growing room: *ma-ai,* the distance in time and space between two people, two events, or two energies. Aikido relies on the interval between an action and a response, between one person's energy and another's. Seeing the larger patterns, we know when to pause, when to move, and when to blend. Moving in too soon is just as unproductive as waiting too long.

There are intervals of *ma-ai* in all areas of life: the rhythms of *yin* and *yang,* action and contemplation, society and solitude. After a busy day out in the world, there's nothing so pleasurable as a quiet evening at home with mellow music and a good book. After a day working alone at my desk, I enjoy the contrast of a good aikido workout. There's always the balance, the rhythm of contrast: *ma-ai*.

Pacing is another aspect of *ma-ai*. Have you ever ruined a race by starting out too fast or a good relationship by doing too much too soon? Impulsiveness and instant intimacy are symptoms of impatience. The wisdom of *ma-ai* allows for natural momentum and room to grow.

We can have too much of a good thing. A phone call from a new friend or a visit from a neighbor can be delightful, but not when it happens so often you can't get anything done. Committee meetings are essential for shared governance, but too many meetings wear us down. A Tao person remembers the importance of balance. The *Tao Te Ching* reminds us that

> *Knowing when enough is enough*
> *Is wealth of spirit.*

> **(Tao, 33)**

Time Bandits and Boundary Violations

As a leader, you become a public person. With increased responsibility comes the increased challenge of maintaining *ma-ai* in your life. As more people make demands on your time and energy, how do you maintain your balance?

Successful leaders develop effective strategies for maintaining their boundaries. California Assemblyman John Vasconcellos's political challenges could easily engulf his entire life. There are always constituents with pressing concerns who are clamoring to see him. But after a massive heart attack and bypass surgery in the 1980s, he learned to schedule regular time for racquetball and relaxation to help him stay balanced. He can do so because he has dedicated staff members in his capitol and district offices who share his vision and commitment to service. He knows he can count on them to help him serve the needs of the hundreds of thousands of people he represents. Part of maintaining *ma-ai* is knowing how and when to delegate.

We maintain *ma-ai* for ourselves not only by establishing boundaries for ourselves, but by enforcing them against "time bandits," individuals whose demands consciously or unconsciously hold us up and drain our energy.

Time bandits have different motives. Some are anxiety ridden, some are lonely, some wish to dominate, and some apparently have more time than we do, along with highly developed verbal skills. But their behavior is easy to identify. Here we are working on a hot project with a tight deadline, and a time bandit interrupts us with a phone call about something much less important or suddenly drops by for a chat.

Most time bandits don't know any better. And being a time bandit is a matter of context. One person's time bandit is another person's pleasant diversion. I'm sure I've probably been a time bandit myself, stopping by to socialize and robbing busy people of the precious time they needed to complete a project.

Instead of gritting our teeth to be polite and resenting the time bandit for holding us up, the best choice is to be honest. We cannot expect another person to honor our needs unless we affirm them ourselves.

Tell the person that you can't talk now because you're up against a deadline. Then reschedule your talk if you need to. You can also affirm boundaries by closing your door and having your secretary hold your calls until you accomplish your task. The important thing is not to be reactive.

Tao leaders maintain *ma-ai,* a balance of action, contemplation, and interaction, in their lives. They know when to be flexible and can change their plans to meet a crisis, but they are not reactive. They keep moving forward in the direction of their goals without letting another person's frantic energies or loquacious personality throw them off balance.

Patience with the Process

Along with *ma-ai,* another lesson of summer is patience. To let things grow, we need to have faith in the process. In the past I was never good at doing so. When I was in graduate school at UCLA, my friends used to grow beautiful plants from avocado seeds, so I thought I'd try it myself. I planted a seed in a clay pot, watered it every day, and waited. Weeks went by, but nothing happened. I waited some more. Finally, I dug up the plant to see what was happening. The seed had sprouted, put forth roots, and was nearly ready to emerge from the soil. But my impatience killed the plant.

We need patience to see projects through to completion. A hard lesson is that different projects, like different plants, have different time lines. In my vegetable garden, green beans spring up quickly, while carrots take a long time to harvest.

Many of us are impatient with problems, eager to solve them quickly. No one can fault us for our good intentions. We care, we want to help, we want to improve things—now. Our society has reinforced us for quick fixes and instant solutions. But some complex problems cannot be solved by riding to the rescue like the Lone Ranger. As Tao leaders, we benefit from the wisdom of the seasons, which helps us keep our centers throughout times of apparent uncertainty. Knowing that one season inevitably leads to another enables us to smile at challenges, realizing that there is always an answer to every problem, even if we cannot see it yet. Within every crisis lies an opportunity.

The wisdom of summer teaches us not to hurry to completion. For hurry—in any context—makes us narrow our vision and lose our centers. If you find yourself rushing near the end of a project, back off, take a *ma-ai* break, and then come back with a new perspective and fresh energy to see the process through.

A Time to Harvest: The Wisdom of Autumn

The wisdom of autumn lets us know when to complete a project, when to harvest. We do not pick green fruit, nor do we wait too long until the fruit rots. Near the end of a project there's always an optimal moment: a time to harvest. If we finish too soon, we spoil the project. If we wait too long, we may never finish it.

My father, who has taught people to fly for over fifty years, knows that after about twenty hours of lessons, there's an optimal moment when the flight instructor gets out of the plane and tells a student pilot "take it around the pattern by yourself." I remember the exhilaration I felt when I soloed for the first time. Afterward I asked my instructor how he knew it was the right time. He mumbled something. So I called my father. He told me that there's a certain time when a student is ready. If an instructor solos a student too early, it's dangerous, but if the instructor waits too long, the student will become so dependent on the instructor that he or she will never solo.

The wisdom of autumn teaches us to recognize that optimal moment in all our projects. As Shakespeare says, "the ripeness is all." I know that when I get an idea for a new project, I must move with it, work with it, or the energies wane and the project languishes.

I learned this lesson in graduate school. During my first year in the Ph.D. program at UCLA, I felt quite insecure. While I had just finished college the year before, most of my classmates already had their master's degrees. Because one friend's father was a professor, my friend had actually met many of the scholars we were studying, while I couldn't even pronounce some of their names. And as if that wasn't enough, my friend had even begun work on his doctoral dissertation.

I didn't have a clue about my dissertation. I was the first

person in my family to get a college degree. But as I slowly moved ahead, my friend got bogged down. He kept doing more and more dissertation research and postponed writing. My fellowship money was running out, so I juggled two jobs and finished my dissertation in 1973. Over twenty years later, my friend has still not finished. He somehow missed the optimal moment.

In group work, as well as in individual projects, the season of autumn is crucial. Many progressive leaders strive for consensus decision making. But as Carolyn Hennings, director of Santa Clara University's Career Center, admonishes, "Some leaders can get too hung up in consensus building, take too long. Ultimately, you have to move on a decision."[1] After considering the options and listening to people's views, there comes a time for action, a time to harvest before everyone's energies run out.

If the time is ripe for change, but you aren't quite sure about a new policy, Hennings advises that you adopt it on a trial basis and then check back to evaluate it with your group before making a final decision. Lately, I've implemented many draft policies, to be refined by experience and further reflection.

Timing is crucial. Some people fail to complete projects because of insecurity or compulsiveness. Others stay with a process too long for reasons of ego. The *Tao Te Ching* advises us:

> *The wise leader knows*
> *When enough is enough.*
>
> *Stretch a bow too far*
> *And it will snap.*
> *Sharpen a knife too much*
> *And its edge will not last.*
> *Fill your house with gold and jade,*
> *And you cannot defend it.*

Exalting in your success
Invites a certain fall.
When your work is done,
It is time to move on.

(Tao, 9)

The moment of harvest, the moment of satisfaction at the end of a successful project, is glorious, but staying around to gloat spoils it all. "When your work is done," the Tao tells us, "it is time to move on," time to step back, take stock, and then begin a new cycle.

A Time to Contemplate: The Wisdom of Winter

From many of the process descriptions I've read, it seems that Western society recognizes only three seasons: spring, summer, and fall—the beginning, middle, and end. The wisdom of Tao reminds us of the fourth: the season of winter, during which little happens on the surface.

During the winter, many plants are dormant, apparently dead. But beneath the surface, within the earth, a great deal is going on. My Japanese maple and peach trees are storing up energy for a spring of rebirth. Pruning and special feeding are essential during this quiet season.

Winter is a natural time for slowing down, for contemplation. At the end of any project, a wise leader pauses to take stock, to go over notes and evaluations, to ask what worked and what didn't, learning from the experience. This final phase is essential so that our new beginnings can be wiser. Tao leaders bring forth deep wisdom from the roots of winter to initiate a new spring of possibilities and a more abundant harvest in the future.

When you plan your next project, leave time at the end to administer a brief evaluation to the people involved. Remember to include these basic questions:

What worked?
What didn't?
What could have been done better?
What are some specific suggestions for improvement?

Then take time to read over the answers, asking what you learned from the experience. Before beginning your next project, reflect on these lessons and include them in your plans.

As we have seen in this chapter, the Tao moves in dynamic cycles. Its lessons can seem elusive, for they reflect a world of change. Yet the cycles and principles of timing endure throughout all creation. The wise leader follows the Tao, aware that

> *Looked at, it cannot be seen.*
> *Listened to, it cannot be heard.*
> *Reached for, it cannot be held.*
> *Beyond all description,*
> *The three blend as one.*
>
> *It is neither dark nor light.*
> *Returning to its essence,*
> *It is the form of the formless,*
> *The image without image,*
> *Beyond all definition.*
> *Meeting it, there is no beginning.*
> *Following it, there is no end.*
>
> *Hold to this timeless pattern*
> *Throughout the time of your life,*

Aware of the eternal cycles,
The essence of Tao.

(Tao, 14)

Aware of the dynamic cycles within and around us, we learn to blend with them and lead with the Tao, becoming more successful in all the seasons of our lives.

CHAPTER 4

Respect

Those who would govern wisely
Must first respect life.

(Tao, 75)

The *Tao Te Ching* is not a prescriptive guide to behavior with rules for every occasion. Rather, it affirms a few fundamental principles that can light our path in leadership and in life.

One major principle of Tao is respect: for ourselves, for one another, and for life itself. Knowing the principle, we need not worry about the particular action to take in a given situation. Wise actions flow naturally from right principles. When respect directs our daily choices, all our policies and interactions are in harmony with Tao.

Isabel Briggs Myers, one of the founders of the Myers-Briggs personality-type indicator, said that no matter how much people differ in background or temperament, three qualities underlie any enduring relationship: understanding, appreciation, and respect.[1]

Eastern philosophy has upheld this lesson for centuries. Buddhism teaches compassion for all living things. Confucianism upholds *jen*, "humanheartedness," respect for others as the foundation of all virtue. The Japanese word for conscience, *honshin*, combines the characters for true *(honto)* and heart *(shin)*. Living with respect unites our hearts with nature and the way of Tao. The *Tao Te Ching* tells us:

> Tao leaders live close to nature.
> Their actions flow from the heart.

> **(Tao, 8)**

Respect as Power

Living respectfully is an essential leadership principle. Modern psychologists have called it the key to personal power. Psychologist Jerry Lynch, who coaches Olympic athletes, says that "your real power as a person comes when you relate to others from your heart rather than your head."[2] Our energies contract when we concentrate on ourselves and the impression we're making. The Tao tells us to reverse this direction, to let our energies flow out from our center in greater respect and appreciation for the people around us.

Instead of self-consciously posing and performing, Tao leaders concentrate on others. Remember this lesson in your interactions. Take time to listen, observe, and discover the spark of greatness in the people you know. As a Tao leader, you inspire others by making that spark come alive.

Soft Is Strong

Tao leaders draw on a power much greater than the stereotyped strength of celluloid heroes. The violent hero stereotype is flashy, tough, emotionally repressed, and ultimately unreal. Real strength is strength of character. Combining courage and compassion, Tao leaders live respectfully, transcending difficulty to create new possibilities.

Affirming the strength of Tao, Jerry Lynch says to ask ourselves how we "can be more kind and gentle. This is true strength and power, as the Tao teaches: 'Soft is strong.'"[3]

The Power of Trust

The *Tao Te Ching* says:

> *Who gives from the heart to all the world?*
> *Only one who leads with Tao.*
>
> **(Tao, 77)**

In this competitive, confusing world that emphasizes the "bottom line" of short-term economic gain, many leaders rise and fall with the cycles of change. Those who rise above mutability, who endure, draw on deeper principles, inspiring trust and commitment in the people around them. As over a decade of management research with nearly two thousand managers in North America, Mexico, Western Europe, Asia, and Australia has shown, the quality people most desire in leaders is credibility, grounded in mutual respect.[4]

Without respect, life is a crazy roller-coaster ride from one sensational experience to the next. Relationships remain superficial, and people can become ruthless, using one another as a means to an end. Unless we work together respectfully, the alchemy of cooperation and creativity cannot exist. Without the trust that respect engenders, we will not risk exploring the unknown. The new paradigm of cooperative leadership is impossible without respect.

This chapter examines the power of living respectfully. At first glance this principle of Tao may seem hopelessly naive, for we are told to

> *Live the Tao:*
> *Giving not only to those*
> *Who affirm the good,*
> *But also to those who do not;*
> *Respecting not only those*
> *Who respect you,*
> *But also those who do not.*
> *For respect increases respect,*
> *Creating essential harmony.*
>
> **(Tao, 49)**

In an Eastern articulation of the Golden Rule ("Do unto others as you would have them do unto you"), the Tao tells us that only by respecting others will we build respect around us. Doing so obviously involves a risk. Some people will disappoint and betray us. But by *not* respecting others, we risk perpetuating a Hobbesian world, in which life is inevitably "nasty, brutish, and short." The Tao dares us to live our beliefs and thereby create a better world.

Far from being naive, Taoism is pragmatically idealistic. Lao-tzu developed his philosophy in the midst of massive social upheaval, during the warring-states period in ancient China. Respect—for self, for others, and for the cycles of nature—was his courageous response to the chaos around him. Instead of surrendering to the violent status quo that defined life as an endless power struggle, he realized that our response to a situation is filled with tremendous creative power. "What is"—the current state of things—does not have to continue. The Tao teaches that we are not passive victims of external circumstances. We can begin a new cycle of creation at any time by acknowledging and redirecting the energies around us.

Tao leaders are realistic. They confront difficult situations with courage and resourcefulness. Living respectfully, they can transform even negative situations into new possibilities.

Dealing with Negative Situations

So, how do Tao leaders deal respectfully with apparent misfortune? Leading in prosperous times is one thing; leading in an unstable economy is something else. In a leadership class not long ago, one women told me that at Monterey Community Hospital in northern California, management policies are based on respect. When the hospital keeps a patient waiting too long, it gives that person a message of appreciation and a bouquet of flowers. When recent cutbacks forced the hospital management to lay off some of the staff, managers held open meetings, told people the truth about the situation, gave them two months' notice, and called in an outplacement service to help them find new jobs. Margaret, the woman in my class, was one of these people. Happily settled in a new job, she still looks back fondly on her former employer.[5]

A policy of respect creates good corporate karma. People

who work in a respectful atmosphere give better service. Clients come back, and business increases by referrals. Realtors Lyle Farrow and his daughter Bonnie Farrow have transcended the ups and downs of the California economy with their personal policy of honesty and respect for clients. No matter what the news says about the real estate market, they have a consistent record of sales because of the principles they live by.

When Respect Is Missing

The Tao tells us:

> *When people lack respect,*
> *Trouble follows.*

(Tao, 72)

The Tao reminds us of the subtle energies that make up all existence. Consciously or unconsciously, people sense these energies and know when respect is missing, when they are being devalued. Morale and productivity suffer. A company that does not respect its clients will not keep them, and an atmosphere that lacks internal harmony invariably drives people away.

While finishing graduate school, I worked in a new Creole restaurant in Santa Monica, California. With its spicy food and upbeat atmosphere, the restaurant made a promising start. Many employees were aspiring actors, who would spontaneously burst into song and exchange lines from popular shows. My job as cashier was a pleasant diversion from my studies. But then the two owners had an argument, refused to speak to one another, and things fell apart. First, we didn't get our paychecks on time, and shortly thereafter the customers stopped coming. How did they know? I wondered. The place looked the same, the staff was the same, and the food seemed just as good, but something was wrong with the energies. In three months, the little restaurant sadly closed its doors. The lack of respect between the owners had destroyed it.

Theory X

Many companies still treat clients like commodities and employees like replaceable parts. This is what management expert Douglas McGregor called "Theory X," an outmoded hierarchical approach to management that considers the institution more important than its employees. In a corporate version of the caste system, managers look down on workers, expecting them to subordinate and sacrifice themselves for the common good.[6] Corporate propaganda reinforces this unhealthy behavior, disguising disrespect and denigration of individuals as dedication to the institution.

For leaders who follow the Tao, such a concept is ridiculous. The Taoist vision is holistic: We cannot separate the parts from the whole. For Tao leaders, the individual members *are* the institution. Supporting their continued personal and professional growth also ensures the growth of the corporation. Reducing employees to mere functionaries not only stunts their growth as human beings but makes the institution stagnate as well. Just as a lake is the sum of many drops of water, an institution is only as healthy as the individuals within it.

It pains me when people believe Theory X's unhealthy propaganda, considering themselves less important than the work they do. There are many examples of this belief. Betty, an administrative assistant in a New York publishing firm, decided to retire because her arthritis was getting progressively worse. The pain in her right hip was slowing her down, making it increasingly difficult for her to walk. She told her boss, "I won't be much use if I can't get around any more."

Her supervisor responded that he valued her not merely for what she did but for who she was, that a disability did not make her less valuable as a person. Furthermore, he said, Betty's logic made no sense. If she retired, she would still have to "get around" in her own life (Betty lives alone with her cat in a modest apartment). She would also lose her health benefits when she needed them most. He suggested that she take time off for surgery and then consider her options. Betty has since returned to work with a hip replacement and a healthier outlook on life.

Wise leaders know that if an individual doesn't count, the institution doesn't count for much either. Put mathematically, if the individual is a zero, together a lot of zeros add up to a whole lot of nothing.

Some leaders in Silicon Valley and in other regions or industries that are part of the emerging knowledge-based economy refer to their employees as "assets" and "human capital." One CEO of a leading software firm remarked recently that "my most valuable assets walk in and out of the front door every day."[7] The monetary metaphors may seem awkward and reductive, but the more we value the people around us, the more value we create in our world. As we know from the Tao, that value—emotional, spiritual, environmental—includes but far exceeds the economic level.

Without respect for ourselves and others, everything falls apart. Jack, a manager in a Boston computer firm, had a crisis nearly every day around five o'clock. He'd rush in, announcing an unexpected deadline, a broken piece of equipment, or a conflict in the office, and someone had to stay late and help him deal with it. His staff complained among themselves, and Marge, who lives near Jack, discovered the underlying cause.

Jack put work above human worth, neglecting his home and family. His wife withdrew in depression and his teenage children grew troubled and confused. Without a nurturing, respectful atmosphere at home, Molly and Jim could get their parents' attention only when they were in a crisis. In what became a self-perpetuating negative cycle, a succession of troubles at school, drugs, delinquency, and juvenile offenses took over their home life, producing more daily drama than the six o'clock news. The whole family used crises to get the attention they craved. But what they really needed was respect.

Since Jack didn't want to go home, he created crises at work. Like the ripples on a pond, the negative energies spiraled out and affected many people.

But the ripple effect can also work in a positive direction. When our actions are guided by a deep core of respect for ourselves and others, the energies of healing, joy, and empowerment radiate out to the world around us.

The Tao of Self-respect

Like everything in the Tao, the lesson of respect is holistic. We can give only what we've got. We must first respect ourselves before we can respect others. The Tao reminds us that leadership involves a lifelong commitment to self-mastery:

> *Analyzing others is knowledge.*
> *Knowing yourself is wisdom.*
> *Managing others requires skill.*
> *Mastering yourself takes inner strength.*
>
> **(Tao, 33)**

An often-quoted maxim tells us: "As it is within, so it is without." To develop our leadership abilities, we must first look within. And what do we see? Writer and educational consultant Sunny Merik admitted, "Sometimes we treat ourselves like things. We should strive not to be that way. Work, work, work . . . trying to be perfect . . . never giving yourself a rest."[8] Does this sound familiar? Conscientious people too often fall victim to compulsive work habits, treating themselves like machines. This unhealthy paradigm is out of harmony with nature. It is not the wisdom of Tao.

The Tao upholds the lesson of balance. We cannot sleep all the time, eat all the time, *or* work all the time. We must harmonize our different needs. Rev. Richard Green of Orlando, Florida, used to tell people that four qualities are necessary in human life: work, play, love, and worship.

Sometimes when we're living creatively, all four qualities come together as one. I've seen this combination in my friend Richard Burdick, an Oregon-based composer and pianist. Richard loves his work, blending words and music into new compositions with a spirit of playful discovery. When he performs, he radiates a joy that inspires his audiences.

Music is an important part of his life, but no matter how satisfying, our vocation alone cannot become our whole life. To maintain his balance, Richard makes time for his family, their shared community service, and his own spiritual growth.

Tao Question

For each of us to experience the fullness of life, we need to work, play, love, and worship in ways that meet our own special needs. How do you provide for this balance in your life?

Specifically, how do you express yourself:

in work?
in play?
in love?
in worship?

If you've been neglecting some vital area, make a plan now to include it as a regular part of your life.

Leveling Up Our Self-concept

Whenever we confront a new challenge, we often wonder "Can I do it?" Have you gotten a promotion recently or started a new job? In today's rapidly changing world, you're probably dealing with a new challenge in at least one area of your life.

New experiences test us in many ways: drawing on our internal resources, our knowledge, skills, and evolving sense of self. My friend Tina Clare, a northern California minister and spiritual counselor, learned this lesson years ago when she went to Peru. As she climbed the mountains, she paused periodically to survey the majestic view and reflect on her life. The progressive ascent became a process of self-discovery. And what was her lesson? To work on her sense of self.

"Self-esteem!" she thought to herself. "I thought I had that one handled years ago." She had already overcome many challenges, building one successful career in public education and another as a spiritual counselor. Then she realized that she was embarking on a new phase of life that was to become her ministry. She needed to "level up" her self-concept to meet the new challenge.[9] This leveling up is part of the ongoing process of life, but it doesn't always come easily. When I arrived at Santa Clara University after four years of college and five years of graduate school, I was a little insecure in my new role as a college professor. My colleagues looked so scholarly, and I still felt like a student. The first day I walked into the faculty club and saw these distinguished professors sitting there in their tweed sport coats, I felt totally out of place. I walked back out again and ate lunch by myself in the student union. I had moved my books and baggage to Santa Clara to begin a new life, but my self-concept hadn't caught up with me.

The Tao reminds us that life is

> *Greatness evolving*
> *In infinite cycles,*
> *Reaching and returning.*

(Tao, 25)

The leveling-up process happens throughout life. Whenever we grow into a new job, a new challenge, or a new relationship, we need to face our momentary insecurity, realizing that even though we've never done this particular thing before, it's only another step on the path.

In Search of Excellence—Not Perfection

Conscientious people are usually their own worst enemies. While others recognize our strengths and accomplishments, we alone remember all our mistakes and often zero in on our slightest flaw. We habituate to what is acceptable in ourselves and don't even notice those things any more. Instead, we see the one detail that doesn't measure up to our expectations. Focusing on it with the zoom lens of our consciousness, we give it undue emphasis.

It is, of course, important to be honest about areas we need to work on, but it's unrealistic to expect perfection of ourselves (or anyone else, for that matter). The Tao tells us that perfection is not natural, not human. What *is* natural is to keep on growing throughout life.

To illustrate this point, a friend of mine tells a hypothetical story about a talented baseball player. As a batter, this man was phenomenal: He always got a hit, and every hit was a home run. And as a pitcher, he struck out every batter. But what would the effect of such a player really be? Simply to ruin the game. The moral is that like baseball, the game of life is not for perfect people. If we somehow managed to become perfect, no one would let us play with him or her. What makes any game exciting is the process of discovery, the unexpected, the probabilities. Perfection is static. The Tao reveals that life is dynamic. Our destiny is to grow, to evolve, to learn, always becoming more of who we are.[10]

I'm Learning

My aikido teacher, Sunny Skys, reminds his students not to get impatient with themselves when they're learning something new. The other night, after introducing a complicated technique, he stopped to ask how we were feeling. Most of us were self-critical, awkward, and confused, except for the youngest person in the class, twelve-year-old Harris Tran, who moves without the self-consciousness of adulthood.

"The next time you feel confused or awkward," Sunny said, "instead of telling yourself 'I can't do this. I'm no good at it,' affirm to yourself simply: 'I'm learning.'"

We're all learning. As young children, we didn't worry about falling down when we learned to walk or making mistakes when we colored outside the lines. These feelings came later.

Learning is an essential part of our nature. What carries us through life is our ability to grow, to discover new possibilities in ourselves and our world. Successful artists, inventors, scientists, or leaders in any field never lose that spirit. When they don't know what they're doing, they embrace the experience, realizing with every fiber of their being that they're learning and that learning is what life is all about.

TAO AFFIRMATION
The next time you find yourself doing something new, remember to break through self-doubt and self-criticism with the wisdom of Tao. Affirm to yourself:
"I'm learning"
and enjoy the process.

Transcending Ourselves

Tao leaders recognize their unlimited capacity for growth. They cast away the proverbial demon of self-doubt with the joy of ongoing discovery. The *Tao Te Ching* tells us:

> *Tao leaders, unaware of their virtue*
> *Are truly virtuous.*

The lesser person tries hard to look good
And is therefore not virtuous.

(Tao, 38)

Tao leaders have no time for self-consciousness and self-doubt. The path is too compelling, the journey too rewarding, for that. While "the lesser person" tries to keep up appearances, "to look good," Tao leaders transcend themselves by embracing the process and living with heart.

Respect as Discipline: The Lesson of Bonsai

But transcending self-doubt is not automatic. We must unlearn our self-limiting habits by replacing them with healthy ones. Self-respect requires discipline. Tao leaders cultivate self-mastery as an expert gardener tends a treasured bonsai tree.

For centuries in the Far East, bonsai have represented the spirit of nature while reflecting the spirit of the person who tends them: a perfect metaphor for living the Tao. Bonsai (or *pun jai* in Chinese), existed in China before the Chin Dynasty in A.D. 317. They spread to Japan during the Tang Dynasty (A.D. 618–906) and have long been revered by both cultures.

Bonsai are miniature trees that are trained to recall the look of a venerable tree on a windswept mountainside. Their trunks and branches are carefully pruned and twisted to duplicate the effects of great age and the contentious elements. Bonsai may not be as old as they look, although some treasured trees are handed down in families for a century or more.

My interest in bonsai developed when my students Eric Charles and Brendan Riley gave me a Japanese maple for my birthday in 1988. Other friends have given me bonsai for birthdays since then, so now I have a small collection.

All bonsai need careful treatment: regular watering; the right balance of fresh air and sunshine; and careful pinching, training, and pruning to retain their shape. Every two or three years they also require a major root pruning. I must lift the plant out of its pot, exposing the roots, then cut out the larger ones at the sides and bottom, filling the pot with fresh soil to allow room for new growth. Otherwise, the tree will get pot bound, sicken, and die.

Cultivating the Tao in our lives involves the wisdom of a master gardener. Self-respect requires time for regular tending. We must give ourselves the right amount of nutrients, fresh air, and sunshine and take time to study the pattern of our life, discerning the main branches from the unnecessary details. Every so often we must prune our roots, assessing our choices, renewing our priorities, making the necessary cuts to allow ourselves room to grow.

TAO EXERCISE

The Japanese train bonsai to affirm a threefold balance. The trees grow in an asymmetrical triangle with the highest point representing heaven; the lowest point, the earth; and the midpoint, humanity.

We can use this threefold pattern as a means to assess the shape of our lives. Ask yourself what you need to do to develop the three following areas. Does one of them need pruning or further cultivation?

- How do you affirm your *spirituality*—your connection with heaven?
- How do you affirm your *physical health*—your connection with the earth?
- How do you affirm your connection with *other human beings,* at home and at work?

TAO AFFIRMATION

Words are powerful tools for self-cultivation, subtly influencing our thoughts and choices. I discovered some interesting changes in my life when I put the word *respect* out where I could see it every day. When I brushed my teeth in the morning, there was the word on my bathroom mirror. I began to treat myself with greater respect, remembering to eat healthier foods and exercise more often.

Try it and see that happens in your life. Put the word *respect* out in front of you: on the mirror, on your calendar, on your desk at work. Feel the subtle influence of this powerful Tao affirmation.

Healing with Respect

Respect for other people has made one of my former students an exceptional doctor. In 1974, during my first year at Santa Clara, I had a bright young man named Randy Peoples in my freshman composition class. Randy excelled in his studies, but it was his response to a series of medical crises that determined the course of his life. When he was twenty, both his grandfathers died. Reflecting on the range of medical care his family had received—from the impersonal technicians to the supportive healers—Randy promised himself he would become a doctor who related to people with empathy and respect.

Randy graduated from Santa Clara University with a major in biology; got a master's degree in immunology at the University of California, Davis; and went on to Loyola University of Chicago's School of Medicine. We lost touch over the years. In 1991, he picked up my book, *The Tao of Inner Peace,* in a Chicago bookstore, called to say hello, and told me he'd be out for a visit. A few months later, there was a knock on my office door, and Dr. Randal Peoples, now a neurosurgeon, caught me up on what he'd been doing.

Randy has become a Tao leader in the medical field. Practicing medicine with respect, he "talks to people at their level"—both literally and metaphorically. Leveling with patients about their condition in words they can understand, he creates an atmosphere of trust. Instead of standing and looking down on his patients in their hospital beds, he makes it a point "to sit on the bed and see eye to eye with them." Randy says he's always the last familiar face his patients see before they go into surgery, and he's had many people reach for his hand and look into his eyes before they go under anesthesia.

Randy believes in telling people the truth about their condition, even in the worst situations. With something as frightening as a malignant brain tumor, he lets people know their options, reassuring them that whatever course they choose, he's there for them. "Either way," he says, "we're going to go down fighting, together, as a team."

As a neurosurgeon, in what is commonly known as the most coldly impersonal specialization in medicine, Randy's personal commitment is extraordinary. He developed this commitment through a personal initiation into healing.

In December 1991, as he was finishing his neurosurgical residency training, Randy got a frantic phone call from a family he knew in California. His friend Joe, who had visited him only the month before, now lay helpless in a faraway hospital, after breaking his neck in a freak accident in Maui.

With all his knowledge of trauma and spinal injuries, Randy knew only too well what this accident meant: His friend Joe, a young man so proud of his physical fitness, so dynamically alive, charismatic, and committed to living on the edge, now faced the grim prognosis of lifelong paralysis. Alone in his apartment, Randy sat down on the kitchen floor, put his head in his hands, and the tears flowed.

In what he considers part of his "final exam" as a neurosurgeon, Randy flew out on the next plane and went to his friend's bedside. His medical training and personal commitment were simultaneously put to the test.

Randy realized that the first few hours after trauma are critical. He checked to make sure that Joe's doctors had administered massive amounts of steroids to reduce spinal-cord swelling—a relatively new treatment. When he arrived, he found the hospital didn't have the "halo brace" used for broken necks, so he had one flown out and had to put it on his friend himself. He then had Joe flown back home to the University of California, San Francisco, Medical Center, where he could get better treatment, and then spent days by his friend's bedside.

Randy had learned all the technical details of trauma and spinal-cord injuries. Now he experienced the personal side, realizing, firsthand, "the anguish and discomfort of feeling so dependent." Joe had always been "the most *in*dependent, invincible person I knew," he said. The hours and days went by with his friend unable to move. A succession of nurses and doctors came and went, dozens of Joe's family and friends came to visit, and Randy remained by his side, sleeping on a cot in his hospital room. He was there to help his friend, who couldn't even roll over to keep from getting bedsores or perform the simplest functions like scratching his face.

One night, long after midnight, Joe told Randy that he wanted to die. "You know me. You know I don't want this. It's time for me to go," he said.

Randy had seen this happen with other patients, especially young men with spinal-cord injuries. He knew how closely mind and body are connected, that when people lost the will to live, they inevitably died.

"I knew he would die," Randy said. "I had seen it too many times." He sadly told Joe, "I know you'll die if you want to, but I'm going to miss you, buddy."

It was Christmastime, and beside the small Christmas tree in Joe's room, they started talking about their lives, about issues most young men never admit, not even to themselves. They looked back on their childhoods, examined the roots of why they lived as they did, why Joe had always taken risks and lived on the edge, why Randy had always worked so hard. The hours went by as the questions and insights came. They talked all night in what was a major catharsis for them both.

Finally, Joe said in a husky whisper, "Doc"—he always called Randy Doc—"don't think I'm queer or something, but . . . I really love you, buddy. I've decided I want to live."

And he did live, slowly regaining much of his function. Joe still uses a wheelchair; one arm and leg have partial function, he can drive, hold a job, and he was recently engaged to a woman he's known since high school. With wisdom and insight, Joe admits that the accident probably saved his life. Living on the edge would have killed him. Now he appreciates every moment of life from a much deeper perspective.

One month later, when Randy had begun his practice in Las Vegas, his grandmother called. She was having trouble with her vision. For the past few years, ever since his grandfather's death, she had become less and less active, and even her personality had changed. The family said that somehow she just wasn't herself. Randy spoke with her doctor and suggested a brain scan. When the test revealed a frontal-lobe tumor, her doctor asked Randy to tell her about it.

Randy did more than tell his grandmother. He flew her to Las Vegas and had his partners perform the operation, while he did the post-op care. It was weird, he admitted, seeing his grandmother as a patient, "with her head shaved and an incision from ear to ear." But she recovered and went back to being herself again.

These experiences, he says, "gave me the last push into being the kind of doctor I am with my patients."

Randy's vision of healing is holistic. He treats his patients with honesty and respect, seeing their illnesses or injuries as another step in the ongoing journey of their lives. And he celebrates their lives, staying in touch with many of them after recovery. Many former patients are in show business in Las Vegas, and one manages a sushi bar he visits often.

Drawing on his background in immunology, Randy emphasizes the crucial mind-body connection to his patients and gives lectures on "Healing and the Mind." In his own busy life, he makes time for friends and maintains his practice of physical fitness. While finishing his residency, Randy ran the Chicago marathon. In Las Vegas, he works out regularly at a favorite gym.

As a surgeon, he operates with precision and grace, making split-second decisions during critical operations. And he loves what he does. Constantly learning and living from the heart, Randy is a Tao healer who respects his patients and the evolving cycles of life.[11]

Political Healing

Healing with the Tao comes in many forms, but always begins with basic respect. In 1978, the world community took the first tentative steps toward peace in the Middle East, when President Jimmy Carter met with Anwar Sadat and Menachem Begin to negotiate the Camp David Accord.

With Carter as mediator, the two leaders had met for a number of days with no success. Begin was all packed up and ready to return to Tel Aviv, when he stopped to say farewell to his American host. Carter thanked him, wished him well, and asked to see some photographs of his grandchildren he'd mentioned earlier. Begin took out the photos and shared them with Carter and Sadat, who spoke about his own family as well.

Suddenly a flash of insight arose between Begin and Sadat, two men who had been bitter enemies for so long: There was something more valuable to them than the battle of egos, the history of terrorism, and the old animosities. Their children represented a future they were both willing to work for. Their love for their families, their common humanity, created a new foundation of respect. They sat down with Carter and negotiated the Camp David Accord, one small step on the torturous path toward peace in the Middle East.

Since he left the White House, Jimmy Carter has not retired from public life, but has exercised his moral leadership in many ways, building houses for Habitat for Humanity, witnessing elections in Latin America and South Africa, and negotiating an arms agreement with the North Koreans and a peaceful resolution of conflict in Haiti.

At a local press conference in 1988, I saw Carter's attitude of respect in action, as he responded graciously to a throng of insistent reporters. The light of kindness shining from his blue eyes was balanced by the power and clarity with which he articulated his principles. Rare in political life, his respect for others builds a foundation of trust, enabling him to move effectively through world trouble spots, as he does his own quiet work for peace.

By living with integrity and respect, people like Jimmy Carter transcend the darkness of conflict and confusion, holding out the light of hope, leading with the Tao.

CHAPTER 5

Yohaku

Thirty spokes meet at the wheel's axis;
The center space makes the wheel useful.
Form clay into a cup;
The center space gives it purpose.
Frame doors and windows for a house;
The openings make the house useful.
Therefore, purpose comes from what is there
Because of what is not there.

(Tao, 11)

An old Zen Buddhist legend tells of an accomplished young man who came to a teacher seeking enlightenment. The young man introduced himself, and the master poured tea. He spoke of his life and his achievements. The master continued to pour. As the man talked on, the tea spilled over the sides of the cup.

"Stop," said the young man. "Don't you see what you're doing?"

The old master smiled, his eyes twinkling as he replied, "You cannot fill a cup that is already full."

The young man was full of himself. To learn, to receive anything new, he would have to empty his cup. Likewise, as Tao leaders we must empty ourselves of preconceptions, suspend judgment, clear away the clutter of our minds. We must learn the vital lesson of *yohaku*.

Yohaku is the Japanese term for the "white space" or background in an ink painting. Adding balance to the whole, the empty space is as important as the image itself. *Yohaku* is a version of *yin,* the "empty space" so much a part of the Tao. In the quote that begins this chapter, it is the space at the center that makes wheels, cups, houses, and our own minds useful. The space of *yohaku* invites us to participate in the creative process, to draw on our imagination. *Yohaku* is the space of insight and creativity.

Yohaku: *the Key to Creativity*

Recent research on creativity has underscored the significance of *yohaku*. Researchers describe the creative process as a period of conscious work, then a pause, followed by another period of conscious work. They divide this process into four stages: preparation, incubation, inspiration, and verification. A writer, artist, or scientist first takes notes, makes sketches, or does preliminary research. Then he or she puts the work aside for a time and lets the unconscious go to work. A sudden insight occurs, followed by a period of recording, verifying, and fine-tuning.

It is the period of incubation—*yohaku*—which leads to the flash of inspiration. This period may be an hour, a day, a week, or longer, but it must occur to allow our unconscious minds to process the information and come up with new insights, inventions, and inspirations.[1]

Many creative minds of the past have benefited from *yohaku*. Samuel Taylor Coleridge wrote his poem "Kubla Khan" after awakening from a dream, Dimitri Mendeleyev awakened with a vision of the periodic table of the elements, Mozart's best inspirations came to him on solitary walks, and Friedrich Kekulé saw a vision of the benzene ring while dozing off before the fire.

When faced with a troublesome problem, the last thing most conscientious people can imagine is walking away from it. Yet taking a *yohaku* break and returning with a fresh perspective may be exactly what we need to discover the solution.

For compulsive workers, it seems hard to believe we can perform better by scheduling regular periods of *not* working. But this principle certainly holds true for physical exercise. Weight training is more effective when we rest our muscles for a day between workouts. A marathon runner I know alternates periods of hard training with light runs and takes a two-day break before a big race. Knowing when to exert effort and when to pause can help us become more effective leaders, bringing greater joy and renewal to our lives.

We can create more *yohaku* for ourselves by being mindful of the space around us, the way we spend our time, and how we use our senses. This chapter will show you how, adapting traditional Taoist principles to modern living.

Yohaku *in the Space Around Us*

The samurai of old Japan drew their esthetic of simplicity from Taoism and Buddhism. These philosophies stress the importance of staying centered in the present. It is difficult, if not impossible, to be centered when our consciousness is fragmented, our attention going off in many directions.

The Tao tells us:

> *If we had the highest wisdom,*
> *We would walk the path of Tao.*
> *The path of Tao is simple,*
> *Yet people take many detours.*
>
> *Foolish leaders indulge themselves,*
> *Leaving their fields untilled*
> *And their storehouses empty.*
> *They wear impressive clothes,*
> *Brandish sharp words and weapons,*
> *Are addicted to food, drink, and possessions.*
> *This is the road of excess,*
> *Not the way of Tao.*

(Tao, 53)

Following Taoist principles, the samurai lived simply and deliberately, believing that excess weakened the spirit. They did not clutter their lives with many possessions, nor did they waste anything. They practiced economy not out of financial need, but because they knew that discipline in small things builds strength of character.

Many people today could benefit from the example of the

samurai. Confusion, conflict, addiction, and feelings of power-lessness come from excessive self-indulgence, which dissipates our vital energy or *ki*. Wanting many things takes us away from our center, undermining our strength.

Like the samurai, Tao leaders maintain power by removing clutter, creating more open space, clearing our minds, and giving ourselves room to breathe.

TAO QUESTION

This week, look around and ask yourself: "How can I bring more *yohaku* into the space around me?"

Can you create more open space by clearing off your desk and work tables? (Do all those stacks of paper really need to be there?)

Organizing your work more effectively?
Delegating more of the paperwork?
Setting priorities?
Building in regular time for long-range planning?
Anything else?

Yohaku *in the Time of Our Lives*

For a number of reasons, many of us try to do too much. There are books for people who love too much, give too much, or work too much.

Ours is a society that keeps score. Recently, I've noticed my students talking about how late they stay up, how many hours they work writing a paper or studying for a test. They talk about how long they've worked more than about what they've learned. Like modern-day Cartesians, their motto seems to be, "I work, therefore I am." Many professors, as well, tell each other how many hours they spend grading papers or working on projects. Why? Do we believe that when the great recorder comes to write against our name, the hours we spent and the sleep we lost will make us win the game?

Tao leaders know that success is more than keeping score and that life is much more than accomplishments scattered on a résumé. They know the importance of open time and the lesson of focus.

Like a Zen archer, to be effective we must be focused. Our intention, like the arrow, must be aimed at one target, one goal at a time. When our minds are focused, we cannot miss the mark.

In the nineteenth century, Ralph Waldo Emerson wrote that "society everywhere is in conspiracy against the manhood of every one of its members." A student of Eastern philosophy, he recognized the thousands of daily temptations that threaten to pull us off course. Organizations, he believed, too often become authoritative forces that undermine our adulthood, reducing us to childlike subservience. "You will always find those who think they know what is your duty better than you know it," he warned.[2] Friends, family, colleagues, and corporate officers are always asking us to do things, important things, and we must make hard choices. Being Tao leaders means deciding for ourselves where to focus, where to aim our intention.

The Importance of Planning

In his books and seminars on leadership, Stephen Covey stresses long-range planning, helping people set goals and priorities for themselves.[3] Long-range planning enables us to be more creative, less reactive. Like *yang* and *yin,* creative and reactive are two polarities: one active, the other passive. When we're creative, we choose how to structure our lives. When we're reactive, life chooses for us.

Yohaku time does not just happen. Nature abhors a vacuum. Unless we consciously choose open time for ourselves, someone or something will invariably fill it up.

This is why setting goals and priorities is so important. As Tao leaders, we are, first of all, the architects of our own lives, building skills and character strengths that will help us make a significant contribution to the world around us. The habits we establish for ourselves give shape and substance to our lives. The *Tao Te Ching* tells us:

> *Frame doors and windows for a house;*
> *The openings make the house useful.*
> **(Tao, 11)**

When planning a house, architects naturally allow for doors and windows. When planning our activities, we must remember to allow for *yohaku,* the essential open space that allows our souls to breathe, our imaginations to soar, and our hearts to rejoice.

Facing Tsunamis: The Tidal Waves in Life

But sometimes, no matter how carefully we plan ahead, life hits us with a tsunami. When an unexpected tidal wave of demands and deadlines comes at us all at once, how can we keep our balance?

TAO QUESTION

When you face an impossible set of conflicting demands, you can cut through the confusion and see more clearly by asking simply: "If I *don't* do it, will it still get done?"

A friend recently had a conference to attend, a series of committee meetings, and a press deadline on her book. She could not possibly do everything in the time allotted. We used the Tao question. The conference would go on without her, and others could take her place at the meetings, but no one else could write her book for her. The choice was obvious.

Yohaku *as Deviant Behavior*

As a child growing up in the Far East, I learned to love contemplative time, finding a private place beneath a flowering hibiscus bush or climbing a flame tree to watch the changing panorama of the sky.

Sometimes we're all so busy that I wonder if some people really notice the sky. With its glorious clouds and colors, it is nature's masterpiece, a forever changing fresco right above our heads.

But in the context of industrialized society, *yohaku* is often perceived as deviant behavior. One summer, after graduation, a colleague and I took two students, Mike and Kelly, out to dinner to celebrate their accomplishments and Mike's departure for medical school. After dinner we walked across the parking lot to a nearby field to watch the sunset on that summer evening. The four of us stood by a fence near an open field watching the clouds change colors, the streaks of pink turning to gray. Gradually, the sky became a deeper blue, and the first few stars came out.

Suddenly, our reverie was broken by a uniformed security guard, who walked up and told us we had to leave. "You can't be here," he said. "You're loitering, and that's against the law."

I was amazed by the absurdity of his accusation. Loitering, literally spending time in idleness, is suspicious behavior in a society in which compulsive action and conspicuous consumption have become the norm. Standing in a field talking with friends and watching the sunset seemed innocent enough to me, but since we didn't want to be arrested, we went back to the car. I later reflected that Emerson and Thoreau, Robert Frost, and Lao-tzu would all be similarly accosted for stopping by a field on a summer evening. What is natural and what is normal are two different things in our fast-paced culture, but I will risk occasional censure to enjoy the serenity of a summer sunset and the enduring spirit of *yohaku*.[4]

Chanoyu:
The Tea Ceremony and the Practice of Yohaku

For centuries, the practice of *yohaku* has been part of the culture of the Far East, where the traditional tea ceremony draws its roots from Taoism. Legend has it that twenty-five centuries ago Lao-tzu's disciple Kwanyin gave him a cup of tea at the gate of the Han Pass.[5]

Tea was later adopted by Buddhists, who drank the beverage to stay awake during long hours of meditation. By the twelfth century, drinking tea had become a ritual. Monks shared a bowl of tea before a picture of Bodhi Dharma, founder of Chinese Buddhism.

Southern Buddhism, or Zen, highly influenced by Taoism, spread to Japan, and along with it, the tea ceremony, which developed into a highly ritualized art form perfected by the renowned sixteenth-century tea master, Sen Rikyu. The traditional Japanese tea ceremony, or *chanoyu,* was designed to produce harmony, respect, purity, and tranquillity.[6]

From the time of the samurai to the present day, busy Japanese leaders have found solace and serenity in the tea ceremony. They meet in a small tea house or *sukiya*. Only ten feet square, the traditional tea house, known as the "abode of vacancy," is a place of *yohaku*.[7] Bare except for one painting or piece of calligraphy, a single flower, and the tea utensils, the *sukiya* becomes a quiet sanctuary. People leave their cares and egos outside to focus on the simple ritual, the perfection of the present.

Before the ceremony, the host carefully cleans the *sukiya* and sweeps the garden path outside. *Misogi,* or purification, is an essential part of the process. Every item, every corner, is scrupulously scoured and scrubbed. Then, shortly before the guests arrive, the host sprinkles water on the path, which leads from the confusion of the outside world to the serenity of the *chanoyu*.

The guests enter the courtyard, carefully taking in the surroundings: the dewy path, the scent of pine needles, the stone lantern that marks the way. The samurai were required to leave their weapons on a rack outside the *sukiya,* for the tea house was a house of peace.[8]

The door to the tea house, only three feet high, requires guests to bend down in humility to enter. One at a time they come in, silently bowing and taking their places. The only sound is the water boiling in the tea kettle. The subdued light, the antique tea utensils and cups, the subtle colors, and the silence calm the mind.

The guests share a light meal and then the traditional green powdered tea. Every gesture is focused, no movement wasted. An exercise in tranquillity, the tea ceremony cleanses the senses. The overstimulation of the outside world is dispersed by the subtle fragrance of incense, the beauty of a single flower, the feel of the teacup, the taste of the tea. The silence is broken only by the humming of the kettle in the background. Together all these sensations focus the mind. Here is *tadaima*—only now.

The Power of Silence

Essential to the tea ceremony, silence clears away the clutter of the mind and focuses attention in the present.

Too often our Western minds are uncomfortable with silence. Anxious during these times of *yohaku,* we rush to fill the gaps with idle chatter. But the *Tao Te Ching* reminds us that

> *Those who know do not speak.*
> *Those who speak do not know.*
>
> **(Tao, 56)**

The Tao leader guards against idle chatter, knowing that actions and awareness are often far more eloquent than words.

Far from the serenity of the *sukiya,* we live in a busy, noisy world. There are cars, radios, telephones, television sets, and conversations all around us. Silence is hard to find.

Those who follow the spiritual traditions of Christianity, Buddhism, Taoism, and Hinduism have long observed the power of silent meditation. Monastics in different corners of the world have chosen lives of silent prayer. Silence can be an aid in the secular world as well. Gandhi kept every Monday as a day of silence to center himself for the demanding task of liberating India. If someone came to visit, he would write notes, but he would not break his silence.

What would it be like if we could keep regular periods of silence, perhaps take a solitary walk at lunchtime or a quiet run after work?

Creating Your Practice of Yohaku

Most of us cannot readily participate in a *chanoyu,* and loitering around town may not be the best way to commune with nature. Our employers would look dimly on our efforts to emulate Gandhi by taking a day of silence each week. But we can still create our own practice of *yohaku.*

Dr. Shu-Park Chan, professor of engineering and founding president of International Technological University in California's Silicon Valley, is also an accomplished artist. His art is his *yohaku.* He says: "Whenever I'm troubled by something, I set aside some time to paint. Once I concentrate myself on the strokes and making the painting beautiful, I can ignore everything else." Painting, he notes, "helps me keep my sanity and come back with renewed vigor."[9]

I find my *yohaku* in the garden. I like to watch things grow, from the tiny buds on my gardenia bush to the annual cycles of my peach tree and Japanese maple. Watering and tending my small plot of ground clears my mind. New insights come and with them a radiant sense of peace.

Wherever we find it, *yohaku* puts us in touch with the ineffable power of Tao. The *Tao Te Ching* tells us:

> *The greatest virtue seems unreal,*
> *And strength of character appears like folly.*
> *Great space has no boundaries.*
> *The greatest skill is developed gradually,*
> *The greatest music rarely heard.*
> *The great Tao is without form,*
> *Elusive, undefinable,*
> *Yet the source of all life.*

(Tao, 41)

TAO QUESTION

What is your practice of *yohaku?*

CHAPTER 6

Joy

Treasure this knowledge:
The Tao leader
Wears common clothing
And precious jade
Close to the heart.

(Tao, 70)

Those who walk the path of Tao know that joy is a vital source of power. It renews our energies as the gentle rain renews the land. It helps us cope with the pressures of our stressful lives. Joy releases tension, defuses conflict, and inspires and heals us.

The "precious jade" worn "close to the heart" is a joyous outlook, the sense that beneath all the surface difficulties life is still worth living, filled with moments of rare beauty. Keep this precious jade close to your heart and don't let anyone or anything take it from you. It is a vital source of your personal power.

The Energy of Joy

Have you every wondered how some people keep smiling as they tackle one demanding task after another? Their secret is just that: They keep smiling. Tao leaders deal with challenge and change without succumbing to exhaustion. The energy of joy sustains them.

Tao leaders remain calm and centered in the midst of a storm, moving with what often seems effortless grace. The energy of joy differs greatly from the energy of compulsiveness, anxiety, and fear that motivates so many people. Compulsiveness produces short-term results but ultimately wears us down.

I recall the intensity of my college years as my friends and I gathered for study sessions, fortified with coffee and cigarettes. We worked our way through term papers and finals, driven by adrenaline and caffeine. Then I'd always collapse after my last exam.

My sore throats and bronchitis attacks were so predictable that one quarter I went to the student health center before finals, asking for medicine because I knew I'd be getting a sore throat. "But you don't have any symptoms," said the nurse. "I will in a week or so," I said. "I thought I'd come in now while I have the time." When she refused to recommend treatment, I told her, "I'll be back." And I was. I knew how to study hard but understood nothing about holistic health and keeping my own system in balance.

Dealing with Stress

In the past three decades, our concept of health has changed dramatically. Whereas we once associated diseases with germs, fighting them with a succession of "miracle drugs," today we focus more on prevention and stress management. Recent research has found that up to 75 percent of all diseases are stress related.[1] Stress has been linked to everything from sore throats, colds, and flu to heart attacks, stroke, cancer, asthma, high blood pressure, muscular pain, migraine headaches, backaches, arthritis, ulcers, digestive problems, diarrhea, colitis, and insomnia.

The stress response served our species well in earlier times, preparing us for physical emergencies. As medical experts tell us, stress sets off an elaborate chain reaction in our bodies. A part of the brain, called the hypothalamus, sends a chemical signal to the pituitary gland, causing it to release large amounts of ACTH (adrenocorticotropic hormone) into our bloodstreams. The ACTH travels to the adrenal glands, causing them to secrete epinephrine (adrenaline) and norepinephrine, which prepare our bodies for fight or flight. Our hearts beat faster, our muscles tense up, our lungs expand, our pupils dilate, and our sweat glands become more active. To meet the immediate threat, our digestive and immune systems temporarily shut down.

But the chronic stress of modern living offers few opportunities for fight or flight. Our conflicts at home and at work are usually not physical. We cannot literally fight with our boss or a troublesome colleague, nor can we flee from a budget crisis, stressful deadline, or traffic jam. In such cases, our stress response works against us, wearing down our health and subjecting us to the constellation of psychosomatic illnesses mentioned earlier.[2] Diseases, such as arthritis, asthma, ulcers, colitis, and heart attacks, were rare in earlier, more rural societies.[3] Like environmental pollution, these disorders are caused by our high-stress modern civilization.

The Power of Positive Emotions

The Tao returns us to the way of nature, affirming our need for balance. If negative emotions, such as fear and anger, set off the stress response, then positive emotions should counteract it. This was Norman Cousins's theory in 1964, when he was beset by an incurable degenerative disease. "Is it possible that love, hope, faith, laughter, confidence, and the will to live have therapeutic value?" he asked.[4] Cousins went on to answer this question for himself in his account of his dramatic recovery, described in *Anatomy of an Illness*. Scientific research has since revealed the powerful interrelation of our emotions and immune system.

Taking a cue from medical research and real-life examples, this chapter explains how joy can relieve stress, renew our minds and bodies, and help us relate to others. You'll learn how the power of laughter can improve your health and overall effectiveness. Reinforced by examples from modern science, the ancient Taoist message of joy contains a valuable lesson for today's leaders.

Misogi: Rituals of Joy and Renewal

Facing an endless stream of challenges, we often get so caught up in the task at hand that we omit time for personal renewal. *Yohaku,* as was mentioned in the last chapter, is essential for restoring our creativity and peace of mind. Also essential are regular rituals of *misogi*.

The samurai of old Japan, who followed Taoist practices, knew that no matter how deep their loyalty to their liege lord, their first duty was to their own spiritual growth. Without a strong core of personal integrity, they could not function effectively and could not maintain loyalty to the cause they believed in. Thus, their daily lives were structured by rituals of empowerment. One of these rituals was an essential *misogi,* or cleansing practice: polishing their swords.

The swords of the samurai are legendary for their power and precision. They were made by swordsmiths who performed sacred chants while forging the many layers of tempered steel. Known as "the soul of the samurai," these swords were strong but mutable, requiring daily polishing, or they would rust in Japan's humid climate.

So it is with our consciousness, an essential tool in leadership. Like a samurai sword, our awareness can cut through layers of deception, clearing the way for new possibilities. But like the sword, unless our consciousness is given daily attention, polished and renewed, it will lose its edge or rust away from neglect.

Without regular *misogi,* leaders can overidentify with their roles. Becoming stuck in rigid adherence to duty and self-abnegation, their health suffers and their work becomes less effective. Exhausted and beaten down by routine, they cannot see new possibilities. *Misogi* brings us renewal, as well as greater vision and creativity. We live better and work better, empowered by the energy of joy.

EXERCISE AS *MISOGI*
The *Tao Te Ching* tells us:

> *The truth is often paradoxical.*
>
> **(Tao, 78)**

One such paradox is the renewing power of exercise. Many busy people think that they have neither the time nor the energy for regular exercise. Little do they know that exercise will give them *more* energy and focus, enabling them to make optimal use of their time. Research has shown that exercise makes us feel better, physically and emotionally, while counteracting the effects of chronic stress.

Aerobic exercise stimulates the release of norepinephrine and endorphins, both of which are associated with joy. Norepinephrine, excreted by the adrenal glands, produces feelings of euphoria and elation. Studies have found that running can increase norepinephrine levels up to four and a half times the norm. Endorphins are chemicals produced in the brain that suppress pain, help process sensory information, and produce deep feelings of joy and well-being.

Research has shown that regular aerobic exercise—such as running, swimming, dancing, playing tennis, or training in the martial arts—can produce a dramatic decrease in anxiety and depression. Exercise releases tension, counteracting the negative effects of stress with healthy physical exertion, relaxing our bodies, lifting our spirits, and sharpening our minds. Studies have found that people who engage in regular exercise are less affected by stressful challenges.[5] We can remain centered in the midst of challenging circumstances if we perform the *misogi* of regular physical exercise.

Tao Questions
What is your physical *misogi,* your exercise?
Do you perform it regularly?

If not, make a commitment to yourself to begin—this week. But don't be compulsive about it. Your exercise should be an enjoyable outlet, not another stressful obligation.

Start slowly. The *Tao Te Ching* reminds us that "a journey of a thousand miles begins with a single step." (Tao, 64) Step out—literally—with a program of running, jogging, or walking. Join a swimming club or sign up for an exercise class. Whatever you do, make your exercise fun and begin to feel more alive.

Many people like to begin their day with exercise. I'd rather exercise after work. If you're feeling tired and sluggish at the end of the day, exercise will relax and energize your body, polishing your mind and spirit.

I train in aikido three times a week, but lately this doesn't seem to be enough exercise. So on the days I'm not training, I've been swimming laps in my neighborhood pool. The first day I went to the pool, I felt like I was on vacation. To me, swimming doesn't feel like exercise. My body glides through the water, almost without effort, without impact, without working up a sweat. A half hour in the pool, embraced by the sparkling blue water, is like a moving meditation. I emerge relaxed, renewed, ready to read, write, or celebrate life.

Adrenaline Addiction

Too many people today are addicted to excitement. They rush from one adrenaline high to another, creating crises at home and at work to fulfill their need for emotional stimulation. I know because I've been there. I used to be drawn to people with problems. Charging to the rescue, empowered by the adrenaline rushing through my system, I put my life on hold to minister to their emergencies. Someone's car broke down repeatedly; someone else's abusive boyfriend was after her again, so she spent the night on my couch while I faced him down at my front door. Another friend had a fight with her neighbor, then called me at 3:00 A.M. in a suicidal depression. After leaving a dysfunctional relationship, I found all these friends in crisis, so I could continue the unhealthy pattern I'd set up. It's a wonder I ever made it through school.

Unconsciously, I was hooked on the adrenaline rush. On the

conscious level, I kept thinking I could help, that I could make things better for people by solving their problems. But the problems just kept coming, one after the other, until I got burned out from all the stress.

The Healing Power of Tranquillity

Studying the *Tao Te Ching* helped me find my center. I learned I could care without becoming a caretaker, that I could be responsible *to* people without being responsible *for* them. When I no longer needed the overstimulation of recurrent drama, some friends began to solve their own problems. Others drifted away to find new rescuers.

Eastern philosophy helps us substitute dharma—spiritual truth—for drama. We learn that "small is beautiful" and "less is more" as we appreciate the subtle but profound beauties and lessons all around us. The Buddhist term, *jaku,* means the awareness that extinguishes blind passions to bring tranquillity of spirit. The Tao helps us develop this tranquillity, the opposite of adrenaline addiction, telling us:

> *The traveler is drawn*
> *To good music and food*
> *But the Tao is much more subtle.*
> *Looked for, it cannot be seen,*
> *Listened to, it cannot be heard,*
> *Yet its power is inexhaustible.*

> **(Tao, 35)**

TAO QUESTION

Have you become caught up in adrenaline addiction, chasing after drama in some part of your life?

If so, what pattern does your drama take?

What payoffs, what hidden rewards are there for you? Do you use crisis as an excuse for not facing something?

Are you willing and ready to change this pattern?

Restructuring your life to include more time for personal renewal, more *yohaku* and *jaku,* will help shift your motivation from the energy of anxiety to the energy of joy. The *misogi* of regular exercise and meditation produces biochemical changes that can help create a healthy new pattern in your life.

The *Misogi* of Meditation

Abraham Maslow, one of the founders of humanistic psychology, said in 1962 that "the Taoists and Zen Buddhists . . . were able a thousand years ago to see what we psychologists are only beginning to be aware of."[6] The Tao brings us a vital shift in perspective, helping us transcend the limited values of competitive capitalism, returning us to the value of our own integrity and peace of mind.

> *The Tao leader practices detachment:*
> *While others are collecting things,*
> *I alone have nothing,*
> *In their eyes a fool.*
> *While they are clever, confident,*
> *I appear indifferent,*
> *Drifting at sea*
> *Without a compass.*
> *They march forward with purpose*
> *While I remain detached,*
> *Delighted by distant harmonies,*
> *Nourished by the source.*
>
> **(Tao, 20)**

Meditation, which helps produce this sense of detachment, also reduces the adverse effects of stress. As clinical psychologists have found, meditation produces the exact opposite of the fight-

or-flight response. Our breathing and heartbeat slow down, our blood pressure lowers, and our brain waves settle into the alpha pattern associated with deep relaxation.[7]

During the 1960s, two Japanese psychiatrists, A. Kasamatsu and T. Hirai, studied monks in a Zen Buddhist monastery. Connecting their subjects to an electroencephalograph, the researchers found that the monks' alpha waves rose dramatically during meditation and that the more Zen training the monks had, the greater the amount of alpha they could generate.[8]

In addition to altering our brain waves, meditation reduces our blood lactate level, which rises to unhealthy levels during periods of stress, fatigue, and anxiety. Some studies have even found that meditation is more refreshing and energizing than is deep sleep.[9] Meditators are better able to deal with life's challenges and crises. They are calmer, more centered, and less vehemently aroused by stress. More stable physiologically and emotionally, they see themselves less as victims and more as participants in an ongoing creative process.[10]

Meditation comes in many forms, from the ancient yoga sutras of Patanjali to today's updated versions. Some forms, like transcendental meditation (TM), assign a special mantram, a word chanted silently to oneself to relax and quiet the mind. Others, like the *misogi* practiced in aikido dojos, ask people simply to concentrate on their breathing, to slow down and let the healing waves of relaxation flow through the body and soul.

You can practice meditation right now, any time you step outside your active routine to follow your spiritual practice.

TAO EXERCISE: *MISOGI* MEDITATION

Set aside a private time and place for your meditation. It can be as little as fifteen minutes.

Make sure you won't be disturbed. Shut off the phone, close the door, and post a Do not Disturb sign if necessary. In time, your friends and family will respect your meditative practice.

Then, take a seat either on the floor or in a straight-backed chair, keeping your spine straight. Close your eyes and gently relax your body, focusing on each part as you slowly breathe *out* tension, breathe *in* peace—first to your toes, your feet, your ankles. Feeling your attention as a warm glow or seeing it as a golden light, gradually move it up to your calves, your knees, your thighs. Feel your muscles relaxing.

Breathing slowly and deeply, move your attention up to your abdomen, breathing in relaxation to all your internal organs. Now breathe in to your back, feeling the glow of relaxation climb up your spinal column, one vertebra at a time. Relax your lower back, middle back, shoulders, and neck, where so many of us store our daily tensions. Gently shrug your shoulders and move your neck from side to side. Feel your facial muscles relax. Open your mouth and yawn, releasing any tension there. Feel the relaxation move down your shoulders to your arms and hands, flowing from your fingers like golden rain.

Now, completely infused with the golden light of relaxation, breathe into your center, release that breath and feel the energy flow through your body. Remain this way as long as you wish, completely centered and connected, breathing in to your center and outward again to your world. Know that you are a center of peace, power, and joy.

When you're ready, open your eyes, stretch, and gradually return to your activities, empowered and transformed by this brief meditative vacation.

The Relaxation Response

Confirmed meditators practice at least once a day, but research has shown that structured meditation is not the only way to reduce stress. Harvard doctors Herbert Benson and Joan Borysenko found that not only traditional meditation but any activity that focuses our attention produces the "relaxation response," a natural pattern of renewal in the body.[11] This response is produced by the ancient Taoist and Buddhist practice of mindfulness, available to us whenever we slow down, pay attention, and live more fully in the present. This is the awareness at the heart of Tao, as immediate as our heartbeat, as close to us as our breathing, a natural gift of healing.

The more we incorporate a mindful practice into our lives, the more this joyous sense of presence flows into all we do. Some people practice traditional meditation, while others take quiet walks by themselves, tend their gardens, or spend time reading a favorite book. Whatever gives you that peaceful, expansive feeling of *jaku,* joy, is your meditative practice. Take time to do it regularly. It is vital for your personal health and effectiveness as a leader.

The Tao tells us:

> *Close the door,*
> *Focus your senses,*
> *Untangle the problem,*
> *Balance sunlight and shadow,*
> *Blend with the path.*
> *This is the way of Tao.*

(Tao, 56)

The Power of Attitude

Remember the old question, "Is the glass half full or half empty?" The difference is not in the glass but in our attitude. And to a great degree, our attitude determines our possibilities. Studying the *Tao Te Ching* helps us expand these possibilities, liberating us from limited vision by revealing nature's evolving patterns. We learn that

> *Through detachment, we see the larger patterns.*
> *Through compassion, we perceive the particulars.*
> *Their source is the same,*

Though they differ in name,
The mystery of life,
The infinite Tao.

(Tao, 1)

Coping with Change: Challenge or Catastrophe?

Following the Tao, we learn that life is dynamic, continuously evolving in cycles. Mindful of these cycles, we see change as a natural process, not a catastrophic threat to our security. This shift in perception makes a tremendous difference to both our immune systems and our success in life.

Researchers have found that a positive attitude reduces the severity of the stress response. When we see change as a meaningful challenge instead of a threat, we're more able to cope with it successfully.[12]

The ability to cope, the sense of being in charge of our lives, releases norepinephrine into our systems, creating optimism, euphoria, and a sense of well-being. In such cases, not only does challenge produce no adverse effects on our health, it can actually make us feel more vital, more fully alive.[13]

Optimism and Health

Our emotional response to challenging situations, whether positive or negative, is based on underlying assumptions about ourselves and our world. A fragile self-concept sets us up for reactive mood swings. If we define our sense of self-worth by external events and the approval of others, we're at the mercy of people and events.

Recent studies have found an amazing correlation between attitude and health. Psychologist Chris Peterson studied 150 college students at Virginia Tech.[14] Over the course of an academic year, he discovered that those who took negative events personally and globally (concluding that the problem was all their fault and would ruin their lives) got sick twice as often and saw doctors four times as much as did those with more positive attitudes.

A pioneer in this field, Martin Seligman, of the University of Pennsylvania, found that people perceive negative events in three ways.[15] They can explain them either (1) *personally* (feeling guilty and responsible) or *externally* (recognizing external causes), see the consequences as either (2) *pervasive* (ruining their lives) or *specific* (having more limited consequences), and consider the time frame as either (3) *permanent* (feeling "this always happens to me") or *temporary* (as a single incident).

To a great extent, our attitudes and expectations structure our lives. People who perceive negative events as external, specific, and temporary solve their problems and move on in life. Others feel personally defeated, seeing themselves as helpless in the face of life's challenges. In a powerful self-fulfilling prophecy, perceiving ourselves as victims actually makes us so. Furthermore, a sense of worthlessness and helplessness undermines our immune systems, making us more susceptible to disease and less likely to recover.

In a study of over 670 managers, University of Chicago psychologists found that leaders who faced stress with a positive attitude of challenge, commitment, and control remained much healthier than did their pessimistic counterparts.[16] Research suggests that a positive attitude can even slow down the aging process. In a thirty-five-year Harvard study, Chris Peterson, Martin Seligman, and George Vaillant found that optimists suffered far less from chronic degenerative disorders and lived longer, healthier lives than did their pessimistic peers.[17]

I've always been impressed by the youthful vitality of optimistic people. Etta Palmer, a remarkable woman in my church, just ran her 100th marathon. She's trim, attractive, vibrant—and in her seventies. A number of years ago I met Norman Cousins for an interview in his office at UCLA. Charming, witty, and energetic, he appeared about fifty. I found myself looking in disbelief at his official biography, which put him in his late seventies. Both these people radiated more energy than do some people in their twenties. The difference is in their attitudes.

The Healing Power of Joy

Joy renews us in wondrous ways. Norman Cousins told a story about his visit with Pablo Casals, then nearly ninety. Every morning at eight o'clock, he saw Casals emerge from his room, crippled and bent over with rheumatoid arthritis, breathing with difficulty because of emphysema.

As he watched Casals walk painfully across the room to the piano, Cousins said, "I was not prepared for the miracle that was about to happen. The fingers slowly unlocked and reached toward the keys like the buds of a plant toward the sunlight. His back straightened. He seemed to breathe more fully" as he played Bach's "Well Tempered Klavier" with precision and grace. Casals then rose, straight and tall, walked briskly to the kitchen, enjoyed his breakfast, and went out for a walk before tackling the day's paperwork.[18] Casals's love of music, the joy he felt in playing, filled his body and soul so completely that there was no room for pain or weakness. His daily ritual was a repeated demonstration of the healing power of joy.

The Tao of Laughter

The Tao is filled with playful paradox, beckoning for us to look beneath the surface of our "civilized" values and assumptions and to take our cue from nature, whose rhythms are often punctuated by arresting surprises. Conventional minds cannot understand these apparent contradictions for which the only response is laughter. We are told that

> *Without laughter,*
> *There could be no Tao.*

(Tao, 41)

Laughter is an essential part of our nature. As far as we know, it is unique to our species. It is a built-in relief valve for our highly developed frontal lobes, which make us so sensitive to life's ironies. The medieval theologian Thomas Aquinas said that the two defining aspects of human nature are being "reasonable" and being "risible"—being able to reason and to laugh.[19] In the Renaissance, Erasmus wrote *In Praise of Folly,* portraying laughter as a powerful coping tool. Throughout the ages, wise individuals have always known that we *need* to laugh to bring balance to our lives.

Laughter is healing. Norman Cousins told of his remarkable recovery from a rare and purportedly incurable collagen disease, ankylosing spondylitis, using his own regimen of vitamin C and therapeutic bouts of laughter. "I made the joyous discovery that ten minutes of genuine belly laughter had an anesthetic effect and would give me at least two hours of pain-free sleep," he realized, prescribing for himself a combination of humor books and films of old Candid Camera shows and Marx brothers movies. The laughter not only relieved his pain but significantly lowered his blood-sedimentation rate.[20]

For today's leaders as well, laughter is an important survival tool. Not only is it a better analgesic than aspirin, with none of the harmful side effects, but it also functions as a helpful preventive, reducing stress and warding off many psychosomatic disorders. It can help us make better decisions. Two Canadian psychologists, Rod Martin and Herbert Lefcourt, suggested that a sense of humor allows us to shift perspective, enabling us to distance ourselves from the stress of a problem, regain our equilibrium, and more readily discern solutions.[21] Research on stress has shown that the fight-or-flight response leads to poor decisions because it narrows our focus, reducing our ability to consider all the available options.[22] Laughter apparently provides the very release of pressure we need to see more clearly.

Like a Zen koan, humor snaps us out of our rigid thinking,

opening up our minds and stabilizing our emotions. Many of our nation's leaders benefited from the power of laughter. Their well-developed sense of irony helped them deal with personal crises and the weighty responsibilities of the presidency. Abraham Lincoln responded to his critics with a keen wit and folksy humor. Able to laugh at himself, he told people that if he ever met someone uglier than he was, he would "shoot the wretch and put him out of his misery." Lincoln spent many evenings exchanging humorous stories with a congenial circle of friends. He also frequented the theater, responding to his favorite Shakespearean comedies with laughter and witty comments.[23]

Franklin D. Roosevelt's courageous response to the crippling effects of polio gave our nation hope during the Great Depression and World War II. His fireside chats revived people's spirits with his invincible optimism. Roosevelt's wit and good humor served him well in many contexts. His White House staff and personal friends became an extended family with whom he shared meals and witty anecdotes. He used humor to distract people's attention from his disability and to deflect criticism. Turning on detractors with mock outrage, he accused them of criticizing him, his policies, his wife, Eleanor, and his little dog Fala. He said he and Eleanor could deal with the criticism, but that Fala had been very upset.

John F. Kennedy charmed reporters during his press conferences and adroitly defused criticism with his quick wit and congeniality. Revisionist historians have pointed out the flaws in Camelot, but more than any other leader in our time, Kennedy imparted a renewed hope and energy to this country. He did so, in large part, with his own vigorous optimism, which helped him cope with Addison's disease and recurrent back pain, as well as the many challenges of his presidency.

Kennedy once said at a press conference, "This is a damn good job," and he seemed to enjoy the challenge of high office.

He playfully bantered with the press. In response to a reporter's complaint when he read a prepared text and refused to go into further detail, he quipped, "I am not a textual deviant." After a demanding day, he often sat up with his friend Dave Powers, exchanging amusing stories and anecdotes.[24]

Enduring Joy: The Power of Social Support

The life patterns of these presidents demonstrate that even dedicated leaders cannot be on duty all the time. Our life is more than our work. If we overidentify with our jobs, we lose our perspective and fail to see new possibilities. If we never take time to relax and cultivate supportive relationships, we miss one of the most joyous aspects of life, as well as a powerful antidote to stress. Feeling loved, understood, and appreciated, being able to trust someone enough to share our concerns and frustrations, assures us that we are not alone in this world, no matter how insistent the demands, no matter how great the responsibilities, we face.

All leaders need someone to whom they can bare their souls, someone with whom they can share life's frustrations and celebrations. Remember the importance of companionship as you face your many leadership challenges. Lincoln, Roosevelt, and Kennedy had their circle of friends and family with whom they could be more fully themselves. We, too, can regain our perspective and find enduring joy in our inner circle.[25]

TAO EXERCISE: SMILING
This is probably the easiest Tao exercise in the book and the fastest way to lift our spirits. Meditation, exercise, and developing a personal support system take time. Smiling can be done anywhere, any time—right now.

The smile is a universal symbol, common to all cultures. We all know that people smile when they're happy. But research has shown that a smile not only results from positive emotions, but it can *cause* them. All those songs about smiling when you're feeling low actually bear some truth. Research psychologists have found that smiling sends a message to our brains to stimulate positive emotions. When people smile, they naturally feel better.[26]

Furthermore, smiles are contagious. When you smile at someone, chances are that person will smile back, beginning a whole new cycle of positive emotions, which reduces stress and improves his or her outlook on life as well.

Smiling can be an incredibly effective leadership tool. Encouraging people, smiling at them with a word of personal support, brings out the best in them. And there's nothing like the power of positive reinforcement.

In Japanese, the word for joy or delight is *yoroko,* a word that seems to convey the sound of rippling laughter. Whether you are smiling, laughing, or feeling enthusiasm or quiet serenity, the energy of joy is the most powerful motivator there is. Maslow saw it as one of the self-actualizing emotions.[27] It leads us to seek more than merely to satisfy our appetites, establish our security, or fulfill our material needs. Joy calls us to live more fully, to follow the Tao and walk the "path with heart," making of life not a task, not a duty, but a glorious adventure.

PART II

The *Yang* of Leadership in Action

CHAPTER 7

Building Community

The Tao leader creates harmony,
Reaching
From the heart
To build community.

(Tao, 49)

In an ancient Chinese fable, Han Fei Zi tells of one man who made outstanding arrows and another who made exceptional bows. Each man praised the excellence of his creation but accomplished no more until the master archer Yi showed them how to use the bow and arrow together to hit any target.[1]

The folklore of the Far East is filled with stories emphasizing the importance of community. Without community, we're isolated individuals, separate pieces, unable to reach beyond our own ability. As this fable demonstrates, by combining the bow, the arrows, and the skill of archery, we achieve a greater purpose. Such a vision of cooperation inspires the work of the Tao leader.

Community: The Leader's Responsibility

The Japanese word for community, *wa,* means unity of spirit or group harmony. In Japan, leadership has always meant responsibility for maintaining *wa*. This is why Japanese corporations spend so much time in elaborate dinners and social events with prospective business partners before they begin negotiations. Their American counterparts often grow impatient, shifting on their heels, checking their watches, wondering why it all takes so long. Used to negotiations in the West, they expect to fly to Japan, sign a contract, and leave in a day or two. With smiles and bows, their Eastern hosts tax their Western patience with elaborate socializing. But there's a reason. In the philosophy of the East, business is more than the exchange of goods and services: It's a relationship. The Japanese leader allows time to develop *wa* before signing any contract.

Group harmony is an archetypal value in Japan. This message comes through in a folktale my aikido sensei tells about the difference between heaven and hell. Hell is a vision of suffering and frustration. There, it is said, people are seated at a great banquet. Their fingers are bound up and tied to chopsticks, or *hashi,* three feet long. Angry, miserable, and emaciated, the people are surrounded by abundant food but are unable to feed themselves.

Heaven, by contrast, is a vision of delight where everyone has enough to eat. But the situation is exactly the same: the banquet, the bound fingers, the long chopsticks. The only difference is that in heaven, the people are feeding each other. Group harmony marks the difference between heaven and hell.

Transforming competition into cooperation, creating heaven from its opposite, Tao leaders promote group harmony in their organizations. They cultivate community much as a master gardener tends a meditation garden: by preparing the right environment, being mindful of group energies, and facilitating unity.[2]

A Common Place: Cultivating the Environment

As a good gardener prepares the soil, so a wise leader creates an environment that promotes community. In San Leandro, California, when Tom Melohn and Garner Beckett bought North American Tool and Die in the late 1970s, they made it a successful corporation within eight years by setting three corporate goals: to make a profit, to share the wealth with the staff, and to have fun. The second two goals helped them achieve the first by building a strong team spirit. The company became a community in which workers strive for quality and continuous improvement, celebrating their successes with monthly "Super Person" awards. Through free stock options, employees become joint owners of the company. They share coffee and doughnuts at morning meetings and can check out company trucks to use over the weekend.

Cultivating community has made North American Tool and Die a more successful company by anyone's standards. By 1990, when Tom Melohn left the company, it had grown by over 20 percent. Between 1990 and 1994, sales continued to increase by 25–30 percent a year. Quality also continued to improve, with the defect rate of 1,000 parts per million in 1990 dropping to only 50 to 200 parts per million in 1994. As this example demonstrates, greater community produces higher-quality products—as well as a greater quality of life.[3]

Another progressive leader, Jimmy Treybig, CEO of Tandem Computers in Cupertino, California, offers his employees flexible work hours and a health club on the premises. He hosts weekly Friday afternoon get-togethers, with popcorn, beer, and soft drinks, and gives people six-week paid sabbaticals to pursue personal growth or community service. In these two cases, and many more throughout the country, successful corporate leaders have realized that building community helps people work together more effectively, with increased personal and financial rewards.

Being Mindful of Group Energies

The Tao leader works with group energies. A staff member at an academic organization that works with department chairs told me at a recent conference how he got people to work together. "The leader provides the structure," he said. "Every group needs to spend a certain amount of time deciding they want to be a group." Sometimes a leader stays in the background, setting up a congenial environment. For example, on the morning of the conference, we were greeted with a table full of coffee, tea, sparkling soda, fresh fruit, yogurt, and muffins. Some time was set aside for people to introduce themselves, get their morning snack, and make themselves comfortable before the meeting formally began.

High-powered controlling leaders with a heavy content agenda consider such time wasted. But this open time was scheduled into the workshop. Before we began working together, it was important for us all to settle in and decide we wanted to be part of the group.

Careful planning, paradoxically, paves the way for greater spontaneity and group interaction. The Tao leader not only establishes a congenial environment—food helps—but sets agendas that open people up to participate. Essentially, the leader encourages members of the group to take responsibility. Taking responsibility is hard. People are reluctant to take responsibility because it means reaching out, taking a risk, and being vulnerable if they're later proved "wrong." Establishing a comfortable atmosphere, Tao leaders promote synergy, which gives people the momentum to take on greater responsibility. They get people working together, helping them to reach out and develop new plans of action.

A November 1993 article in *Time* magazine noted that in the 1990s, more women than men are starting companies; the 1992 incorporation statistics were 1.5 women to every man. As more women assume leadership roles, researchers say we can expect more decentralization of decision making, more community in the workplace. Nadja Aisenberg and Mona Harrington's extensive study, *Women in Academe,* showed that when women become administrators, they rely more on consensus and committees to help them make decisions.[4]

Faith Gabelnick, provost of Mills College in Oakland, California, calls this attention to group energies "a radical reframing of how we work together." A Tao leader in academe, she teaches professors to build community in the classroom, believing that "people learn through cooperation and consensus, making meaning together." With careful attention to group process, she has broken away from the old lecture method, in which the student is a passive recipient of information, and moved on "to get students to take up authority in the classroom." As in the foregoing example of the conference, she first establishes a comfortable atmosphere, setting up introductory exercises that she calls "preaffiliative activities." Then she gives people small-group assignments, emphasizing careful listening and attention to differences as they work to find solutions.

Gabelnick's small-group approach to solutions is shared by progressive corporations. Apple Computers relies on close-knit task forces to get the job done. Corporate leaders in Apple's Cupertino, California, plant set their goal of creating a new electronic message pad, then let engineering teams work out the details. For two years, the Apple Newton Group brainstormed, experimented, shared meals, and even pulled occasional all-nighters, bringing in their sleeping bags so they could continue the work in shifts. They assessed their progress periodically, redesigning the project many times before completing the Newton in summer 1993. Apple introduced the Newton at MacWorld in Boston on August 2, 1993, flying the teams there for the official project launching and celebration banquet.

Decentralize and Empower

As a familiar quote from the Tao reminds us:

> *With the best of leaders,*
> *When the work is done,*
> *The project completed,*
> *The people all say*
> *"We did it ourselves."*

(Tao, 17)

Whether in the world of computer corporations or higher education, the process of community building follows the same Taoist principles: decentralize and empower. The leader

1. gives the small group an assignment
2. gets the members to commit to a shared goal
3. has them agree on a way of measuring their progress
4. lets the team work out the details together, combining their differences to create successful results.

Instead of giving orders, the Tao leader works with group energies to facilitate solutions. Gabelnick offers a challenge to leaders in every field, asking "can you be a leader in terms of the *structure* of your group?"[5]

TAO QUESTION

How can you apply these principles of Tao to your own group?

Think of a new goal at work.

Design a Taoist structure to achieve it, planning how to get commitment from your group about

1. working together as a group
2. cooperating to achieve this goal
3. agreeing on a way to measure their progress.

Creating new patterns of cooperation, Tao leaders, men and women, draw on greater power and wisdom than the old top-down leadership pattern could offer. The more points of view included in a decision, the more possibilities that emerge and the more the potential for error is eliminated. Community involvement not only ensures greater quality control, it also builds greater commitment. The more actively engaged people are in making the decisions, the more committed they'll be to the actions that follow and the less they'll complain about the results.

Cultivating the Spirit of Teamwork

The *Tao Te Ching* tells us:

> *All life springs*
> *From* yin *and* yang
> *As they blend forever*
> *Into patterns of harmony.*
>
> **(Tao, 42)**

Aware of how *yin* and *yang* combine throughout nature, the Tao leader combines individual differences into new harmonies.

Team sports teach us this lesson of Tao. When I became chair of the English department at Santa Clara University, I'd been exposed to twenty years of hierarchical leadership in universities, preceded by another twenty years growing up as the daughter of an air force colonel. But I had also learned another way, long ago, as a ten-year-old child at Clark Air Force Base in the Philippines. Living on a tropical island had its exotic side. Bananas, pineapples, and papayas grew outside our door. But like most children back home, we played games—kick the can, hide-and-seek, and touch football. Touch football taught me a wonderful secret about leadership.

My neighbor Jim Foley would take our team into a huddle, discussing strategies and drawing football plays in the dirt with his finger. Leaning down, we watched the patterns emerge as we designed our next play together. All of us were important. We each had different talents. Some of us were little, but we could hand off the ball. Some of us were skinny, but we could run. Jim's hefty brother Pat couldn't run fast, but he was a great blocker. Everyone was important. Together we were a team, and together we could make a touchdown.

The Tao leader is mindful of group energies and abilities. He or she recognizes the diverse talents of the people in the group, combining them into an effective team to reach a common goal.

TAO EXERCISE
Stop for a moment and think about your team.

This team can be a department at work, a class you teach, a community organization, your family—any group with a common goal.

Think about the personalities involved, the people in your starting lineup.

Who's good at initiating projects? at kicking things off?
Who's good in the middle of a project? Who can you
  depend on to carry the ball?
Who are the idea people?
Who's good with details?
Who's a good offensive lineman, able to tackle problems and
  solve them effectively?
Who's good at going the distance? Who can you count on
  to finish the job?

When you begin your next project, make sure all the people on your team use their special talents to advantage.

Communication and Purpose

The Tao leader realizes that community involves a common place, a common time, and a common purpose. Just getting people in the same place at the same time does not produce a team. Community requires a common vision. In our touch football game, Jim's diagrams in the dust helped us see how we all fit into the pattern.

Community requires effective communication. To achieve

it, Tandem Computers has frequent unit meetings. The corporation involves a whole department in the hiring process, links all employees to an electronic bulletin board, and connects separate divisions through teleconferencing. Tandem's CEO, Jimmy Treybig, is on a first-name basis with the employees. He has a modest office with an open-door policy, and takes frequent walks around Tandem's Cupertino plant to keep up with what's going on.

Combining advanced technology and interpersonal communication, Tao leaders of the twenty-first century will stay in touch with their people. They will use better communication to help them make more effective plans, adjusting and changing when necessary.

Common Problems Can Be Powerful Resources

Lao-tzu tells us:

> The Tao is the source
> Of ten thousand things,
> The good person's treasure,
> The lesser one's salvation.
>
> **(Tao, 62)**

Tao leaders are resourceful, finding hidden opportunities in everything. They know that solving problems together can build a stronger sense of community. In September 1992, my department held a one-day retreat to address the five problems we'd been complaining about for years—everything from staffing to the lack of coherence between upper- and lower-division courses. By the end of the day, we'd assembled five task forces, one to address each issue. By December, the task forces had met repeatedly, brainstormed, and come up with proposed solutions. We voted on these proposals as a department, then met with the dean to ask for administrative support. The department not only solved some chronic problems, but by working together so closely, we also developed a greater appreciation for one another, a stronger bond of solidarity.

Leaders throughout history have realized that a common purpose can unite a disparate group, but all too often this common purpose has been a common enemy. Niccolò Machiavelli's *The Prince* tells how to use a common enemy to advantage, and Shakespeare's *Henry V* tells prospective leaders to "busy giddy minds with foreign quarrels," advice that all too often becomes a foreign-policy norm.

A common enemy can indeed unite people. In academic circles the faculty often unite against the administration. In business, labor can unite against management or people in one company can unite against the competition. But instead of uniting *against* some enemy, why not establish a more enduring bond by uniting *for* something? In the former case, when the enemy disappears, no common purpose remains. But when a group works together to achieve an initial goal, the members can build on it, moving on to future accomplishments together.

Tao Exercise
Ask yourself: "What can my group unite *for?*"
This is the Tao, the larger purpose that connects you all.

What will you do to help bring it about?
Do you feel energized by this thought?

If not, ask the first question again later.
If so, then share this thought with others. Brainstorm and take action, building unity and empowerment with the Tao.

Confucian and Taoist Communities

There are two contrasting concepts of community that are as old as the philosophies of ancient China: Confucianism and Taoism. Confucius taught that social harmony is based on the dutiful performance of social roles and conformity to external expectations. Lao-tzu saw harmony as being true to one's nature, resisting any such conformity. *Te* in the *Tao Te Ching* means character, or essential nature.

The Taoist sage Chuang-tzu tells of a prince of Lu who welcomed a lovely bird into his home and entertained it with an elegant banquet, fine wine, and classical music. But what was pleasure for a man was torment to the bird. In three days the bird died.[6] The prince killed the bird with kindness because he did not respect its nature.

A Tao leader respects the nature of everyone in the group, realizing that harmony comes not from repression but from the balanced *expression* of who we are. Leading with the Tao is inclusive and dynamic. Unlike Confucian leaders who treat their employees like military troops or machinery to be used, transferred, and moved around, Tao leaders relate to their employees as whole people.

The wisdom of Tao is holistic. Tao leaders recognize that the common good must involve the good of individual members or it is not the common good at all. Confucian communities make demands on people from the top down, inhibiting creativity. Tao communities emerge from the grass roots. Affirming a dynamic vision of life, Tao leaders emphasize growth and self-actualization, supporting the highest good of everyone involved.

In a Confucian community, a person feels obligated to attend prescribed "community" events. Small towns and churches frequently subject their members to Confucian duties and social obligations. For example, while trying to finish her new book, Peg is often interrupted by well-meaning neighbors who like to talk. Her church expects her to participate in the bake sale, teach Sunday school, volunteer in the office, and work at a fund-raising auction.

A Tao community would encourage Peg to grow and prosper. Instead of pressuring her to conform when she's up against a deadline, her neighbors could support her desire to write by respecting her privacy, perhaps even dropping off a casserole so she wouldn't have to cook dinner. At work as well, a Tao community does not expect us to conform to the same cookie-cutter roles, but encourages us to express our unique strengths.

Leading with the Tao means supporting everyone's personal growth and realizing that the collective must necessarily be the combination of everyone's individuality. Leading with the Tao during my first year as chair of Santa Clara University's English department meant supporting the professional growth of all my colleagues. At their annual evaluations, I asked them to set goals for the coming year and to propose strategies for reaching the goals. I also asked what I could do to help support them in reaching their goals.

The department flourished. Many people achieved new levels of accomplishment in teaching, scholarship, or service, and the department attracted a record number of students. But three part-time teachers left our institution, which had no full-time positions to offer them. Two women returned to graduate school to get their Ph.D.s, and one went on to a full-time tenure-track job in Los Angeles. With conversations, letters of recommendation, and phone calls, I supported their plans and celebrated their successes. The Tao reminds us that we are all part of a larger whole. My friends have gone on to enrich the field of education. To have stayed in their part-time positions when they needed to move on would have stunted their growth and left us all the poorer for it.

Rituals of Community

Every world culture has its rituals of community. Anthropologist Margaret Mead described the richness and variety of these rituals in the South Sea Islands. My Chinese and Japanese friends tell me of moon festivals and Lunar New Year celebrations, many Jewish friends observe the Passover seder, and some Italian friends make nearly every meal a celebration. Literary scholar C. L. Barber used to explain how Shakespeare's comedies end with a wedding or a feast, a formal ritual of unification.[7] These concluding celebrations are no coincidence. The spirit of community heals us by reuniting us with ourselves and one another.

Whether with holiday meals, ritual banquets, or more casual fare, feasting together has always been a ritual of community. When I was in graduate school at UCLA, my women friends and I celebrated each other's birthdays together in nearby Westwood Village. With congeniality, laughter, and surprises, we treated each friend to a festive luncheon on her special day, which proved to be a renewing occasion for us all, a sudden holiday amid the demanding routine of classes, papers, and exams.

Tao leaders make effective use of feasting and ceremonies to build community at work. Apple gave the Newton Group a banquet in Boston, but community feasting is not always such an elaborate undertaking. Our department celebrates the beginning of each academic year with a "New Year's brunch" of fresh fruit, orange juice, bagels, and pastries in the department office. People gather around the buffet table, sharing greetings, anecdotes, and plans for the year ahead.

TAO EXERCISE
Ask yourself: "What ritual feast can I create for my group? What will I celebrate?"
Visualize your group experiencing this feast.
What will you need to bring this feast about?
Make your plan and make it happen.

Community as Security in a Changing World

The *Tao Te Ching* tells us:

> *Without the One, the heavens would fall,*
> *The earth would die,*
> *The spirits would mourn,*
> *The valleys dry up,*
> *The ten thousand things perish,*
> *The leaders fail.*
> *Therefore, wise leaders depend upon their people,*
> *Without whom they are lonely exiles.*
> *When the parts are separated,*
> *There can be no harmony.*
> *Do not think yourself precious jade,*
> *But wind chimes made of stone.*
>
> **(Tao, 39)**

When we follow the Tao, we know that we are not alone. We're part of the oneness of life. When we recognize our oneness with nature and when we're part of a supportive team, we no longer cling to a rigid status quo. In his classic text, *Leadership and Motivation,* Douglas McGregor explains how community in the workplace provides people with a strong sense of security.[8] With community, we become more creative, more willing to take risks and try new projects. The Tao of community helps us become more adventurous and more productive.

A Community of Learners

Mitch Saunders, director of programs for California Leadership, consults with public and private agencies to promote new patterns of decision making. He says that more attention to group work, collaboration, and shared governance is changing the way we perceive ourselves and one another. "It's part of the belief that I'm not an island," says Mitch, a recognition that we are all part of the larger whole that hearkens back to the Tao. Mitch mentioned a group of physicists involved in a research project. "All fifty of them signed their names on a landmark paper because they so deeply appreciate the collective inquiry that informed their individual insights. That articulation is rooted in a community of learners."[9]

"A community of learners" is a vital part of leading with the Tao. Together we can discover what none of us could find alone. In 1991, California state legislator John Vasconcellos put together a group of legislators and business leaders to come up with innovative solutions to California's economic problems. The group's report, published in 1992, explains "that traditional ways can no longer suffice in today's complex global economy. Neither the standard stereotypical Republican *laissez-faire* model nor the standard, stereotypical Democratic command and control model works any more. . . . We learned that only a third force—the way of trust, partnership, and collaboration—offers us any hope for our future."[10]

The Vital Lesson of Community

We all have our stories of community, memories of a time when we felt our lives enriched by participating in a vital group. My friend George Sullwold used to tell about the time he and his colleagues at St. John's College in Shanghai were imprisoned in a Japanese internment camp during World War II. "We couldn't do anything about the food and living conditions," he said, "so we concentrated on our studies." With their precious few books and active minds, the professors and students taught each other courses: Latin, Greek, history, geography, theology, poetry, and drama, whatever someone wanted to learn and someone else could teach. In their simple bamboo shelters, they created an academic utopia. They had poetry readings, philosophical discussions, and plays. In fact, George would say, with a tinge of regret, that they were all ready to perform Shakespeare's *Twelfth Night* when the camp was liberated and the war was over.

George returned to the United States and taught at American universities for the rest of his career. But he always said that his internment had been "the best time of my life." Why? Certainly not for any of the reasons we commonly equate with success: fame, fortune, or material comfort. No, it was the close-knit community who saved one another from despair by continuing to learn together. It was the community forged in crisis that provided the vital connection we all require to become more fully realized, more fully human.

TAO QUESTIONS
What is your story of community?
What lesson does it hold for you?
How can you apply this lesson to your leadership role?

As Tao leaders, we know that the power of community can release a tremendous force for creativity and innovation. It offers us a new form of security amid the challenges of our complex world. With community we become part of a dynamic team, exploring new possibilities together. Learning together, living together in new and vital ways, we lead into the future with the collective power of Tao.

CHAPTER 8

Vision, Empowerment, and Growth

Can you lead your people
Without seeking to control?
Can you open and close the gates
In harmony with nature?
Can you be understanding
Without trying to be wise?
Can you create without possessiveness
Accomplish without taking credit,
Lead without ego?
This is the highest power.

(Tao, 10)

Many Americans are complaining about a crisis in leadership. But throughout our history, whenever we've faced challenging times, strong leaders have emerged to help us meet the challenge. Our country was founded by leaders like George Washington, Benjamin Franklin, and Thomas Jefferson. The signers of the Declaration of Independence were courageous individuals who pledged their lives, their fortunes, and their sacred honor to their new vision of government.

The dark days of the Civil War brought us Abraham Lincoln and the two great generals, Ulysses S. Grant and Robert E. Lee. The twentieth century brought not only political and military leaders but the lone eagle, Charles A. Lindbergh, whose solo flight across the Atlantic led us into a new age of aviation. The Great Depression brought the courage and creative vision of Franklin and Eleanor Roosevelt. During World War II, strong leaders arose on both sides of the conflict, with Roosevelt joined by Winston Churchill, Charles de Gaulle, and strong-minded military leaders, including General George S. Patton and Field Marshal Bernard Law Montgomery. The turbulent 1960s brought America into new frontiers. But our leaders, John F. Kennedy, Robert Kennedy, and Martin Luther King, Jr., fell to assassins' bullets, and we haven't seen the likes of them since.

The current crisis in leadership is part of a larger paradigm shift, a redefinition of power at almost every level of life. Our leaders aren't like they used to be because leadership itself is changing. As California Assemblyman John Vasconcellos said, "We won't have a healthy society because somebody—whether it's Ronald Reagan or John Kennedy—comes riding a white horse and tells us how we ought to be."[1] We must find that power of leadership within ourselves.

The *Tao Te Ching* teaches that we are all leaders. If you're reading this book and dealing with the issues it raises, you're a leader. Some of us exercise leadership in our careers, and some of us do it in our homes and neighborhoods, in grassroots political action or community work. Together, we represent a new form of leadership that is re-creating the world as we know it.

Whatever your field, leadership is a matter of vision, empowerment, and continuous growth. It involves courage and strength of character. Who we are ineffably imprints on what we do. The many small choices we make each day add up to a major difference in the world around us.

Exercising Leadership

At a recent leadership conference in Idaho, my friend Dr. Liahna Babener asked a crucial question. Throughout the conference, we'd heard two competing concepts of leadership: (1) the leader as facilitator and (2) the leader as decision maker. What does it really mean, she asked, to exercise leadership?[2]

In the old definition, the leader led the charge and people followed. The more progressive leader is expected to facilitate decisions, to develop a consensus. Yet both polarities blend into the Tao leader's approach, which combines the *yin* and *yang* of vision and empowerment.

Leaders are in a better position to see the overview, to recognize how their units function as a whole. Vision gives their actions direction and focus. But Tao leaders don't impose their vision on the group, acting like Moses did when he brought the stone tablets down from Mount Sinai, although many administrators and CEOs still mistakenly do just that. As Tao leaders, we don't dictate but *direct* the vision-making process, sharing it with others to obtain their advice and commitment. This is the process of empowerment.

The Importance of Vision

A friend tells an anecdote about the importance of vision. An aviation emergency occurred involving the pilot of a private plane and four passengers: the president of the United States, the smartest man in the world, a hippie, and a priest. The pilot announced an unavoidable crash, took his parachute, and bailed out. This left only three remaining parachutes for the four passengers. The president, citing executive privilege, grabbed one parachute and bailed out. The smartest man in the world made a self-serving reference to the bell curve and did likewise. This left the hippie and the priest, who said, "My son, I am prepared to make this sacrifice. Take the parachute with my blessing." The hippie smiled back and said, "That's OK, father. There's one for each of us. The smartest man in the world just grabbed my backpack and jumped out of the plane."

As the Bible says, "Without vision, the people perish"—in this case, literally. Intelligence by itself is not enough. The Tao reminds us to

Be aware of small things
And develop great wisdom.

(Tao, 52)

Studying the Tao makes us more aware of the patterns in the world around us. We see how the parts relate to the whole.

Leadership expert Warren Bennis blames America's recent economic decline on our unwillingness to consider the larger picture. According to Bennis, we've become a nation of short-term thinkers, who have developed a "national obsession" with making a quick profit.[3] Neglecting vital research and development and concentrating only on short-term gain inevitably lead to long-term loss. We must become more conscious of whole systems.

Our Greatest Natural Resource

A few years ago I interviewed Norman Cousins in his office at UCLA. We spoke of many things, from holistic health to international conflict resolution—all involving a Taoist vision of whole systems. To illustrate a point, he said with a smile, "The greatest natural resource of the Japanese people is their minds."[4] An island nation with little land mass, limited agricultural potential, and few minerals, then devastated by bombings during World War II, Japan became a world economic power in a single generation through vision and hard work. Total Quality Management, based on the Taoist principles of whole systems and continuous growth, revitalized the country's economy.

The Tao reminds us that the greatest natural resource of any group or individual is our consciousness: our ability to learn from experience, to look to the larger patterns, and to discover new solutions.

TAO EXERCISE: *YIN* AND *YANG*

At workshops, I often give people a Tao exercise designed to stretch their minds, to develop their vision of larger patterns. You can try it yourself.

Find one larger concept that includes each of the two polarities listed next:

Earth   Sky
Listen   Speak
Open   Closed
Water   Stone

(For some common responses, see note 5.)[5]

Now that you've done the first warm-up exercise, find two polarities in your life and think of a concept that includes both of them. Doing so will give you new insight into your current situation.

At a recent workshop in Monterey, California, a woman

asked me, "What is one concept that includes both yes and no?" I thought for a moment. "Priorities," I said. "You have to say no to one thing to say yes to something else." I thanked her for the insight, a valuable reminder I needed as well.

Leaders as Pathfinders

The Tao leader is a pathfinder whose vision reveals new directions. When people want to get from here to there, the leader helps them chart the course. Phyllis Roth, dean of faculty and acting president of Skidmore College, said recently that a leader is someone who can "convert a problem into an opportunity. Learn to make it happen. Figure out multiple ways to get to your destination." She reminded today's leaders to "hold onto the thought that you're doing tremendously important work."[6]

Where another person sees problems, a leader sees possibilities. Janet Constantinides, chair of the English department at the University of Wyoming, combines vision and resourcefulness. During a recent budget crisis, instead of focusing on what her department couldn't do, she asked, "What areas *do* we have control over?" thereby improving both her program and her department's morale.[7]

Leaders must have the courage to follow their vision, to believe in the invisible, to work for something that's still only a possibility, while others often wring their hands in despair.

Psychologist Rollo May called this "the most important kind of courage." He said, "In our day, technology and engineering, diplomacy, business, and certainly teaching, all of these professions and scores of others are in the midst of radical change and require courageous persons to appreciate and direct this change."[8]

The Inner Leader

Leading with the Tao begins with our own personal vision. In leadership handbooks from the Renaissance to the present day, one thing that has marked leaders has been sovereignty over their own lives. Leaders are not buffeted about by circumstance. They make what *is* into what *might be,* transforming challenging situations by means of courage and insight.

Your Personal Mission Statement

Insight is a quality we can cultivate. Leadership consultant Stephen Covey asks people to exercise greater leadership in their lives by writing a personal mission statement.* Busy as we are, it might seem strange to spend time examining our values and priorities. But, as the Tao reminds us, life is a journey. If we don't chart our course, someone else will surely do it for us.

Set some time aside this week to begin your personal mission statement. It needn't be long and it needn't be a final draft. What it *should* be is one to three sentences telling who you are and what you value in life. Include your career but don't limit yourself to that. Remember to add what you value in your personal life. Here are some questions to get you started:

- What three things make you feel happy, centered, and most strongly yourself?

- Is there one word that stands out for you? A friend of mine came up with the word "freedom"—freedom to learn, to grow, to become more of who she wants to be.

- Think of someone you've always admired. What quality do you most admire in that person? Is this something you'd like to develop more of yourself?[9]

---

*Copyright © 1989, Simon & Schuster, *The Seven Habits of Highly Effective People,* by Stephen R. Covey. All rights reserved. Used with permission of Covey Leadership Center, Inc., 1–800–331–7716.

Fidelity to Your Vision

In Japan, the pine tree is the symbol of fidelity. Throughout the changing seasons, its branches remain green. Your personal mission statement can help you remain faithful to your values.

Tao leaders make their decisions by deliberation, not by default. They know whether a particular action is consistent with their goals. My friend Jerry Lynch, a writer and consultant with a private practice in sports psychology, has a multifaceted life. He's a husband, a father of three active boys, a busy professional, and a competitive runner. When faced with a decision about how to spend his time, he asks a question he learned from Sam Keen, "Does this fit skintight over my spirit?"—his way of saying, Is this consistent with what I value?[10]

You can tell when something fits your spirit and when it doesn't. What does energizes us, what does not exhausts us. In 1994 I was invited to represent my university at a regional conference on higher education. A group of us flew to Los Angeles for a weekend of nonstop meetings. The sessions were well organized, and the topic was important. But I felt tired and restless. My mind kept wandering back to the green hills where I spend Sundays at home. I asked myself, "Why am I doing this?" and I realized that I'd attended the conference out of duty, not because I really wanted to be there. My waning energies gave me away. The event did not fit skintight over my spirit.

Developing Your Group Vision

Leaders are called on to see for the group, to facilitate group vision. But it's important to ask where this vision comes from. Tao leaders, aware of patterns and process, sense what is emerging; they don't impose their will on a group and call it vision. Steve Privett, Santa Clara University's academic vice president, describes the leader as being able to "resonate with the *sensus fidelium*" of a group. Any group has a sense of who it is and what it values, but this sense often remains beneath the surface. A wise leader can discern these unspoken beliefs and articulate them. Sociologist Chuck Powers, who studies new forms of leadership, says that good leaders can "see the group vision, reveal to people what they are in a deeper and fuller way."[11]

Cultivating this vision requires effective time management. We cannot see far if our schedules and desks are cluttered and our days are filled with crises and interruptions. Tao leaders carefully plan their schedules to allow for a balance of routine work, research, consultation with others, and long-range planning.

TAO EXERCISE: LEADERSHIP TIME

How does your schedule look? Do you just let things happen, or do you cultivate your time carefully?

Take a cue from successful people and block out at least one hour of "leadership time" every day to devote to long-range planning. If you work at home, monitor your calls. At the office, tell your secretary to work around these blocks of time, holding off phone calls and appointments.

Try this practice for a month and see if it gives you greater vision and perspective in your life.

Communicating the Vision

A leader not only cultivates a collective vision but also communicates it. Public speaking is one way to do so. Many political leaders have been inspirational speakers. Winston Churchill, Franklin D. Roosevelt, John F. Kennedy, and Martin Luther King, Jr., are some powerful examples. They sensed their people's dreams and eloquently articulated them.

As a leader, you owe it to your people to speak well—not to parade your ego in front of them, but to cast the vision for your group. You're their representative, their spokesperson. Certain public occasions—beginning a new project, facing a serious challenge, celebrating the completion of a project, commemorating someone's retirement—require a leader to speak for the group, to underscore the significance of what you're doing together.

There are many ways to develop your public-speaking ability. One way is to take a class at a local community college. Another is to find good role models. Read biographies and speeches of people you admire and keep a collection of motivational quotes and stories. If possible, listen to recordings of famous speeches. Notice the pacing, the effective use of repetition, the passionate commitment that touches people's hearts.

Leading by Example

Words alone are not enough. Too often, people become suspicious of slick public relations efforts, wondering if any substance lies beneath the surface. The most enduring way to communicate your vision is to live it.

As her husband's valued partner, Eleanor Roosevelt led by example, eloquently living her vision of social justice. In 1936, she invited Marian Anderson to sing at the White House. In 1939, when Howard University tried to arrange a concert for Anderson in Constitution Hall, the Daughters of the American Revolution said that no African American could perform there. Eleanor Roosevelt immediately canceled her DAR membership and arranged for Anderson to sing at the Lincoln Memorial.

That night, Marian Anderson's dignity, her voice, and the setting were magnificent. With a gesture of her hand, a hush fell over the crowd of 75,000 people. She began her concert with "America." Her powerful voice rang out above the multitudes, "My country 'tis of thee, sweet land of liberty / Of thee I sing"—a musical affirmation of human dignity and liberation. Leading by example, each in her own way, these two women transcended small-mindedness and bigotry, affirming the triumphant beauty of the human spirit.

Vision and Empowerment

The Tao repeatedly affirms leadership by empowerment. When a project is completed, "The people all say, 'We did it ourselves.'" (Tao, 17) How different this form of leadership is from that of the authoritative, controlling leader who treats people like children and tries to take credit for everything.

Leadership expert Douglas McGregor explained that these two concepts of leadership are based on opposing definitions of human nature. In "Theory X," people are perceived as basically lazy, so they must be controlled and closely watched to get the work done. "Theory Y" assumes that people can be trusted to meet a challenge and do their best without excessive supervision. This theory is similar to Abraham Maslow's concept of self-actualization, which defines human beings as forever striving to learn, to grow, to develop their potential.[12]

These two theories about human nature and the nature of leadership have alternated over time. According to Mitch Saunders, director of programs of California Leadership, for the past two centuries, "life for most westerners has been built around the industrial factory model." Organizations have become like big machines with the leader doing all the thinking and the workers expected to follow orders. This model parallels the military system in which the officer gives orders and soldiers carry them out. As Mitch reminds us, however, "in some contexts, a command and control style of leadership *may* be the most appropriate approach. For example, if my house were burning, I wouldn't want the firefighters to conduct a dialogue once they arrived at the fire."[13] A crisis demands immediate action, and someone must take charge.

But most of the time we are not in a crisis and could benefit from the more inclusive leadership of Tao, trusting the people closest to the work to make the best decisions. Habitual over-controlling debilitates people:

The more rules and restrictions
The weaker people become.

. . .

Therefore, the Tao leader
Does not give orders
And the people lead themselves;
Keeps a peaceful heart,
And the people achieve harmony;
Does not control,
And the people prosper;
Remains detached,
And the people find
Their own centers.

(Tao, 57)

Leadership Teams

In matters of governance, Zen monasteries have always followed the Tao. The monks share daily work and decision making, organizing themselves into cooperative teams. In Zen there is no hierarchy or elitism. Elders are respected, but they do daily manual labor alongside the newest members.

In today's business world, organizational patterns hearken back to Zen monasteries, although more for economic than for philosophical reasons. Amanda Fox, senior vice president of an executive search firm in Fort Worth, Texas, says that economic layoffs have pared away the layers of middle management, leaving many workers to manage for themselves in self-directed leadership teams.[14]

Leadership teams encourage flexibility. Instead of staying in the same role, one person may play many positions. A colleague of mine characterizes this new form of leadership as a shift from the game of baseball, in which a team member occupies a set position on the field (like first base) to the shifting movements in basketball as the team moves the ball down the court.[15]

Combining the talents and insights of many people in leadership teams is what has become known as Theory Z. The Japanese character *kyo* (to be in harmony) combines the character for "strength" repeated three times together with the character for "ten." The harmony of many people working together multiplies our power, with resulting dramatic improvements in quality and productivity. At a General Mills cereal plant in Lodi, California, productivity increased by 40 percent with the advent of leadership teams.[16]

Exercising the New Leadership

Leadership teams can produce impressive results, but shared governance takes time. People still expect leaders to be decisive, to get things done. Otherwise, they accuse them of weakness and waffling. As leaders, how do we balance empowerment with decisiveness?

The answer lies in being decisive about the goal, selecting a talented team, and then trusting them to run with the ball and get the job done. The Tao leader does not micromanage.

Selecting your team is an art in itself. Who will do what? In any group you'll have a variety of talents. I sometimes see my department as the New York Philharmonic. Some folks are the rhythm section; some are the strings; some are the woodwinds; and others are the brass section, who can overpower the rest if you let them. The trick is to recognize the diverse talents, give the right part to the right musician, and bring all the musicians together to create harmony. A Tao leader must be a good judge of character.

Exploring New Territory Together: A Tao Leader's Action Plan

Once you've selected your team, it's time to set up an effective action plan. The following guidelines will help you get started:

1. *Deliberation:* What are the options? This is the time to communicate and get everyone's input.
2. *Decision:* What do we want to do? Set your goal. Goal setting can be done in one of two ways: Either the team comes up with a goal, or the leader introduces a goal to the team, asking for input and support.
3. *Commitment:* Get your team to commit to the goal and come up with a path to get there. Write down your goal. You may want to post it in a prominent place to keep everyone on track.
4. *Assessment:* Check in along the way. Is the plan working? Do we need to make any midflight adjustments? Modify your plan if necessary.
5. *Completion:* Complete your project and celebrate with your team.
6. *Reflection:* Ask yourself: What did we learn? What's the next step? The end of one cycle leads to the beginning of the next.

Facing the Unknown

Today's leaders are pathfinders, doing things they've never done before. It's only logical that if we've never done something before, we don't know exactly how to do it. So how do we exercise leadership when we don't know what we're doing?

One way—the wrong way—is to fake it. Some leaders shroud themselves in pretense, acting like they know what they're doing. Many people are taken in by appearances, unable to discern fact from fiction, playacting from real life. John Wayne was such a convincing actor in movies like *Flying Leathernecks* that many people believed he was a World War II hero. They named Orange County Airport "John Wayne International" in his honor. But John Wayne actually spent the entire war in Hollywood, exempted by marriage from military service.

Unlike Niccoló Machiavelli's *The Prince,* which tells leaders to dissemble and manipulate people, the *Tao Te Ching* tells us to look for the truth beneath the surface:

> *Truthful words do not flatter.*
> *Flattering words are not true.*
>
> **(Tao, 81)**

Because of all the posing, posturing, and public relations packaging, people are becoming increasingly cynical about their leaders. Words and images are not enough to sustain our faith. While insecure, childlike individuals fall prey to demagogues, adults would rather have a leader who levels with us, someone we can trust.

Integrity and good process skills mark a Tao leader. People don't expect a pathfinder to have a preconceived map of the unknown territory. However, they *do* expect him or her to have the tools and strategies to get them to their destination.

A Politics of Trust

The Tao tells us:

> *If we never dare to trust others,*
> *We will not be trusted.*
>
> **(Tao, 17)**

Progressive leaders emphasize this issue of trust, asking "How can we develop a politics of trust instead of the politics of power?" One way is to involve the stakeholders in the decision-making process. To paraphrase the Tao: When "we dare to trust others, others *will* trust us." Another way to build trust is to be consistent, to "walk our talk," to make sure our actions and procedures reflect our values. If you give speeches about shared governance and consensus and keep on making unilateral decisions, you're not a Tao leader.

Procedures can conflict with stated values when leaders encourage people to work in teams, but their companies' reward structures still reinforce competition and individual effort. Last year Peter Facione, the dean of Santa Clara University's College of Arts and Sciences, came up with a new idea, Collaborative Grants for the Common Good, which rewards team projects. Now instead of merely talking about cooperation, our college tangibly supports it.

Another way a procedure can conflict with stated values is to hand down a "truth" from on high that's supposed to reflect the will of the people. At one company I know, a group of executives went on a retreat to talk about collective goals. They came back filled with excitement, announcing to the employees, "This is your new mission statement."

"No, it's not," responded the workers, who'd had nothing to do with creating it.

Wu Wei: *The Power of Inaction*

The *Tao Te Ching* tells us:

> *From this I learn the power of* wu wei.
> *This lesson without words,*
> *This power beyond action,*
> *This is the highest wisdom.*

(Tao, 43)

Sometimes the most powerful thing a leader can do is nothing. *Wu wei*—inaction—can be an important tool. Michael Herzog, the chair of the English department at Gonzaga University in Spokane, Washington, told me how important he's found what he calls "a period of judicious waiting on some issues. There are times when I *shouldn't* make a decision yet because I really cannot make it."[17] A Tao leader doesn't let impatience overrule judgment. He or she knows when to take action and when to wait. We need to wait when the picture isn't clear, when we need more information, more data, more input from our team.

Effective Delegating: The Wu Wei of Backing Away

Have you ever tried to work with someone else looking over your shoulder? Being watched that closely makes me nervous. I feel like a child with a judgmental parent watching to make sure I get things right. It seems like the other person doesn't trust me, doesn't really believe I can do the job—and that undermines both my self-confidence and my effectiveness.

Yet many insecure leaders micromanage, afraid to release control even when they've delegated a task to someone else. They keep checking up on people, sending a message that they don't trust them. That apparent lack of trust undermines both the quality of work and overall morale.

Micromanaging erodes people's confidence, making them overly dependent on their leaders. Well-meaning leaders inadvertently sabotage their teams by rushing to the rescue and offering too much help. A leader needs to balance assistance with *wu wei,* backing off long enough to let people learn from their mistakes and develop competence.

This leadership error occurs at home as well as at work. Some conscientious parents "help" their children with their homework so much that they actually do it for them. But this practice doesn't help their children develop competence any more than lifting weights on their behalf would develop their muscles. Imagine what happens to such students when they go away to college. I can. As a college professor, I see hundreds of new freshmen every year. I watch the dependent ones collapse in anxiety, suddenly faced with the challenge of college work—without Mom and Dad. I'm grateful to other parents for teaching their sons and daughters self-reliance.

Teamwork: Empowerment in Action

Tao leadership is springing up in different fields, in different parts of the country. Tom Chappell, founder and CEO of Tom's of Maine, is a new leader who sees himself as part of a team of people solving a problem and "a student who learns from the people I work with." Dean Hall, a department head at Kansas State University, takes time before a big vote to walk around his department and talk to everyone individually in their offices. He does so to combat "a feeling of powerlessness," to make people realize that they're an important part of the team. By listening to his colleagues, he shows them that their voices matter.[18]

Instead of specialization and compartmentalization, many companies are using cross-division teams. Combining different perspectives, these teams help create a more holistic vision of the product that aids in troubleshooting and quality control. General Motors' new Saturn was developed, manufactured, and marketed by teams that included representatives from research and development, manufacturing, quality control, and marketing.

The positive effects of teamwork are undeniable. Saturn auto worker Joe Caldwell recalls that in his previous job he "felt just like a body on the [assembly] line, doing the same thing day after day." Now part of a division team at Saturn, Joe says, "You're not bored to death like in the old world. I've grown a lot because I've had the opportunity to get involved with a lot of segments of the business." Joe's team at Saturn is like a small business, which does its own purchasing, budgeting, and maintenance. The team elects its leader, who's a facilitator, not a boss. Democracy, empowerment, and good business go together. Joe's plant in Spring Hill, Tennessee, is outperforming its competitors, and the new Saturn has given a valuable boost to the U.S. auto industry.[19]

Troubleshooting Your Team

There are many success stories about teamwork. Recent books and business journals have been full of them. But sometimes your team doesn't work; the energies aren't right. Then your job as the leader is to find the problem and fix it. Here are some things to consider:

- One person may be sabotaging the team. Can you take the saboteur aside and convince him or her to get back on track, or will you need to send in a replacement?

- The problem may be low morale or misunderstanding. In this case, meet with your team and restate your objectives. Listen to see what's happening, so you'll know whether they need more information or more encouragement and support.

- Perhaps the goal is so big that it overwhelms people. If it is, break it into smaller units. Establish checkpoints along the way, so people can recognize their success. These small successes will give them heart.

Leadership is an art. Your task is to listen, watch for the energies, recognize the patterns, and improvise. Your artistry will improve as you follow the Tao.

Beyond Problem Solving: A Vision of Growth

In any organization, there are at least three kinds of people:

> those who see problems—the victims
> those who see solutions—the managers
> and those who see possibilities—the leaders.

Leadership is more than problem solving. Leaders who define their role this way only go from one crisis to another. Their sense of self (and the concomitant adrenaline rush) revolve around being a Lone Ranger who rides to the rescue. But their organization will not progress. Lone Rangers are always riding off in a cloud of dust, never leaving themselves time to develop a vision and to facilitate growth.

The Tao is a philosophy of growth. Nothing ever remains the same. W. Edwards Deming, the man who brought Total Quality Management to postwar Japan, based his business philosophy on continuous growth. "Improve constantly and forever every process for planning, prevention, and service," he told people.[20] For the Japanese, this maxim translated into *kai-zen,* a philosophy of constant improvement.

Nature teaches us that any healthy system must grow and develop. A potted plant that outgrows its container languishes and dies because it has no more room for growth. Any unhealthy group, whether a dysfunctional family or an addictive organization, confines individuals to rigid roles. Its equilibrium is threatened by any change in an individual, even a change for the better. Family therapists see this phenomenon when an alcoholic goes into recovery and upsets all the other family members.

In nature, human nature, and the nature of business, sick systems resist growth; healthy systems thrive on it. Deming's Total Quality Management approach emphasizes education and self-improvement for everyone, from line workers to management. Progressive corporations have adopted this self-actualizing approach in business. Tandem Computers offers seminars on career skills and health issues on site and gives employees sabbaticals for community service or personal growth. In the 1980s, IBM invested $500 million a year in education and training for its employees.[21] The Tao tells us:

> *The wise leader*
> *Encourages open minds and strong centers.*
>
> **(Tao, 3)**

The more people know about what they do, the better the final result. Continuous growth is not only good for business, it's an affirmation of the human spirit. And as we develop "open minds and strong centers," we can cope more effectively with tomorrow's challenges.

The Tao leader develops a vision of life in which everything is a spiritual practice. Projects, problems, and even crises are not isolated incidents but steps on the path of personal development. Some actions may go unnoticed by anyone else, but for us they can assume deep symbolic value, for even the smallest actions are opportunities for us to develop greater patience, courage, and inner strength. The Tao leader,

> *Aware of small things,*
> *Develops great wisdom.*

(Tao, 52)

Moving Forward

One of my greatest lessons in aikido is to stay centered, undaunted by conflict, confrontation, and the surprise of someone moving in for an attack. "Keep moving forward," my teachers tell me, noticing when I flinch or back away.

The *Tao Te Ching* teaches that everything is related. In our practice of physical exercise, many of us confront the same lessons we face in everyday life. One of my friends is a marathon runner, who impresses me at work with his strength of character, his resourcefulness and endurance, the same skills that enable him to run a grueling twenty-six-mile marathon up and down the hills of San Francisco.

My lesson is to face a challenge with grace and good humor, maintaining my center, so I can move the energies of opposition into new patterns of harmony. I realize that for many leaders in these uncertain times, the task is much the same. We must learn to face the unknown without flinching, move forward courageously, and accept change as part of what makes us grow. By developing greater vision and empowerment, we can create new patterns, even better ones than those that came before.

The Chinese word for "crisis" combines two characters: danger and opportunity. We often learn the most when we are the most challenged, coming up with strengths we didn't even know we had. Earthquakes, floods, and other natural disasters often transform ordinary people into heroes and bring together a community like nothing before.

Challenge mobilizes our resources, increases our awareness, makes our senses more acute. As Tao leaders, we can use challenge to advantage. With vision, we can reassure our people, showing them how this challenge relates to what came before and pointing to new opportunities. With empowerment, we can give them greater hope, affirming that together, we can discover what none of us could find alone.

The Tao teaches that life flows like a river and that the wisest people are like water, fluid yet infinitely strong, able to reach their destination, overcome barriers, as a river cuts through solid rock. A wise friend once told me that "we never cross the same river twice." Because every experience changes us and we change everything we touch, the river, the stream of life, is never the same. In every career, every relationship, every living organism, to live is to grow, to grow is to change, and to change is to go on creating ourselves and our world endlessly, flowing with the cycles of Tao.

CHAPTER 9

◇ ◇ ◇ ◇ ◇ ◇ ◇ ◇ ◇ ◇

Communication

The highest people teach the lowest
And learn from them as well.

Those without appreciation
For the teacher or the lesson
Have strayed from the path.
They may be highly educated,
But lack the deepest wisdom.

(Tao, 27)

The *Tao Te Ching* encourages us to watch and listen for life's patterns, not only in nature but in the world of human interactions. Our ability to communicate, to balance the *yang* and *yin* of giving and receiving, speaking and listening, is essential for leading with the Tao.

Dynamic as the Tao itself, the new leadership requires us to stay in touch with the energies of the people around us. Today's problems are too complex for any one person to solve alone. Now more than ever, we need strong interpersonal skills, the ability to communicate effectively with a diverse group of people. Communication skills are crucial as we move from an industrial to a postindustrial society, in which routine jobs are being converted to automation, leaving people with greater responsibility to coordinate and innovate.[1]

Effective communication helps people overcome their fear of change. Admiral Grace Hopper, who coordinated naval communications until her retirement at age seventy-nine, overcame people's resistance to change with anecdotes from her past. To those who clung to the status quo, she'd point out that there really *is* no status quo. She explained how she'd watched the development of aviation, computers, and modern appliances. She'd tell how some people once rejected the new flying machines and others had refused to touch a telephone, afraid they'd get a shock.[2]

Today's world not only challenges us with continuous change, it has also made many people cynical about leadership. Professor Wayne Booth, of the University of Chicago, recently told a group of academic leaders that "today's citizens are very reluctant to 'follow,' very suspicious of people who purport to lead." In part, he said, this reluctance to follow stems from America's tradition of rugged individualism. "People are convinced that following anyone is a sign of weakness."[3] In a tradition grounded in our pioneer past, Americans are unwilling to surrender their autonomy. This attitude is healthy. But too much individualism prevents people from working together. The Tao challenges us to balance individualism with community, developing our own abilities to the fullest while looking to the larger patterns.

Our nation's growing suspicion of leaders and disillusionment with traditional politics is a sign that the old order is changing, that we need a new, more inclusive vision of leadership. The new leadership requires us to see ourselves and others in terms of dynamic, evolving energies. This chapter shows how to identify and flow with these energies: to listen and learn from the people around us.

Selecting the Right Mode of Communication

Although many leaders in the past were known for their eloquent speeches, today communication on *all* levels is essential for effective leadership. Twenty-first-century leaders have access to many forms of communication: memos, letters, electronic mail, faxes, phone calls, voice mail, and face-to-face meetings. Some companies, like Tandem Computers, also use television, linking management and employees with regular teleconferences.

Communicating effectively means choosing the best mode of communication. Sometimes you'll need an official paper record, so a memo or letter is in order. To get the message out instantly, use the magic of fax transmission. To convey the original document, put the letter in the mail.

But in your own office, a memo is probably not the best way to communicate, unless you want to congratulate someone formally. The general rule is that the more *personal* the routine communication, the greater the morale. In a department with a strong sense of community, colleagues discuss concerns over coffee and in small group meetings. In a department with low morale, colleagues who work in the same building barely speak to one another. Instead, they send memos back and forth like bullets, "cc'ing" the management, documenting their every request and grievance. Conflict is aggravated by the lack of face-to-face communication.

The introduction of voice mail into our department last year has made interoffice communication much more efficient. If someone is out of the office or on the phone, I can still transact business by leaving a message. I can send a message to my entire department with one voice-mail transmission. Voice mail enables me to stay in touch with my office while working at home. It's also an effective way to transact business across different time zones. It may be noon in London, 7:00 A.M. in New York, 4:00 A.M. in San Francisco, and 9:00 P.M. in Tokyo, but voice mail is always there to answer our phone.

Voice mail helps busy people stay in touch. Some of us use it regularly to schedule meetings and lunches, even to check in with friends. But voice mail can also make your customers irritable if they get a recording—not a live person—during regular business hours. A wise leader balances efficiency with personal attention when setting up a phone system.

The right mode of communication depends on both the context and the preference of the person you want to reach. Some of my colleagues detest electronic mail, preferring phone calls, while our busy dean is an e-mail aficionado. Send him a request by e-mail and he'll respond the same day. Send him a memo or set up an appointment, and his response takes much longer. For simple requests, I much prefer e-mail. But when there's something to negotiate, the best way is still a face-to-face meeting.

Face-to-Face Communication: Active Listening

The Tao tells us:

> The spirit of the valley is eternal.
> It is yin, *mother of all life.*
> Its portal is the source of all creation,
> Subtle and yielding
> Yet infinite, strong.
> Blend with its power
> And succeed without effort.

(Tao, 6)

The ability to listen carefully, to yield our attention to another, enables us to seek the truth in any interaction. My friend Carol Rossi, coordinator of Santa Clara University's Leaders for Tomorrow, knows the importance of this skill. "The really energetic leader," she says, "needs to listen, not push ahead so impatiently."[4] I can identify with this lesson. My natural response is to push forward to get things done, an asset in some cases, but a definite liability when it comes to listening. A wise leader knows when to be *yin,* when to listen and exercise patience.

Developing Insight: T'zu Jan

The Chinese character *t'zu jan* means a spontaneous insight into the nature of things. It cannot be acquired by intellect alone or even hard work. It must be found by opening our hearts. The character *t'zu* means compassion or empathy, one of the three treasures of the Tao and a vital aspect of listening. As we open our hearts and carefully listen to the other person, we transcend our limited egos, which keep us from recognizing the subtle energies between us.

As leadership expert Douglas McGregor realized, "leadership

is a relationship."[5] The Tao reminds us that everything in life is a relationship. Communication is a dynamic cycle of *yin* and *yang* between sender and receiver. Together we create something more than either one of us could conceive alone. Listening with heart, we see into the very heart of Tao.

Listening is not easy. The average person remembers only about 25 percent of what he or she hears because we don't pay attention; our minds wander.[6] Since most people speak about 125 words a minute and our brains process information three times that fast, we have a lot of lag time, which we usually fill up by tuning out, daydreaming, or rehearsing our response.

Awareness is power. When we become aware of lag time, we can do something with it. In Japanese, the word *ma* means an interval or pause. Much of the magic of poetry and drama is the effective use of the pause, the space between the sounds. In the art of listening, we, too, can use *ma*, realizing that we have more capacity than words alone can fill. Consciously using this capacity, we can attend to the nonverbal messages the other person is sending. How is this person sitting or standing? Is she relaxed, tense, or nervous? What does the tone of his voice tell us? The words give us the informational content, but what's the emotional content of the message? Often, the emotional content is even *more* important.

TAO EXERCISE: REFLECTIVE LISTENING

We can tune in to the emotional content of a message by reflective listening, using comments or questions to check the accuracy of what we hear. Here are some examples:

Reflective comments: "It sounds like you're————" (fill in the blank with the appropriate feeling and context, such as tired, excited, or angry), as in the following examples:

It sounds like you're angry with Mary for going to the boss behind your back.

You seem worried about the big race.
I see that you're excited about the promotion.

Clarifying questions

Can you explain a little more about this?
Is this what you mean? (and then paraphrase)
What do you really want in this situation?

Reflective comments allow us to pinpoint the feeling behind the words. Clarifying questions help us to get the information we need for greater understanding.

The wonderful thing about reflective listening is that you really can't go wrong. If you say to someone, "You sound angry," and the person isn't angry, he or she will correct you—"I'm not really angry. I'm just disappointed in Mary" or whatever. Like a natural mirror, your reflective listening reveals the truth of what the other person is saying. But reflective listening is more than a mirror. It sends a strong message of commitment and concern, helping to build greater trust between the two of you.

Communicating with Clarity and Integrity

Listening is the *yin* and speaking is the *yang* of effective communication. We must do both to get our message across. Sometimes people don't send clear messages because they're unaware of their audience. We need to consider who we're speaking to, taking into account the person's background and knowledge base.

When I grew up in the Philippine Islands, many of the air force officers' families had Filipino cooks to prepare their meals for them. Our cook, Baltimore, was an expert chef who made elegant Asian, Creole, and French meals, along with unforgettable banana cream pies, but some cooks were not so experienced. One colonel was trying to teach a young Filipino woman how to make spaghetti sauce. "First sauté chopped onion and garlic," he said. She did so perfectly. "Then put in a can of tomato paste and stir." She did this, too—literally, without opening the can. For this young woman from the countryside, cans and can openers were foreign to her experience.

The same lesson holds true in a contemporary context. How many people do you hear complaining that they can't understand the manuals for their new computer programs? For the most part, these manuals were written by engineers, people who already know computers. My friends and I have to go out and buy users' guides, which present the same information in a way we can understand. Like the colonel giving instructions on spaghetti sauce, the engineers skipped some important steps that were obvious to them but mysterious to their audience.

Sometimes, words themselves can be confusing. When I became head of the English department, I wasn't used to giving people instructions. Trying to adopt a democratic tone, I'd tell my secretaries, "We need to get this report finished by next Tuesday." My attempt at diplomacy didn't work very well, however, because they wondered who I meant by "we" and what exactly I wanted them to do.

TAO EXERCISE: COMMUNICATING YOUR ACTION PLAN
Remembering these key words will help you communicate more clearly:

1. Make sure people understand *why* they need to do something. Help them see how their work helps achieve a larger goal.
2. Establish clearly *who* will do *what*.
3. *How?* Communicate whatever specific details you find necessary and leave the rest to the team.
4. *When* do you need the work completed? Set clear and reasonable deadlines.

Communicating with Integrity

One of the most disillusioning phrases I've heard in recent years is "The president misspoke himself." This euphemism dismisses a blatant breach of truth as no more than a slip of the tongue, the spoken equivalent of a typographical error. Political cynicism has skyrocketed because people cannot trust their leaders to tell them the truth. Without truth, we are without trust. Without trust, we can neither live together nor work together harmoniously.

The Tao leader communicates openly, honestly, and accurately. This doesn't mean, however, that you reveal everything you know, from personal matters to state secrets. When Tao leaders need to maintain confidentiality, they say, "I'm not at liberty to discuss this." They never lie or cover up.

Tao leaders also have the humility to acknowledge what they *don't* know and the openness to accept new knowledge. The Tao says:

> *Those who admit that they don't know*
> *Become wise.*
> *Those who conceal their ignorance*
> *Never learn.*
> *Those who admit mistakes*
> *Develop strength of character.*
> *Those who pretend to be strong*
> *Become weak.*

(Tao, 71)

When we don't know something, our egos may tempt us to give some phony answer. But the only honest response is to admit we don't know, get the facts, keep learning, and report back to people.

Being a leader in this dynamic, fast-moving world is a lifetime education. We must stay current in our field, keep up with recent developments so we can make wiser decisions. It's folly for companies to cut back on long-term investment in research and development to save money or make a quick profit. It's equally foolish for professionals in any field to stop learning. University professors conduct research on subjects as diverse as linguistics, economics, chemistry, and neuropsychology, adding to the body of human knowledge while keeping themselves intellectually alive, so they can bring new insights into their classes. What's true for individuals is true for nations. I find it disturbing that our country spent 9 percent of its budget on nondefense R&D in 1965 but it spends only 2 percent today. Individually and collectively, we *must* keep learning to meet the challenges of tomorrow.

TAO QUESTION

What is your R&D? What are you doing to increase your knowledge in your profession?

If you don't currently have a personal program of R&D, ask yourself what you need to know to advance in your field. Then sign up for a course or begin a regular reading program. Find a mentor. Ask someone who knows the subject about the best way to get started.

Keeping Lines of Communication Open

The wise leader keeps lines of communication open. One of W. Edwards Deming's principles of successful management is to "drive out fear with effective two-way communication. For better quality and productivity," he realized, "employees should not be afraid to ask questions."[7]

Dr. Cynthia Brattesani, a dynamic young dentist in San Francisco, told me why her office is so successful. She and her partners regularly attend leadership conferences, bringing back the latest methods to make their practice more effective.

Each day the people in Dr. Brattesani's office have a "morning huddle," going over every patient scheduled to come in that day. They look at each person's medical history and discuss what to expect. Dr. Brattesani and her colleagues emphasize listening—to their patients and to one another. They're committed to working as a team to provide the best possible care for their patients.[8]

Dr. Brattesani's office demonstrates how leaders in any field can structure their work environment to nurture more effective communication. The Tao reminds us of the subtle patterns beneath all that we do, for the Tao itself is

> *The form of the formless,*
> *The image without image,*
> *Beyond all definition.*
> *Meeting it, there is no beginning.*
> *Following it, there is no end.*

(Tao, 14)

The more we study the Tao, the more we realize that leadership is not a science but an art. We work with subtle energies, creating new habits to channel them into more positive patterns.

TAO QUESTION
What procedures does your office have to keep lines of communication open?

If you haven't already done so, set up regular staff meetings. Include everyone and go over the week's projects and goals. Develop a plan. Determine who will do what. Remember to thank people for the work they've done.

Ask yourself what else you can do to increase communication. Do you need a departmental newsletter? A suggestion box?

A lounge? Studies have shown that departments are more productive when they have a place where people can meet informally and talk over coffee or brown-bag lunches.[9]

Remember to get away from your desk and practice "management by walking around." Take some time to see what people are doing. Ask for their advice and opinion on important issues.

In your office, for at least part of each day, keep your door open, so people can drop in with questions and comments. An "open-door policy" breaks down people's defensiveness and encourages them to make suggestions.

When people bring in "bad news," remember that a complaint is often only the flip side of a suggestion. Thank the person who brought up the problem and enlist his or her support. Ask "How can we do this better?"

Communicating for Quality: Leadership Teams

The Tao tells us to

> Hold to this timeless pattern
> Throughout the time of your life,
> Aware of the eternal cycles,
> The essence of Tao.

(Tao, 14)

Like the cycles of Tao, the cycles of communication in progressive organizations are self-perpetuating, leading to continuous improvement.

As Carolyn Hennings, director of Santa Clara University's career services, explains, "leadership has changed. It isn't someone in an old patriarchal system who knows the answers and gets everyone else to do the work. It's not necessarily having the answers but drawing others together, facilitating, consensus-building."[10]

Leadership teams participate in an ongoing process of discovery. Examples of this new leadership abound in many fields from auto production to politics. New United Motor Manufacturing Incorporated (NUMMI), once an abandoned General Motors plant in Fremont, California, now a joint-venture partnership between Japanese and American automotive companies, has developed a reputation for quality—through communication and teamwork. NUMMI employees take pride in their work and have learned effective communication skills and positive ways to deal with problems. The plant manufactures Toyotas and the Geo Prizm, which was rated the best car built in North America in 1994.

Communication and teamwork can also build new political alliances. Bringing together the medical experts in his home district of Baltimore, Maryland, Congressman Benjamin Cardin set up a Health Care Advisory Group, comprised of physicians, nurses, insurance company workers, and advocates for the elderly. Cardin, who serves on the House Ways and Means Committee on Health Care, has held numerous town meetings to discuss health care issues and to obtain valuable information and advice, which he then takes back to Washington to help with strategic planning. If our nation is ever to have a workable national health care plan, it will be because of leaders such as Cardin, who can listen to multiple perspectives and come up with new solutions.

Leadership Evaluations

The Tao upholds an important lesson in trust, telling us:

> *Those who do not trust others*
> *Will never be trusted.*

(Tao, 23)

One way that leaders can demonstrate trust in their people is to ask for regular leadership evaluations. Following the Tao must be holistic. We cannot emphasize continuous improvement for our employees, products, and services without a corresponding commitment to improvement in ourselves.

Leadership evaluations, called "upward performance appraisals," have become increasingly popular across the country. Managers at BellSouth Advertising & Publishing, in Orlando, Florida; editors at the *Hartford Courant* in Connecticut; and other progressive leaders have benefited from such evaluations. Like everyone else, leaders need to know their strengths and weaknesses, so they can continue to improve.

At the end of my first year as department head, I asked my Executive Committee to conduct a leadership evaluation. I wanted to know what people wanted, what was working, what I could do better. Near the end of my three-year term the department will ask for recommendations about the kind of leadership my colleagues would like in the future before electing the next department head. The leadership evaluation will enable me—if my term is renewed—or my successor to develop processes and priorities for the next stage of our collective growth.

Having experienced leadership evaluation firsthand, I encourage you to accept it in the spirit of ongoing discovery and development. Your colleagues will praise your work in some areas and criticize it in others. This is as it should be. Remember to see all the comments in perspective and follow this lesson from the Tao:

> *Nature's way is alteration.*
> *Some things move forward*
> *While others fall back.*
> *Now we reach out*
> *And then we reach in.*
> *Today we're weak,*
> *Tomorrow strong.*
> *Therefore, the Tao leader*

Avoids excess,
Avoids extremes,
Avoids pride.

(Tao, 29)

Communicating Bad News

Not only do Tao leaders need to accept criticism in their own performance appraisals, but they need to communicate bad news effectively to their clients and colleagues.

Communicating Bad News to Clients: Some Pointers

I've spent lots of time in airports, which has enabled me to study the different ways airlines communicate with passengers during flight delays.

A flight delay is never pleasant. Passengers don't like being inconvenienced, and the airline staff doesn't like announcing bad news. Communication skills generally leave a lot to be desired.

The most common practice is to treat passengers like baggage and tell them little or nothing. One China Eastern Airlines flight kept passengers waiting three hours in Los Angeles without telling us anything. We finally took off for Shanghai, then spent an extra hour on the ground in Seattle, never knowing why we were repeatedly delayed.

Even worse was a flight home from Honolulu. Hawaiian airlines kept the passengers waiting from our 8:00 P.M. boarding time until 1:00 A.M. without telling us what to expect. We kept asking, but the gate crew wouldn't tell us what was going on. The passengers grew increasingly restless and irritable. Finally, at 1:00 A.M., we were taken to a nearby hotel while our luggage remained on the airplane. We still didn't know when we'd be leaving. We'd just gotten to sleep when we were awakened at 3:30 A.M. and taken back to the airport to board our plane.

A pleasant contrast occurred recently when my 7:30 P.M. Northwest flight from Minneapolis to San Jose was delayed three hours because of an altimeter failure. The gate crew told us about the problem and gave us twenty-minute updates on conditions, as well as meal vouchers so we could have dinner while we waited. When the instrument was replaced, we were told our new arrival time in San Jose, so we could call friends and family who'd planned to pick us up. The delay was still an inconvenience, but it was an inconvenience we could live with. The airline staff *communicated*—with consideration and clarity. They let us know what to expect.

Most people don't like to communicate bad news, so they practice avoidance, as in the first two examples. But remember: Most of us can handle bad news a lot better than we can chaos and uncertainty.

Even at the risk of disappointing someone, the important thing is to tell the truth. In early August 1993, a local cabinet-maker named Phil, who was referred to me by a friend, came by to give me an estimate on making a storage shed for my deck. Phil's price was reasonable, and he told me the job would take two weeks.

Two weeks went by, and then two months. Phil responded to my phone calls with a series of calamitous stories. He'd finished the shed, but then he got sick, his family members had a series of exotic illnesses, and his truck had broken down. More time went by. Finally, I had my friend call Phil, only to learn that he hadn't even started building the shed. He'd only been stalling and lying. I canceled the order in dismay and later had a shed built by someone else.

I didn't get a storage shed from Phil, but I did get a good lesson. I realized that I wanted the truth, not excuses, and that if Phil didn't want to do the job, he shouldn't have said yes in the first place. A simple, "No, I'm overbooked right now," would have disappointed me—for about ten minutes. Then I would have called someone else. Clear, honest communication is always better than denial or telling people what you *think* they want to hear.

BAD NEWS CHECKLIST

The next time you need to communicate bad news to a client, remember these points:

1. Be *clear*. Tell the truth.
2. Be *concise*. Don't ramble or make excuses.
3. Be *compassionate*. Don't just slam the door in the person's face. Give him some options. If you can't fill his request, what *can* you offer him? Cite some alternatives. If you can't do the work for her, refer her to someone who can.

Staff Evaluations: The Way of the Samurai

Another opportunity that leaders have to communicate bad news is in their staff evaluations. Of course, you'll communicate good news, too. In fact, I always begin with the good news. But you'll need to help people improve in certain areas. How do you do so effectively?

The three words *clarity, conciseness,* and *compassion* hold true here as well. You'll need to exercise compassion in approaching the person. The worst thing a leader can do, according to the samurai tradition, is to shame someone. Shame kills a person's spirit. Do not reprimand or criticize anyone in public. Have a private meeting.

Suppose you need to talk to Jack about his performance. First, tell him clearly what he does well. Emphasize his strengths before you turn to the area that needs improvement. Then be clear and concise about it, as in, "I've noticed that you've been coming in late three or four times a week." Be specific and objective. Remember, it's his *behavior* you're criticizing, not Jack as a person.

Jack will respond with explanations and excuses. Listen reflectively to show respect. Then ask what he intends to do about the problem. Get him to commit to a plan of action. Emphasize improvement and end the review on a positive note.

In your staff evaluations, remember to affirm these qualities of Tao:

> *Honest, as an uncarved block of wood;*
> *Open, as a yielding valley;*
> *Blending, as if earth and water.*
>
> **(Tao, 15)**

Communicating Good News

The importance of communicating good news cannot be overemphasized. Psychologists tell us that people learn best by positive reinforcement, yet most leaders and institutions get so bogged down with daily details that they forget to reinforce what they want most. One of the most common complaints in organizations is the lack of appreciation. People work hard and feel that nobody notices, nobody cares. Morale suffers.

Be a resourceful leader. Come up with creative ways to acknowledge your staff. Tell people you appreciate what they do. Write thank-you notes, take people out to lunch, congratulate them on their accomplishments. Commit to getting them the recognition, raises, and promotions they deserve. Post their successes on a departmental bulletin board or put them in a company newsletter. Plan a celebration. Find the combination of positive reinforcements that works best for your team.

As a leader, your job is to communicate in ways that nurture your team. Keep listening and learning, encouraging others to do the same. As sociologist Chuck Powers once told me, "a good leader has to be able to keep people in discovery."[11]

Your consciousness and your ability to communicate are powerful tools that can transform any situation. The *Tao Te Ching* reminds us that things *never* remain as they seem. Our response shapes the outcome:

> *Success can grow from failure,*
> *Misery from happiness.*
> *Who knows what lies*
> *Beneath the surface?*
> *Complaint and conflict*
> *Can turn to good,*
> *Morale can shift*
> *From high to low.*
> *People have long been confused*
> *About causation.*
> *The Tao leader is*
> *Just, but not judgmental;*
> *Honest, but not hurtful;*
> *Straightforward, but not inflexible;*
> *Bright, but not flamboyant.*
>
> **(Tao, 58)**

With a belief in new possibilities and effective communication skills, we shape our collective future. This is the way of Tao.

CHAPTER 10

Conflict Resolution

Those who responsibly meet
Life's conflicts
Can truly lead the world.

(Tao, 78)

One of the most needed, least known skills in the world today is conflict resolution. We don't learn about conflict resolution in school, at home, in the media, or on the streets. We don't learn it at all, most of us. So we act on impulse, lapsing into fight or flight, turning conflict into combat, perpetuating cycles of misunderstanding and violence in all our interactions, from the interpersonal to the international.

The *Tao Te Ching* teaches that

> *Harsh words and weapons*
> *Bring violence and pain.*
> *The wise leader chooses combat*
> *Only as a last resort.*
>
> *For in combat even victory*
> *Is no cause for joy.*
> *To gloat in victory*
> *Means delight in destroying others.*
> *In destroying others,*
> *We destroy ourselves.*

(Tao, 31)

The Tao reminds us that we are all part of something larger than ourselves, that everything and everyone is intrinsically related. Every violent act constitutes a breakdown of civilization, a violation of the order that unites us all. Working with the natural patterns, the Tao leader upholds a new way of resolving conflict, affirming a spirit of partnership and building a foundation of greater understanding.

Conflict has led to division and discord because two common misperceptions have trapped us in fight-or-flight reactions. We overgeneralize, seeing whoever disagrees with us as the enemy. In a hostile reductionism, we narrow our vision, reducing the richness of human experience to that one thing on which we disagree—and fight over it.[1] Or we flee from conflict, feeling shame for disagreeing. Denying our own concerns, we give in to avoid confrontation. Never communicating our needs, we settle for appeasement and superficial solutions. Either response is dualistic. The Tao tells us to transcend dualism, to

> *Stop arguing and end your worries.*
> *What difference is there*
> *Between agreement and disagreement?*
> *Between correct and incorrect?*
> *Accepting another's opinion*
> *Obscures the dawn*
> *Of your own awakening.*

(Tao, 20)

Instead of succumbing to dualism and seeing the other person or ourselves as "bad," the Tao shows us another way. Conflict becomes the means for greater understanding—of ourselves and one another. It can create a wall to divide us or a bridge to unite us. The difference lies in how we respond to it.

Transcending Dualism

In the Western world, we habitually fall into the logical fallacy of the false dilemma, seeing all life as either-or: win or lose, right or wrong, all or nothing, us or them. The wisdom of Tao reminds us that all creation is comprised of complementary opposites: *yin* and *yang*.

Dualism limits our options and makes us see differences as

threatening. Instead of working together to discover solutions to problems, we waste time blaming others. Fixated on the problem, we cannot see beyond it.

Dualism keeps us stuck, frustrated, irritable, and irrational—often with tragic consequences. Speaking on Martin Luther King Day in 1993, Dr. Raye Richardson, former director of black studies at San Francisco State University, pointed to the violent effects of dualism in our society. "We don't solve a problem," she said. "We just kill it."[2]

News reports are filled with alarming examples. In Gilroy, California, in December 1993, a fifteen-year-old boy brought his father's revolver to school and shot another boy who had been bullying him. In the same year, a survey found that 23 percent of American high school students and 11 percent of their teachers had been victims of violence; 13 percent of the students reported that they regularly carry weapons. To deal with the symptoms of increasing violence, high schools in New York City, Richmond, California, and other troubled districts have begun installing metal detectors.

But metal detectors deal only with externals. They don't address the cause of the violence, which lies deep within us: in our mounting anxiety and frustration because we don't know how to resolve conflict.

The Tao tells us that using force never really solves problems; it only temporarily defeats the opposition:

> *Meeting conflict with force*
> *Overcomes opposition,*
> *But never the conflict.*
>
> *Blame and attack,*
> *Rage and resentment*
> *Perpetuate cycles*
> *Of violence and pain.*

> *The wise leader*
> *Seeks real solutions,*
> *Resolving conflict*
> *With the wisdom of Tao.*

(Tao, 79)

Violent confrontation is not the only way that dualism turns conflict into combat. There are the painful relationships at home and at work, filled with resentment, anger, and frustration because people lack essential conflict-resolution skills. Hurtful arguments, irrational decisions, despair, divorce, and escalating domestic violence are other unhappy consequences.

Dualism also leads to confrontations in the courtroom. Lawyers compete like gladiators, collecting astronomical fees not to resolve conflict but to win legal duels over the guilt of one party and the innocence of the other.

Suing as a means of conflict resolution often reaches absurd proportions. In January 1994, a student at the University of Idaho looked out a third-floor window, saw his friends outside, and decided to "moon" them. As he climbed on top of a heater and pulled down his pants, he lost his balance and fell through the window, injuring his back and sustaining numerous cuts and bruises. His parents have sued the university for negligence to the tune of $940,000.[3]

Blaming others, attacking others, suing others only escalates animosity without addressing the basic roots of conflict. The Tao gives us a vision that transcends dualism. We learn that

> *The Tao leader*
> *Looks beyond friend and foe,*
> *Profit and loss,*
> *Fame and disgrace*
> *And therefore prevails.*

(Tao, 56)

Avoiding *Aiuchi*

Dualism weakens both parties, who attack each other instead of working together to deal with the problem under contention. An archetypal symbol of dualism in my mind is *aiuchi*, a double kill. In ancient Japan, 80 percent of all samurai duels ended up in *aiuchi*. Both samurai stood poised for the attack, swords raised, aggressively assaulting each other's openings, and the result was often simultaneous decapitation. In other contexts as well, dualism makes us lose our heads, ending up in "lose-lose" interactions.

Instead of looking for another person's weaknesses, Tao leaders affirm their own and the other's strengths. Keeping their heads, they work for "win-win" solutions.

Tao leaders keep two important principles of Tao in mind: *oneness* and *dynamic growth*. Building partnership, concentrating on shared concerns, Tao leaders emphasize common ground as a foundation for conflict resolution. Realizing that life evolves in dynamic cycles, they approach a conflict as an opportunity to learn and grow, to strengthen a relationship, and to develop greater understanding.

Knowledge Is Power: Overcoming Fight or Flight

The holistic principles of Tao may be clear when we're feeling composed—reading this book, for example—but what about crisis situations when we experience the physiological effects of stress?

As we learned in Chapter 6, stress triggers an elaborate chain of psychophysiological responses to prepare us for an emergency. Psychological research at the University of Haifa showed that stress can seriously undermine our decision-making skills.[4] The stress response pumps adrenaline through our systems, fills us with anger or fear, and narrows our field of vision, making us likely to revert to dualism and jump to conclusions.

But we needn't be prisoners of our biology. As scientific pioneer Francis Bacon realized as far back as the seventeenth century, "knowledge is power." Knowledge of our body's stress response and some key conflict-resolution skills can make a major difference in our lives. This chapter shows how.

Redirecting Energy

Taoism and the new physics converge in one important insight: that all creation is comprised of dynamic energy patterns. Everything—our bodies, our world, our emotional responses, our movements—is energy. Realizing this fact, we can redirect anger, hostility, or any other negative energy. The Tao says:

> Lead with the Tao
> And negativity has no power.
> The energy is not repressed
> But redirected
> So that it does no harm.

(Tao, 60)

Health professionals, conflict-resolution experts, and martial artists concur with this essential principle of Tao. Dr. Ken Eisold of New York noted, "If you recognize when you're experiencing anxiety, you're less likely to act it out."[5]

Consciously acknowledging how we feel can keep our emotions from running away with us. Dudley Weeks, director of the Conflict Partnership Center and professor of conflict resolution at American University, Washington, D.C., says that it helps when we "know our buttons," are aware of what sets us off. When he feels himself beginning to react, he tightens his muscles and then relaxes them, releasing the tension and coming back to center. Another way, taught in yoga and the martial arts, is to take a deep breath, focus your attention deep in your center, and then slowly breathe out, releasing tension and regaining your equilibrium.

TAO EXERCISE: LEARNING WHAT SETS YOU OFF
Stop for a moment and ask yourself:

"When was I last upset?"
"What was it about the situation that upset me?"
Do you see a pattern?
What can you learn from this situation?

One thing that sets me off is feeling that I'm not being taken seriously. Because I grew up as a skinny kid in pigtails who moved around a lot, trying to make friends in dozens of new schools and neighborhoods, I developed some underlying insecurities. I never seemed to "fit" anywhere and always envied people who did. I was also the first person in my family to graduate from college. Underneath my adult accomplishments, part of me sometimes still feels like that kid in pigtails trying to prove herself.

Being aware of this pattern helps me put things into perspective, making me less likely to overreact.

Do you have a pattern like this in your life?

Lately I've found that uncomfortable situations contain valuable lessons. If I ask what lies beneath my discomfort, I discover more about myself and how I relate to others.

Centering Down

Aikido trains people to center down, relax their bodies, and open their minds instead of tensing up under stress. With enough training, people automatically drop down into center, keeping their balance despite the threatening energies around them.

My friend Sunny Skys, an aikido black belt, once stopped a fight in a fast-food restaurant just by centering down. A retarded teenage employee had spilled a drink on one of the customers, who started yelling and shaking his fist at the boy. Standing on the other side of the room, Sunny automatically dropped down into a centered, relaxed posture and caught the angry man's eye. Instantly, all the fight went out of the man, he backed away, and business went on as usual.[6]

Aikido teaches us to drop down into center, literally to focus our energy into our *hara,* a point two inches below the navel. Relaxation makes us much stronger than does rigid armoring or muscular strength. Centered, we can meet any conflict with power, grace, and flexibility. This, again, is the Taoist paradox of "soft is strong," the strength of bamboo. Able to blend with the energies around us, we can transcend dualism, perceive new creative options, and prevail in difficult situations.

Sunny tells his aikido students, "You need to be centered within yourself to respond appropriately." Centering requires a positive sense of ourselves, which evolves in a Taoist cycle. The greater our self-esteem, the more centered we feel. Conversely, the more we practice centering, the stronger our sense of self.

TAO EXERCISE: CENTERING DOWN

Try this simple centering exercise:

Stand normally. Then in one movement bend your knees slightly, relax your arms, bend your elbows, and hold your hands out in front of you at waist level. Feel your energy move down to your *hara.* Breathe into your *hara.* Then exhale.

How do you feel? Stronger? More in charge?

Remember how this exercise feels and use it regularly to reduce tension. After a while, you'll be able to center down naturally whenever you're under stress.

Psychological Aikido

Drawing on the fluid power of Tao, aikido teaches us a way beyond fight or flight, beyond being either victims or aggressors. Centered and strong, we become more aware of negative energies around us. We learn to move aside and get off the line of conflict, so these energies cannot harm us. Then we move forward to transform conflict, blending with our opponents, redirecting energies.

In physical confrontations, blending means actually moving with the other person's body to redirect the energies of conflict into resolution. The graceful movements of aikido send the other person rolling away in gentle spirals, overcoming aggression without harming the aggressor.

On a psychological level, the same response helps us resolve conflicts in daily life. By centering, getting off the line of conflict, and blending with the other person in empathy and greater understanding, we can redirect the hostile energy into new, more positive directions.

The Tao tells us:

> *The Tao leader honors all energies*
> *So no harm is done*
> *And essential character is affirmed.*
>
> **(Tao, 60)**

Conflict always involves explosive emotions. Many people are intimidated by all this powerful energy, but the Tao reminds us that all energy contains the potential for either good or ill. The determining factor is our response to it. The energy of conflict can bring breakdown or breakthrough, destruction or creation. Like electricity, it can either destroy us or light up our world. "The Tao leader honors all energies" and responds to them wisely.

One Man's Path to Conflict Resolution

Inclusive and dynamic as the Tao, conflict resolution is a process that not only solves problems, but can actually improve relationships. According to Dudley Weeks, resolving conflict effectively is "an essential life skill. The more I've learned about how conflicts are dealt with," he says, "I realize that among the many common human denominators, one is certainly the fact that we *all* have conflict."

In summer 1994, I met with Weeks in Washington, D.C., to discuss his partnership approach to conflict resolution, which is deeply aligned with the Tao. A thoughtful man with kind eyes, salt-and-pepper hair, the hint of a southern accent, and a smile that puts people immediately at ease, Weeks told me why he'd made conflict resolution his life's work.

He grew up in the American South, at the time "a very conflict ridden area—racist and sexist. I was taught that to be a man, you didn't cry. I felt very alien to all of that and spoke out from a very early age, which put me in direct conflict with the dominant paradigm around me."

Then, he said, he reached "a point of choice": whether to continue to do battle with the people who disagreed with him or to see the areas in which they disagreed as only *parts* of a larger relationship. As he put it, "Could I stand up to what I believed in and build a relationship with people?" When he first considered this question, he was only six years old.

In his teens, Dudley became involved in the civil rights, peace, environmental, and women's movements. He realized then how essential it was for people who work for social change to learn about conflict resolution. "Trying to change the existing system," he said, obviously "threatens people committed to that system."

As Tao leaders, we face the same challenge: how to blend different factions into a changing system. Any time leaders work for change, they must decide what to do with the people who are part of the old system. To move forward, we must involve both groups in a dynamic partnership.

Dudley Weeks has served in the Peace Corps and worked as a teacher, paramedic, social activist, and international conflict-resolution facilitator. His work has taken him to all the continents, most recently to South Africa, Northern Ireland, the former Yugoslavia, the former Soviet Union, Tibet, Nicaragua, the Middle East, and Rwanda. When he's not on the road facilitating or conducting workshops, he's a professor of conflict resolution at the American University School of International Services in Washington, D.C. This section draws on his strategies as we learn to resolve conflict with the Tao.

Seeking the One: Redefining Conflict

The *Tao Te Ching* tells us:

> *When the parts are separated,*
> *There can be no harmony.*
> *Do not think yourself precious jade,*
> *But wind chimes made of stone.*

(Tao, 39)

The Tao tells leaders to look for the underlying harmony beyond apparent division and discord, to affirm the Taoist principle of oneness. We can begin to do so by suspending judgment and practicing the *yin* characteristics of patience and presence.

For Taoists and Zen Buddhists, conflict just *is*. It's part of life, part of experience. What it becomes—either good or bad—depends on how we respond to it.

Our culture too often thrusts conflict into the shadows. We're ashamed of it. As Dudley Weeks observed, "Most people perceive conflict as unnerving, a disruption of order, a blemish on a smooth complexion."

Our static concept of success also keeps us from effectively dealing with conflict, which challenges us continually to redefine ourselves and our relations with others. As the Tao reminds us, life is *not* static. It evolves in continuous cycles. Conflict only underscores the dynamic nature of reality. What *was* is never what *is* or what *will be*. Conflict is a symptom of the ongoing evolution of life that moves us out of complacency into discovery.

The pervasive economic paradigm in this country also distorts our definition of conflict. As Dudley Weeks explained, "In the United States, competition is almost made into a god. Therefore, conflict is seen as just one more competition. People then use an adversarial, competitive pattern, rather than a 'partnership' pattern in dealing with conflict. We need to teach and learn *partnership* conflict-resolution skills, especially since we are in the habit of letting the profit motive invade even our relationships. We ask, 'How much can we get from a minimum of effort?'" All together, these pressures lead us to define conflict dualistically as win-lose, which narrows our vision and limits our choice of options.

But there is another way: We can see conflict as a valuable opportunity to learn. Progressive thinkers in many disciplines are beginning to appreciate the new insights conflict can bring us. Anthropologist Mary Hegland told me that one development in her profession is that some progressive researchers have stopped maintaining the illusion of "objectivity" and realized that they bring their own cultural assumptions and expectations into the field. "The conflicts that emerge," she says, "can serve to highlight the cultural differences and create greater understanding."[7] In many ways, in many fields, conflict can serve as a valuable learning tool.

Looking at the Relationship, Not Just the Conflict

One of the mistakes people make is to obsess about conflict, reducing an entire relationship to that one disagreement. We need to open up our perspective, to see the current conflict as only one part of a much larger relationship.

Otherwise we can become trapped in such reductionism that the other person becomes for us only a negative caricature. Hidden agendas can also distort our emotional responses, blowing things way out of proportion. To release their pent-up frustrations, people will often fight over minor issues.

People can get so stuck in a problem that they forget to look for the solution. There's an old Buddhist story about a man who'd been struck by a poisoned arrow. Buddha told the man he could spend his time asking who shot him—or he could pull out the arrow.[8]

We get fixated on a problem because our egos become attached to that poisoned arrow. We get invested in being right, in asking "Why did this happen to me?" in feeling victimized, and in attacking the other person and narrowing our vision instead of resolving the conflict.

From Power Over to "Power-With"

The Tao tells us:

> An open mind brings compassion.
> Compassion builds power.
> Such power is natural
> And nature is one with Tao.
>
> **(Tao, 16)**

An essential step in conflict resolution is to redefine power. Dudley Weeks says that "we're caught up in the belief that to be powerful is to have *power over.* The most powerful kind of power is what I call *'power-with.'"*[9]

Weeks calls the old definition of power "seesaw power." Like two children playing on a seesaw, one person goes up when the other goes down. If one individual makes the other look weak, he or she appears stronger. Power positions may alter, yet no actual increase in power occurs.

Seesaw power is demeaning and counterproductive: I appear powerful to the degree that you are weak, to the extent that I dominate you. Tao leaders see beyond this hierarchical definition, realizing the greater potential of synergy and empowerment. In effective conflict resolution, the people in conflict become partners who are engaged in solving the problem together, without domination, degradation, or loss of power.

Redefining power, we see it not as domination but as maximizing our own potential. Dudley Weeks calls this "positive power." We can increase our positive power without taking advantage of someone else; in fact, we can increase someone else's positive power while building our own. Positive power is a key to effective conflict resolution.

To resolve conflict effectively, we need to move from "power over" to "power-with." When F. W. de Klerk and Nelson Mandela did so in South Africa, they led the way out of the darkness of apartheid into new possibilities of partnership and peace. Looking beyond reactive emotions, thinking mathematically, such a concept of power is only logical. Our power—yours *and* mine—is obviously more than yours or mine alone.[10]

Becoming Conflict Partners: The Process

Once we've done the important inner work of redefining conflict and power, we're ready for the actual process of conflict resolution. In his book, *The Eight Essential Steps to Conflict Resolution,* Dudley Weeks goes into far greater detail. This section focuses on three essential principles, each of which combines the *yin* of patience and receptivity with the *yang* of positive action. The principles are (1) developing a partnership atmosphere, (2) identifying shared needs, and (3) finding stepping stones (which Weeks calls "doables").[11]

Developing a Partnership Atmosphere

As we have seen, we begin to develop the right atmosphere for conflict resolution by working on our own consciousness. We must remember that conflict can improve or undermine a relationship, depending upon our response to it.

TAO EXERCISE: INNER WORK

The next time you find yourself involved in conflict, cultivate a cooperative attitude: See yourself and the other person (or persons) as partners.

Review the essential principles. As experienced as he is, Dudley Weeks does so every time he facilitates a conflict resolution.

Keep an open mind. Remember the strength of bamboo: Flexibility, not rigidity, prevails.

The Importance of Timing

You don't have to react to conflict immediately. As Tao leaders, we know how to let timing work *for* us.

Tell the other person you'd like to work together to resolve the conflict. Then choose a time that is good for both of you—when you've had some time to get centered and to consider your options, when you don't have to rush, and when you won't be interrupted. Select a time when you're both at your best. If your partner's a night person, don't schedule your meeting at eight o'clock in the morning.

Allow enough time. Don't schedule your meeting an hour before you have to catch a train or when people are likely to drop in on you.

Choosing the Right Place

Choose a comfortable place where both of you can relax, free from interruptions. If you outrank the other person, don't meet in your office because this place will only intimidate your partner.

Meet on "neutral territory" if at all possible. I've met with people over tea in a quiet coffee shop, which works fairly well. I wouldn't recommend busy restaurants, where the details of ordering lunch and dealing with gregarious waiters create endless interruptions. Some companies have private conference rooms or quiet gardens that are ideal.

Opening Comments

Set the tone of your meeting by stating your desire to work as partners, to learn from one another and improve the current situation. A positive, nonblaming, nonthreatening opening sets the tone for the entire meeting.

If you're the facilitator and one person wants to bring up a list of grievances, respectfully ask people to put their grievances aside for the moment to concentrate on "shared needs."[12]

Identifying Shared Needs

Needs are the crucial building blocks of conflict resolution. The *Tao Te Ching* tells us:

> *Those who know the needs of the people*
> *Are fit to govern them.*
> *Those who responsibly meet*
> *Life's conflicts*
> *Can truly lead the world.*

(Tao, 78)

Effective conflict resolution moves from the hostile atmosphere of *demands* to the partnership atmosphere of *shared needs*. Demands separate people. Everyone fights for what he or she wants. Shared needs build greater understanding, improving relationships as well as resolving the current conflict. Dudley Weeks asks people to identify and work through four kinds of needs:

1. your needs
2. your partner's needs
3. relationship needs
4. shared needs

Conflicts arise when we ignore any of these vital needs.[13]

Personal Needs: Developing Positive Self-power

Some people are conditioned to be so "unselfish" that they ignore their own needs, never sharing them with their partners. Is it any wonder they feel neglected and misunderstood? Such excessive unselfishness often happens with couples. Dick and Teresa are young newlyweds. Eager to keep the honeymoon alive, Teresa doesn't tell Dick that she hates picking up after him—he's used to his bachelor days when he left his shoes, socks, and clothes wherever he took them off. Resentment seethes inside Teresa each time she picks up a pair of Dick's socks or sees his underwear draped over a chair, but Dick doesn't know she is resentful. He just wonders why Teresa has become so moody and irritable lately.

We owe it to ourselves and our relationships to break through the facade of excessive unselfishness and let the other person know how we feel. For some of us, this means first getting in touch with our own needs. Dudley Weeks calls this step "developing positive self-power": building a healthy self-image based not on what we think other people want us to be, but on our own needs, beliefs, and goals.[14] The more we know who we are, the less of ourselves we surrender to the control of others and the less reactive we are when other people push our buttons.

TAO EXERCISE: WHAT ARE MY NEEDS?

The next time you face conflict, ask yourself:

"What are my needs in this situation?"
"What are my values and priorities?"

Separate your preferences from your needs. Know when you can bend and when you need to stand your ground or risk losing your self-respect.

When you've identified your needs, the next part of the process is alternately listening to your partner's needs and sharing your own. This process of communication builds greater respect and understanding.

Your Partner's Needs

Conflicts often occur because people behave according to assumptions—what they *think* their partner needs—without consulting the other person at all. A case in point: After twelve years of marriage, Imogen returned to college to get her degree. She graduated with honors and was accepted into a highly competitive MBA program. The tuition was steep, but the MBA would increase her prospects for employment, and she knew that her husband Barry, a successful executive, could afford to pay for it. She meant to discuss this opportunity with him after graduation.

Meanwhile, glad that Imogen had finally put the long evenings and weekends of study behind her, Barry decided to celebrate her graduation with a special gift. He had a jeweler design a ruby-and-diamond pendant, let her best friends in on the surprise, and presented it to her at her graduation party. When Imogen later approached him about the MBA program, he said he didn't have the money. He said that he had just spent thousands on her necklace, and now she was "being selfish." Barry felt unappreciated, and Imogen felt misunderstood and accused Barry of sabotaging her.

Never assume you know what your partner needs. Ask:

"What do you need from our relationship now?"

"What do you need to come out of this conflict as a stronger, happier person?"

"What do you need from me to feel more positively empowered?"[15]

You'll often be surprised by the results.

In this stage of the process, you don't need to agree with your partner. Just open your heart and listen. Solutions will come later. Sometimes, the greatest gift we can give another person is our understanding.

Identifying the Relationship Needs

You have needs, your partner has needs, and your relationship has needs. For some people, this is a stunning realization. A relationship is a living, growing process, made up of your combined energies, a gestalt in which the whole is more than the sum of its parts.

To look back at the earlier example, Imogen and Barry were embroiled in a conflict over needs. Barry ignored Imogen's needs, but in pursuing her education, she'd overlooked their relationship needs. Because Barry felt abandoned on evenings and weekends, his feelings of rejection expressed themselves in his manipulative gift. He knew that Imogen wanted to get her MBA and he didn't like it, so while appearing generous and loving, he did his best to control her, to keep her from neglecting him.

Whenever we make changes in our lives, these changes affect the people we're close to. They have to. As the Tao reminds us, nothing in the universe exists alone; everything is connected.

A few years ago, when Barry worked and Imogen stayed at

home, a lot of their couple time happened by default. She was available whenever Barry came home from work. But then her schedule changed.

As she prepared to return to school, the two of them should have sat down together and identified their individual and relationship needs—setting aside time in their busy schedules to spend together, away from work and household duties, to keep the relationship alive.

Busy people need to make sure that their decisions are made by deliberation, not by default. Our needs are too important to leave to chance.

Identifying Shared Needs

Probably the most powerful shift in conflict resolution is to get the people involved to stop arguing about the area of disagreement and to start building a working relationship. They do so by concentrating on shared needs. In every conflict he's ever worked with, Dudley Weeks has built an effective partnership for resolution on the foundation of shared needs.

While working in South Africa in 1986, he asked a group of Afrikaners, "What kind of South Africa do you want your children to grow up in?" They said they wanted peace and a viable economy. Then he asked the same question of another group of black South Africans. They said they wanted to participate as citizens in a country at peace with a viable economy. When these two groups recognized their shared needs, they began building together for the future.

Sometimes groups become so polarized by hate and fear that they can't believe they have *any* shared needs. But as human beings we always do.

Some years back, Dudley Weeks was working in a troubled inner-city community marred by crime and hostile factions. At a meeting with representatives of all the groups, from business leaders to leaders of teenage gangs, he began by asking, "What do you think your community needs?" Everyone wrote down his or her thoughts.

"How many shared needs do you think you have?" he asked. At first, the people said, "None." They thought they had nothing in common. But they had six shared needs, among them a community center and a health clinic.

Recognizing their shared needs, the people began to see each other differently.

Finding Stepping Stones

Conflict resolution is a process, a path we walk one step at a time. As the Tao reminds us, there are no instant solutions:

> *A journey of a thousand miles*
> *Begins with a single step.*
>
> **(Tao, 64)**

Dudley Weeks builds the path of conflict resolution with "stepping stones," or "doables," small actions that people can take to move forward toward the solution. Doables lay a foundation of trust and teamwork, establishing a successful momentum of working together.

In the inner-city community discussed earlier, Dudley Weeks asked people what it would take to accomplish all their objectives. This question was too much for them to deal with. So he asked for a single step: "What *can* you do as a beginning?"

The people agreed on streetlights. The homeowners and business leaders thought that streetlights would make the streets safer. So did the gang leaders, who said that their members had been getting hurt in fights on the dark city streets. To get streetlights installed, everyone had to sign a petition, which became a tangible sign of shared commitment to improve conditions in the community.

"It was a doable, a stepping stone. They learned they *could* work together," he said. When the streetlights were installed, the people painted them bright colors and celebrated their accomplishment. In two or three years, they had a youth center, a health clinic, and a more harmonious community.

A Process of Discovery

Dudley Weeks says that "people think conflict resolution means making a grand design, but it's not." Conflict resolution is an ongoing process of discovery as people learn, one step at a time, to create new possibilities together.

The Tao leader realizes that the best way to explore any new territory is one step at a time, learning along the way. Rigid plans are not the way of the Tao, which tells us:

> *If your plan is inflexible,*
> *It cannot succeed.*
> *Unable to bend,*
> *The tree will break.*
> *Hardness and stiffness*
> *Lead to destruction.*
> *Flow with the process*
> *And live to prevail.*

(Tao, 76)

Openness to process is key. Weeks says that he has learned as a third-party facilitator how the process itself develops greater vision and better options than any one person could reach alone.

Flowing with the Process:
Leaders and Conflict Resolution

As Tao leaders, we can develop a culture of conflict resolution and team building wherever we live and work. First, we can keep learning and practicing conflict resolution ourselves. Then we can sponsor regular conflict-resolution workshops, especially when new people come into an organization. We can emphasize "power-with" in all our interactions, no longer relating to people in terms of roles, which only reinforces old hierarchical patterns.

As Tao leaders, we can make problem solving a team effort, a chance to work and learn together. We can model conflict partnership skills ourselves, not only in conflict but when dealing with any new challenge.

Dudley Weeks's "conflict partnership" process uses skills that both resolve conflicts and build relationships.[16] These skills reinforce trust, group harmony, and empowerment—the atmosphere of the new leadership.

As the Tao reminds us, we can build greater harmony around us by seeking greater harmony within us, by overcoming our anxiety, defensiveness, and hostility in the face of conflict. Coupling the *yin* attributes of patience, process, and empathy with the *yang* attributes of courage and positive action, the Tao leader reconciles opposites within himself or herself to develop the positive power of Tao. We learn to

> *Know the sunlight*
> *While confronting the shadows,*
> *Becoming a leader to all.*
> *As a Tao leader,*
> *You move with infinite power,*
> *Ever drawing upon the source.*
>
> **(Tao, 28)**

As Tao leaders, we resolve conflict in a spirit of partnership, working with essential energies to create new patterns of harmony for ourselves and our world.

CHAPTER 11

Transcending Ego

The Tao leader acts without attachment,
Achieves, but does not take credit,
Transcending ego
With greater harmony.

(Tao, 77)

Tao leaders affirm an inner strength that transcends ego. They know that their current leadership position is just that—a position, not a set role. Like dedicated athletes, they play their positions to the best of their ability. But they don't identify with their titles. They know that who they *are* is always more than what they *do*.

Lesser leaders become intoxicated with power, developing bloated egos. They succumb to hubris, the primal flaw of tragic heroes since the days of ancient Greece. In over two thousand years of recorded history, the literature of both East and West has warned leaders to beware of the pride that blinds them to their own humanity. Far too many leaders have become "high" on power, letting the adrenaline rush, the trappings of authority, and the adulation of followers make them lose their balance and fall to ignominious ends.

Ralph Waldo Emerson told people over a hundred years ago to get their "bloated nothingness" out of the way. Twenty-four centuries earlier, the *Tao Te Ching* asked if we could transcend ego, the crucial lesson of this chapter.[1]

Beyond Self-indulgence and Self-abnegation

Transcending ego does not mean self-abnegation. The teachings of Buddha tell how Prince Siddhartha became an ascetic, mortifying the flesh, fasting, and practicing strict self-denial. But this was not the answer. Then he immersed himself in worldly riches and sensual delights, but found no fulfillment in self-indulgence either. Finally, as he stood by a river in utter despair, he realized that while practicing the two extremes of self-denial and self-indulgence, he had remained self-centered. The way out of his misery was to escape from self-centeredness by developing an expanded awareness of the world around him. His lesson of mindfulness and compassion became the dharma, or teachings, of Buddhism.

Transcending Ego, Affirming Character

Taoism shares many spiritual practices with Buddhism, while emphasizing the importance of character. The Tao tells us:

> *All actions flow from the Tao*
> *Character* (Te) *shapes them,*
> *Circumstances complete them.*
>
> **(Tao, 51)**

By building character, we transcend ego, overcoming the false by affirming the true. As Emerson realized from his studies of Eastern philosophy, "character is higher than intellect." What we think takes us only so far. Who we *are* ineffably imprints on what we do.

According to Washington, D.C., writer Charles Peters, Presidents Lyndon B. Johnson and Richard M. Nixon lacked strength of character in administering American foreign policy. They surrendered to "the need to appear tough," which kept us embroiled in the Vietnam War.[2] Concern with their image narrowed their vision, causing thousands of unnecessary deaths.

A Taoist definition of character takes us beyond the need for approval and applause. We are told:

> *The Tao leader*
> *Does not try to appear great*
> *And thereby achieves*
> *True strength of character.*
>
> **(Tao, 34)**

Whether arrogance or insecurity motivates our concern with our own image, the result is the same: We become fixated on ourselves. Full of ourselves, we have little room for anything else. We shut ourselves off from new sources of information, becoming deaf and blind to advice that could lead to wise decisions. Self-centeredness is a fatal flaw in leaders.

Leadership Is More Than Being Well Liked

Our culture's values too often neglect substance for surface. Willy Loman, the misguided protagonist in Arthur Miller's *Death of a Salesman,* spent his entire life trying to be well liked. Men and women of character set their compass by a higher standard than this. They know that externals—fame, fortune, and fancy titles—do not constitute leadership. Leadership involves strength of character, which means making tough decisions, doing things not because they're popular but because we believe in them.

When we take an unpopular stand, people are bound to criticize us. We will not always be well liked. Tao leaders work to transcend their own hurt and defensiveness, so they can listen to criticism and learn from it.

TAO QUESTION
How do you respond to criticism? Do you feel wounded? rejected? defensive?

If so, remember that no one is perfect. Like everyone else, you're a human being, here to learn and to grow.

Most criticism isn't a personal attack. When people criticize you, look beneath the surface. Ask yourself what action, policy, or behavior they're criticizing, whether the criticism is justified, and what you can learn from it.

This exercise will help you develop greater detachment and strength of character.

•　　　•　　　•

Tao leaders don't take criticism personally. They know it is part of our collective search for truth. They don't expect to have all the answers or to proceed without error. In fact, they welcome people who can be honestly critical—for the greater good of us all.

How Do You Perceive the People Around You?

Another sign of character is how leaders perceive the people around them. I once heard a woman say, "I have ten people working under me." Under her? This phrase sounded odd. I don't think of people working *under* me unless they're working in the basement. I work *with* my colleagues—we're on the same team.

Our language often reveals outmoded attitudes. Some people speak in the language of hierarchy, of "superiors" and "subordinates," of working "under" or "over" someone. As we learned in the last chapter, they're still living in a paradigm of "power over," not "power-with."

Insecure leaders are often threatened by excellent people in their midst. With their limited concept of power, they see someone else's success as diminishing their own. There's a Native American legend told by the Quakiutl people on Vancouver Island about two mask makers, an accomplished master and his protégé. The young man learned his craft so well that his skill threatened his mentor. The older man couldn't accept the excellence of his protégé, so he killed him. The master was condemned to be a river and never to rest because in life he'd been driven by the currents of envy and ambition.[3]

Practicing Detachment

The Tao tells us:

> *In leading others and serving the universe,*
> *The greatest lesson is detachment.*

Detachment means transcending ego.
This comes from years of building character.
With strength of character
Nothing is impossible.

(Tao, 59)

Until we give up attachment to our self-image, we spend lots of time and energy defending it. Detachment brings liberation. All the energy we've spent preserving our image comes back to us, and our time expands as well. Our lives become more enjoyable, less of a struggle.

In detachment, we perceive the recurrent patterns in our lives, the subtle energies within and around us. Greater awareness gives us greater freedom of choice. Aware of our patterns, we can move with them or work to change them.

Have you ever been a prisoner of envy? I have. I found myself becoming increasingly uncomfortable around a successful woman I know. To see what was happening, I wrote down my feelings about her for a few days. The lesson was fascinating. I found I envied all the qualities I admired in her. I'd been relating in the old seesaw paradigm of power. What she had made me feel less.

I didn't like the way I'd been feeling, so I decided to make peace with her. We had a pleasant lunch together, and I felt much better, no longer drained by the negative energy of envy.

This experience taught me that whatever other people say or do, whatever happens on the outside, I value my peace of mind far too much to engage in competitive ego games.

Mushin—the Power Beyond Ego

The Japanese have a word for what happens when we clear away ego blocks. They call it *mushin;* in Chinese, the word is *wushin* (literally "no mind"). The word means a mind crystal clear, able to perceive all the beauty and significance on life's horizon.

In the traditions of Zen and the martial arts, we create a *suki*—an ego block or opening—whenever we become fixated on a person, object, problem, or conflict. These openings are places where we don't see clearly, where we become reactive and vulnerable to manipulation. Zen meditation is designed to help heal these areas of vulnerability so we can become more whole, more totally present.

Anger, envy, resentment, insecurity, trying too hard—all these create *suki* within us. We develop a split consciousness, which takes up valuable energy.

Overcoming *suki* gives us a new level of power. Have you ever seen an Olympic athlete perform so well, so naturally, that the technique seemed easy? Or a musician play as if he were one with his instrument? Or a ballerina dance as if all the steps came naturally? Or an aikido master move with effortless grace? It all seems like magic. It is *mushin,* the art beyond art, when we transcend self-consciousness to become one with what we do. This is the mind of Tao, which makes leadership a joyous dance and life a work of art.

Transcending *Suki:*
The Threefold Way of Detachment

The Tao tells us to

> *Know fame and glory,*
> *Yet remain humble as a valley,*
> *With potential*
> *Vast and undiminished*
> *Like an uncarved block of wood.*

> *When the wood is carved,*
> *It is used by others.*
> *Wise leaders*
> *Are mindful of wholeness,*

Not letting themselves
Be carved into pieces.

(Tao, 28)

Tao leaders strive for the wholeness of *mushin,* the integrity of the uncarved block, overcoming the *suki* that carve them into pieces. Three common areas of *suki* are role identification, emotional reactions, and attachment to outcome. The following pages will show you how to overcome them.

Avoiding Role Identification

Many dedicated leaders fall prey to role identification. Our jobs become so central to our lives that everything else loses significance. Many companies encourage this imbalance, subtly discounting our personal lives, our need for rest and recreation. People equate their worth with their work, at the expense of their health, their happiness, their humanity. Perhaps this extreme behavior grew from our Puritan roots or perhaps from our Western emphasis on activity and distrust of contemplation. Whatever the cause, conscientious people by the hundreds of thousands overidentify with their jobs.

This pathological behavior can be fatal. I sometimes call it the "King Lear syndrome." King Lear, in Shakespeare's play, retired, dividing his kingdom among his daughters. Suddenly without crown or country, he suffered an identity crisis. "Who is it that can tell me who I am?" he cried in despair, went mad, and died, taking many people with him. When he was no longer king, Lear felt he was without worth, and his two heartless daughters confirmed his estimation.

King Lear is a dramatic fiction, but similar real-life dramas occur when role-identified people lose their jobs to retirement or layoffs. A wave of suicides followed the layoffs of aerospace engineers in Seattle some years ago. Without their jobs, these men, like Lear, did not know who they were.

Marge, a woman in her early sixties, told a friend recently that she was afraid to retire because "Who will I be then?" She has been a wife and a mother and is now CEO of the family business. Because she has role identified all her life, her future prospects seem sterile and bleak.

Role-identified people can become hostile and defensive, afraid of change because it threatens their security. Sociologist Kichi Iwamoto says that "when a leader stays in one position too long, it becomes almost personal property."[4]

Tao Insight: I Am an Evolving Soul

The Tao gives us greater perspective, helping us overcome role identification, reminding us that nothing in the universe stands still. We're all here to develop our potential.

One way to overcome fear of change in your career—whether a layoff, a promotion, or retirement—is to affirm to yourself:

"I am an evolving soul."

Another way is to keep growing. Tao leaders are self-actualizing people who embrace change as a process of discovery, a means of becoming more of who they are. With our sights set on the horizon, we cannot become fixated on the present.

As we continue to learn, we increase our knowledge base, our competence, and our joy in life. John F. Kennedy realized that "Leadership and learning are indispensable to each other."[5]

TAO QUESTION

"In a world that is constantly changing, how can I keep learning?"

Detaching from Emotional Reactions

Successful leaders are not reactive. Even when faced with conflict, they don't let their emotions throw them off balance.

A friend once told me, "I don't get angry with people because I can see where they're coming from." A leader in his profession, his wisdom and compassion keep him from being reactive. As a result, his mind is as clear as a mountain lake, his judgment and perception of detail truly remarkable. I have seen him remain steady, daring to speak his truth, affirming integrity in many turbulent situations. "You have the qualities of a samurai warrior," I once told him, deeply impressed with his strength of character.

The samurai would never fight when they were angry. They knew they would lose their center, their judgment, and their honor. Succumbing to anger, they could not maintain their edge. The Tao tells us:

> *The best leader does not use force.*
> *The best warrior does not act in anger.*
> *The best officer does not fight petty battles.*
> *The best managers seek to understand their people.*
> *This is the practice of detachment*
> *Which brings the power to lead others*
> *And is the highest lesson under heaven.*
>
> **(Tao, 68)**

TAO QUESTIONS

"What can I learn from this lesson of the samurai?"
"How can I apply it to my life?"

Detachment from Outcome

Detachment from outcome is a lesson that spans many spiritual traditions, from those of the Native Americans to those of the Taoists of ancient China.

Life in the industrialized West makes us impatient with process, addicted to the illusion of control. We punch the remote to change the channels on our television sets. A phone call brings us a broad assortment of consumer goods, available twenty-four hours a day. But all this control is only an illusion. We cannot control the moon, the tides, the cycles of nature, or the seasons of our lives.

Whenever we blend our energies with those of anyone else, we lose exclusive "control." And the Tao reminds us that nothing in the universe exists alone; we are always blending our energies with others: at home, at work, in relationships. We creatively coexist with all the people, plants, and animals on this planet. Because of the complex tapestry of life, our intention can be only *part* of any outcome.

To relinquish the illusion of control, to detach from the outcome, does not mean to surrender our goals and become ineffectual. Mahatma Gandhi, who liberated an entire subcontinent from colonial oppression, made detachment an important part of his spiritual practice.

Gandhi used to say that we were not responsible for the outcome. Our duty is to make sure that our motives are pure and our means are consistent with our beliefs. If we take care of our motives and means, the rest will follow naturally.[6]

Gandhi knew what one committed individual can do. "My life is my message," he said. When beset by challenges and blocked by confusion, remember this lesson from Gandhi: Your life is your message, your personal testament of what you believe.

No matter how dark and foreboding a situation may seem, your task is only to walk the path with heart. Set your goal, then take one step at a time on that journey of a thousand miles, making sure that your motives are pure and that you are acting with integrity. The universe will do the rest.

TAO EXERCISE: THE PRACTICE OF DISIDENTIFICATION

If you feel overwhelmed by any aspect of your life, try this practice of disidentification:

Take a deep breath. Slowly release it, and say to yourself:

"I *have* a job, but I am not my job."

"I *have* emotions, but I am not my emotions."

"I *have* a goal, but I am not my goal."

(For any other area of your life in which you feel "stuck," simply fill in the blank: "I *have* ——— but I am not my ———." Some possibilities are: family, children, love, home—or any other area you choose.)

Once you have disidentified, *then* remind yourself of what you are. "I am a child of the universe." "I am an evolving soul." "I am a conscious spark in the galaxy of universal light." Make up your own expansive definition of all that you are.

Leaders Produce Results, Not Excuses

To disidentify and detach from outcome does not mean to relinquish results. The focus and flexibility of Tao leadership always produces results, results we can live with.

Some people get results; others give excuses. They're always missing deadlines or arriving late. Then they waste people's time with elaborate alibis.

I've learned a lot by watching the people around me. Leaders don't want to hear excuses, nor do they make them. In the past, when running late, I used to greet people with a dramatic list of "reasons," convinced that I had to earn absolution.

Over the years, my precision has improved. But when I do run late, there are no more elaborate confessions, just a brief apology, and then I get on with what we're doing. Leaders don't want excuses. They want action.

Maintaining Perspective

In our busy lives, it's important to maintain our perspective. In the nineteenth century, Henry David Thoreau said, "Our life is frittered away by detail. . . . Simplify, simplify." His own efforts to simplify, to seek the essentials, made his book *Walden* an enduring record of one man's spiritual quest.[7]

Cultivating Vision and Precision: Yin *and* Yang

A leader needs the complementary qualities of *vision* and *precision*. Overwhelmed by extraneous details, the structure of our lives can become obscured by clutter. We need vision to guide us into the future. On the other hand, we must be mindful of important details or we'll make costly errors.

Both vision and precision flourish when we detach from ego, seeing beyond ourselves to perceive the scope and detail of our lives. Precision is nurtured by the practice of mindfulness, which will be explored later. Vision is nurtured when we get away from the incessant details, the daily deluge of paperwork long enough to see what it's all about.

Cultivating Vision

The Tao tells us:

> *Empty your mind of clutter,*
> *Maintain an inner peace.*
>
> *Ten thousand things move around you.*
> *In detachment, perceive the cycles.*
>
> **(Tao, 16)**

When pruning my Japanese maple recently, I experienced just how this process works. To prune a tree in the Japanese manner, you must study it with your heart–mind, removing any leaves and branches that are not part of the essential design.

What is the essential design? It gradually reveals itself as you look for it.

The same lesson is true in our lives. Every so often, we need to do some pruning, to eliminate everything that is not part of our essential design. One day, while I was working at home, I called in to check my voice mail at work. There was no emergency, nothing requiring my immediate attention. All the administrative details could wait until the next day when I was back in the office. Saving those messages, I returned to my work. When I checked in later that day, one person had called back to say that she had answered her own question. I smiled and thought how refreshing it was not to be interrupted—as I am in the office—with details, minor crises, questions, and routine paperwork.

TAO QUESTION

As life presents you with a continuous stream of invitations and opportunities, remember to make your choices affirm your essential design. Ask yourself: "Is this activity central to me or peripheral?"

Peripheral choices are not wrong in themselves. What is peripheral to you may be central to someone else. Recently, I was asked to give a workshop on a subject that was peripheral to me but of central interest to a friend. I declined the invitation, recommending my friend instead—a choice that benefited both of us.

Tao Time

It's important to set time aside regularly to gain perspective. Whatever field we're in, as leaders we all do research of one kind or another, developing new projects and learning more about the implications of our decisions, our directions, our lives.

A clear vision can save us weeks, even months, of wandering through details and debris. It can reveal new solutions to pressing problems. For example, in November 1940, Franklin D.

Roosevelt came up with his lend-lease plan while on a two-week Caribbean cruise on the USS *Tuscaloosa*.

Although people agreed that the president deserved a rest after the recent election, many complained that with Britain's survival hanging in the balance, this was hardly the time for him to take two weeks off. But it was. The time away—the rest, renewal, and *yohaku*—was just what Roosevelt needed to see beyond traditional politics and to come up with a daring new idea. His innovative lend-lease policy provided ships and supplies to Britain, helping that beleaguered country survive during the grueling winter of 1940 until the United States entered the war and the Allies defeated the Axis powers.

Take your cue from Roosevelt and remember to renew yourself—and your vision—with well-timed vacations and regular breaks from work. During the dark days of the Great Depression and World War II, Roosevelt kept up his country's morale with his own buoyant optimism, which he continually recharged by vacations and visits from friends. He recognized the importance of time off for renewal, no matter how great the challenges of his presidency.

Remember the importance of *yohaku* in cultivating long-range vision. Give yourself some "Tao time" every week. Take a walk. Get away from your desk. See an old friend. Shake the cobwebs out of your mind and let the insights come.

Knowing Yourself: Perceiving Your Patterns

The Tao tells us:

> *Tao leaders*
> *Respect themselves*
> *Without needing approval,*
> *Know themselves*
> *Without self-consciousness.*

(Tao, 72)

Gaining greater perspective, detaching from ego, you'll recognize some of your recurrent patterns and learn more about your talents, strengths, and weaknesses. This inner work is a vital responsibility for leaders.

Strengths and Weaknesses: Yin *and* Yang

Years ago, while teaching Shakespeare, I realized that all the heroes in his tragedies make their fatal choices because of character. Who we *are* inevitably determines what we *do*.

As I studied these heroes more closely, I noticed that their greatest strengths were also their greatest weaknesses. Hamlet and Othello are polar opposites. Hamlet is the thinker who is unable to take action, whereas Othello is the man of action who never stops to think things through. One man's character was molded by his study of philosophy, the other's by a lifetime on the battlefield. In both cases, their extremes led to tragic errors: their greatest strength was their greatest weakness. It is so for all Shakespeare's tragic heroes, and it is so for us.

Think of someone you know. What is his or her character strength? One of my strengths is high energy. The upside of this strength is high motivation; the downside is impatience. I've been wrestling with impatience all my life. My impatience to complete projects tempts me to rush when I get near the end. This tendency can produce hasty actions and unnecessary errors. My greatest strength is my greatest weakness.

My friend Kim has lots of empathy for others. As a division manager in a computer start-up company, she has won the trust and loyalty of all her employees. That's the upside. The downside is that she empathizes so much that she often finds it difficult to take a stand.

Leon, a top-flight executive, has a great deal of confidence, which gives him the courage to take risks, to chart new courses for his company. The downside is that his equally strong ego keeps him from listening to the people around him, which makes it hard for him to practice the principles of inclusive decision making he says he believes in.

In each case, self-knowledge can help us affirm our greatest strength. Being mindful of the downside can keep us from falling into our greatest weakness.

TAO QUESTION
What is your greatest strength or weakness?
How about some of the people you know?

Mindfulness: Cultivating Greater Precision in Your Life

Along with vision, wise leaders cultivate precision, focusing on the important details of their lives. The teachings of Buddhism help us stop being caught up in recurrent dramas by becoming mindful of what is happening within and around us. We turn from drama to dharma by following the Buddhist practice of mindfulness, which is also the way of Tao.

TAO QUESTION
When you find yourself swept up in a challenging situation, instead of reacting emotionally or turning away, look more deeply at it. The wise leader uses every challenge as an opportunity to grow.

Ask yourself: "What can I learn from this?" Then watch and listen.

Being Mindful
Living mindfully makes life an ongoing meditation, a continuous opportunity for discovery. When you detach from ego, you

become more aware of important details. No longer turned inward in emotional turmoil, your senses become more acute. You'll find lessons everywhere, as Shakespeare put it, "Tongues in trees, books in running brooks, sermons in stones and good in every thing."

TAO EXERCISE

Spend a short time each day simply being mindful. You may begin with ten or fifteen minutes. Turn your senses outward. Notice, really notice, the colors, textures, and patterns around you. Look at people's eyes. Become more aware of their energies. Don't judge. Merely observe.

After a while you can practice this exercise while waiting in a bank line, riding the subway, sitting in a meeting, or relaxing during your lunch hour. Being mindful subtly expands your awareness, building greater detachment and strength of character. It also increases your enjoyment of life.

You can reinforce your practice of mindfulness by saying an affirmation every morning, such as "I am mindful of my life today" or recording your insights in a journal.

Being Mindful at Work: Avoiding Isolation

The Tao warns leaders to remain centered and mindful or

> *Losing touch with our hearts,*
> *We fall into confusion*
> *And fools try to sell us*
> *Their answers.*

(Tao, 38)

One common problem for leaders is becoming isolated, losing touch with what's happening around them. Sociologist Kichi Iwamoto says that leaders become isolated when they rely too heavily on advisers, some of whom may not be trustworthy. When leaders start believing what people say about them, "believing their press clippings," as he put it, they're headed for trouble. Isolation can lead to inflated egos and poor decisions.

The greater the leader's authority, the greater the possibility of isolation and the greater the danger. "Johnson didn't have a clue about the public's feelings about Vietnam until too late," Iwamoto noted. Carter was insulated by his staff, and Nixon "wasn't kept informed about the dangers or the consequences of the Watergate break-in."

Leaders become isolated because members of their staff often shy away from criticism, not wanting to be the bearers of bad news. At best, such people mean well but are conflict avoiders; at worst, they are conscious manipulators. Either way, they sabotage their leaders by concealing the truth.

For centuries, in both the East and the West, handbooks for leaders have described the dangers of isolation. In Renaissance Italy and England, Baldassare Castiglione's *Courtier* and Shakespeare's history plays warned leaders of "flatterers," the yes-people who swarm around a leader like flies around honey. Attracted by the trappings of power, flatterers manipulate leaders to advance themselves politically. In Japan, the samurai warned of flatterers, calling them *nei-shin,* followers who could not be trusted. The *Tao Te Ching* of ancient China warns us to look beneath the surface of charming rhetoric, for

> *Truthful words do not flatter.*
> *Flattering words are not true.*
>
> **(Tao, 81)**

How can leaders avoid isolation? One way is to be mindful enough to recognize the cloying sweetness of false praise and centered enough to avoid it. As a friend told me recently, "a leader is someone who's learning to do without narcissistic gratification."

You can avoid isolation if you keep learning. Don't rely on your advisers as your only channel of information. John F.

Kennedy read three newspapers every morning to keep up with national and international affairs.[8] What do you do to keep up in your field?

Another way to avoid isolation is to choose advisers you can trust to tell you the truth. Following her coronation in 1558, Queen Elizabeth I made her chief adviser, William Cecil, Lord Burgley, promise he would always tell her the truth, no matter how disagreeable. True to his word, he remained her loyal adviser for forty years.

Franklin D. Roosevelt had his own "loyal opposition" in his wife Eleanor, who became a valuable source of information, traveling around the country, and later the world, keeping the president informed about the plight of his people. Two strong personalities, Franklin and Eleanor became loyal partners in a cause that transcended their individual differences. She reflected in her memoirs that "He might have been happier with a wife who was completely uncritical. That I was never able to be, and he had to find it in other people. Nevertheless, I think I sometimes acted as a spur,"[9] reminding him of difficult problems to solve, important work to be done.

Do you know someone whose commitment to truth transcends ego and partisan politics? Integrity makes this person a rare gift, priceless as an adviser, friend, and colleague.

Affirming Integrity

The Tao tells us:

> Tao leaders live close to nature.
> Their actions flow from the heart.
> In words they are true;
> In decisions, just.

(Tao, 8)

The Tao leader lives with integrity, building power through strength of character. The samurai code held that a *gishi,* or person of integrity, was greater than an accomplished master in any art. The samurai lived by an intrinsic concept of honor, which once violated, required them to perform *seppuku,* ritual suicide, because they could not live with the shame of dishonor. *Bushi no ichi gon,* the word of a samurai, was an oral contract, a promise based on personal honor. A liar, *ni gon* (literally "double tongued"), was punished by death and disgrace.

Western Europe had its parallel in the *comitatus,* the Germanic code of loyalty that bound a knight to his liege lord and held the fabric of society together in the early middle ages. Honesty and trust were everything. One who broke his word was reviled as an animal, an outcast, outside the bounds of civilization. In the Renaissance, Edmund Spenser's epic, *The Faerie Queene,* upheld Arthur as the model of magnanimity, the combination of all the knightly virtues: greatness of soul.

In our century, one whom the Hindus called "great of soul"—Mahatma—Mohandas K. Gandhi, changed the history of India without money, armies, or political position, armed only with the personal power that radiated from his integrity.

In today's cynical world, where economic values often distract us from deeper truths, we have a tremendous need for leaders with integrity. In the late 1980s, four top administrators from some of California's most prominent institutions of higher education—Stanford University, the University of California, the California state university system, and the California community colleges—lost credibility and power over issues of integrity.

These administrators were intelligent, well-educated, committed individuals. But they faltered. How many of us would have done the same?

A 1994 article in the *Washington Post* reported that over one hundred students at the U.S. Naval Academy were caught cheating, violating their honor code, which states: "Midshipmen are persons of integrity; they do not lie, cheat, or steal." As disappointing as the cheating itself was the slipshod disciplinary action taken by the administration. Only six students were expelled, and many of the ringleaders were released. Annapolis superintendent, Rear Admiral Thomas Lynch, said that the U.S. Naval Academy must revise its curriculum to emphasize character development. However, the students were already following a four-year integrated ethics curriculum. Up until then, however, their knowledge of ethics apparently had been more theory than practice.[10]

Integrity may be hard to find, but it is much desired. No matter how many disappointments and disillusionments they have suffered at the hands of scoundrels, people still want to trust their leaders. Management experts James Kouzes and Barry Posner found, in more than a decade of research with over 15,000 managers worldwide, that the number one value people look for in a leader is integrity.[11]

Developing Integrity: Four Stepping Stones

Leaders are, of course, only human. We do not come into this world as perfect beings. Other species are physically stronger than we are. They can run faster, dive deeper, swim farther, and even fly under their own power. But as humans, our greatest asset is our ability to learn. We can build ourselves up in any area—our aerobic ability, muscle mass, communication skills, or integrity—with conscious training.

Four stepping stones on the path to greater integrity are

1. to live your values consistently
2. to maintain a spiritual practice
3. to tell the truth
4. to practice openness.

Let's consider these steps in greater detail.

Consistently Living Your Values

The Chinese classical writer Meng-tzu told a story about a man who used to steal a chicken every day. When someone told the man that stealing chickens was wrong, he agreed to cut down. He stole only one chicken a month and planned to stop completely the following year.

What's wrong with this story? If stealing a chicken every day is wrong, it's also wrong once a month. The fable highlights a common failing in ethical behavior. Many people persist in stealing an occasional chicken, rationalizing with situational ethics or a promise to cut down.

Dr. Marcia Pearce, pastor of the Valley West Church in Campbell, California, reminds her people: "Never compromise principle, not even on special occasions."[12]

Her statement is a great affirmation about consistently living our values. With consistency comes greater strength of character. When we backslide, even if no one else finds out, *we* know, and it weakens us. When we affirm integrity, we also know, and it strengthens us. Tao leaders realize that they can never fool themselves—or the universe.

Maintaining a Spiritual Practice

The Tao tells us:

> *The greatest virtue seems unreal,*
> *And strength of character appears like folly.*
> **(Tao, 41)**

The way of integrity runs contrary to prevailing norms in our society, which are based on competition and short-term economic gain. These popular values may be normal, but they're not natural.[13] Nor are they healthy. But because they're so prevalent, we need a regular spiritual practice to counteract their aversive effect on us.

Steve Privett, academic vice president of Santa Clara University, says that the main responsibility of a leader to himself or herself is to maintain integrity. A Jesuit committed to social justice, he stays in touch with his values through prayer and meditation, regularly reflecting on what's important to him. If you keep your values in the forefront of your mind through your spiritual practice, he says, you notice and "seize the opportunities which arise. If the concern is only for your career, then you grab those opportunities."[14] By pursuing a regular spiritual practice, what you value determines at a deep level the daily choices you make.

TAO QUESTIONS
"What is my spiritual practice?"
"How do I remind myself of my deepest values?"

Your practice can be anything that affirms your own deepest values—prayer, meditation, devotional reading, a centering exercise (such as yoga, tai chi, running, or aikido) or getting in touch with nature. Find something that speaks to you and reinforces what you believe and pursue it regularly.

Telling the Truth

The Tao exhorts us to live and speak our truth. Telling the truth builds integrity. The word *integrity* (from the Latin, *integritas*) literally means wholeness. Every half-truth or act of dishonesty divides us, leads to *dis*integration of our essential self. Every act of honesty leads to deeper integration, making us stronger and more whole.

A commitment to honesty doesn't mean telling everything you know. As a leader, you need to keep some things confidential.

A commitment to honesty *does* mean avoiding "diplomatic dishonesty," or white lies. Resorting to such untruths may seem like the easiest thing to do at the time, but these untruths build walls between people, one brick at a time, and divide us from ourselves.

Challenge yourself to combine honesty with compassion in

all your interactions. Small acts of honesty are the spiritual equivalent of isometrics. Each time you perform them, they'll become easier and you'll grow stronger.

Practicing Openness

Open communication builds integrity and nurtures trust. Keeping information hidden behind closed doors creates distrust, even if there's nothing unsavory going on. Whenever I'm faced with a routine choice between openness and secrecy, I choose openness because of the healthy atmosphere it engenders.

I learned this lesson from my state assembly representative, John Vasconcellos. When I visited his Sacramento office in the early 1980s, John received a phone call that most politicians would handle in private. I got up to leave, but John shook his head, while telling the person on the phone in no uncertain terms how upset he was about his stand on a current bill. In public or in private, John stands by his word, practicing the openness he believes in.

He has also been open about his ongoing therapy and involvement in the human potential movement, which has shaped his values and his politics. A number of years ago, the news that Senator Thomas Eagleton had seen a therapist destroyed his political career. John, on the other hand, had nothing to expose simply because he had nothing to hide.

Following John's example, I try to be more open about my life, my decisions, and my opinions. Openness cuts down considerably on stress. You don't have to worry about people finding out, since in an open atmosphere they already know.

Surviving Adversity and Success

The Tao asks:

> *Which is greater,*
> *Fame or peace of mind?*

Which is more valuable,
Peace of mind or wealth?
Which brings more problems,
Gain or loss?

(Tao, 44)

In the Hindu classic, the *Bhagavad Gita,* Arjuna learns that a person with the highest consciousness is free from anger, free from fear, unshaken by adversity. Even the way this person moves conveys composure and peace of mind.

The *Tao Te Ching* also reminds us to stay centered. With classic paradox, it tells us that success and failure can often produce opposite results:

Some win by losing
Others lose by winning.

(Tao, 42)

After an unpromising early life—he was called "Useless Grant" by many people—Ulysses S. Grant overcame a series of failures to emerge as Lincoln's commanding general, leading the Union to victory during the Civil War. Overcoming adversity, he won while losing, becoming a national hero. But then he lost by winning. As president of the United States, he was an abject failure.

His inauguration in 1869 ushered in an era of graft, corruption, and nepotism, known as "Grantism." Grant gave away cabinet positions to unqualified men who'd done him special favors. Adolphe Borie, of Pennsylvania, who knew nothing of naval affairs, but had given Grant fifty thousand dollars for a new house, was named secretary of the navy, and Alexander Stewart, a rich New York merchant, who had given the first lady a new wardrobe, was named secretary of the treasury. Two dozen of Grant's relatives were appointed to the civil service and foreign ministry. The influence of financial opportunists Jay Gould and Jim Fisk over Grant's ambitious brother-in-law brought about "Black Friday," a disastrous drop in the national gold market.

Totally out of his element, Grant was a hero on the battlefield, but a failure in the White House. His state dinners were opulent affairs, with thousands of dollars spent on rare delicacies. Surrounded by the trappings of success, Grant made bad decisions, trusted the wrong people, and lost his center. And our country lost a valuable opportunity to rebuild the nation during Reconstruction, leaving the South to unscrupulous carpetbaggers.

The Tao tells leaders not to be distracted by success:

> Foolish leaders indulge themselves,
> Leaving their fields untilled
> And their storehouses empty.
> They wear impressive clothes,
> Brandish sharp words and weapons,
> Are addicted to food, drink, and possessions.
> This is the road of excess,
> Not the way of Tao.

(Tao, 53)

Keys to Surviving Challenge and Adversity

The Tao reminds us to stay centered, trust the process, detach from outcome, and take the longer view. Successful leaders are unmoved by extremes of crisis or success. They can tolerate high levels of anxiety.

Flexible as bamboo, they don't hold on so tightly to one option that they can't recognize alternatives. When faced by challenge, they keep moving forward. Sometimes this means the equivalent of tacking into the wind, sometimes taking one slow step at a time on a path that feels bogged down by mud. Never losing heart, Tao leaders stay the course at those times when life seems to be testing them. When they've proved themselves and the resistance clears, they move ahead with a quantum leap in the direction of their dreams.

Dealing with Immature People

As you work to transcend ego, you'll see people around you who are still drawn into the mire of flattery, ego intoxication, and manipulation. Like some unfortunate dinosaurs drawn into primeval tar pits millions of years ago, these emotionally immature people are caught in a sticky mass from which they cannot extricate themselves. Sometimes these people will betray and disappoint you, offering you another powerful lesson on the path.

Emotional Immaturity and Corporate Politics

As a new manager in a computer company, Dale worked hard to create an atmosphere of cooperation and teamwork. To meet a proposed budget cut, Dale called together the department's senior members to draft a cooperative plan designed to protect their junior colleagues from the next round of salary cuts and layoffs.

But a chain of cooperation is only as strong as its weakest link. After Dale submitted the plan to Nick, the division head, a junior employee named Wilma met privately with Nick to lobby on her own behalf. He flattered her, took her out for a drink after work, and pumped her for information, promising that whatever happened to the rest of her department, *she* was special, and her job was not in danger. Instead of increasing her duties and reducing her salary and staff support, he promised her a raise.

Her ego intoxicated by flattery, Wilma laughingly undermined her department's cooperative plan, calling it "silly" and "illogical." She discredited her senior colleagues, whom she secretly envied, and exulted in this opportunity to exercise power over them by playing up to Nick.

So intoxicated was she with power that she bragged to some of her colleagues about her "influence" over Nick. "He listens to me," she said. "The senior members of this department are out of touch. They're just a bunch of old fogies."

Instead of going through channels, Nick began meeting with Wilma, inflating her ego by letting her in on confidential information. Meanwhile, Dale wondered why it was taking so long to hear about the cooperative plan. Was Nick stalling?

When Wilma's betrayal was revealed, Dale was angry and disheartened. Her end run had sabotaged months of careful work and put many junior people, even Wilma herself, at risk.

Why had Wilma betrayed her colleagues, sabotaged her department, and worked against her own best interest? Nick was notorious for isolating people, promising them special favors, using them to get what he wanted, and then discarding them. Dale realized that the only way to overcome such corrupt practices was to affirm a larger vision by establishing democratic procedures and consistent policies. Otherwise, corporate life can become a Hobbesian nightmare, "nasty, brutish, and short," in which unscrupulous people manipulate others to their advantage with all the tricks in Machiavelli's book, *The Prince*.

The Tao encourages us to transcend self-centered politics and affirm a larger, inclusive vision. But even if we transcend ego ourselves, this doesn't mean that people around us won't succumb to short-sighted and self-centered behavior. End runs, sabotage, and self-centeredness are still quite common, even in progressive organizations, and present a powerful challenge to Tao leaders. What would *you* do in this situation?

Staying Centered: Overcoming Fight or Flight

The wisdom of Tao asks us to look beneath our anger and disappointment, to see that often underneath the gossip, end runs, and back stabbing, there's an insecure person in there. Insecurity makes us vulnerable to flattery and manipulation by those we think have the power to give us what we want. It can make people lose their centers and compromise their integrity.

The important thing when dealing with these insecure people is not to let them make us lose *our* centers. Overreacting to their behavior can throw us into fight or flight. The stress response—adrenaline rushing through our bodies—can easily make us lose perspective. We fall into a *fight* mode, seeing the immature person as the enemy, becoming fixated on him or her, losing our balance and peace of mind. Or we fall into a *flight* mode, becoming disillusioned with the system. Our energy drained by disappointment, we feel like giving up. Either way, we surrender to negativity, letting someone else's immature behavior drag us off center.

Disheartening as such behavior may be, don't let it sabotage you. If you do, then that misguided person will have won, overpowering you with negativity. Then you'll be unable to exert your positive energy to make a difference. Remember the wisdom of Tao: Look to the larger patterns. This event is only an unruly wave. It is not the ocean. The cycles of *yin* and *yang* show us that ultimately nature achieves its own balance. For every action, there is an equal and opposite reaction. For every excess of *yang,* there's a corresponding extreme of *yin.*

People who play destructive political games ultimately isolate themselves and lose what power they have because no one trusts them.

Following the larger vision of Tao, progressive leaders affirm the power of honesty, integrity, and truth, the force that Gandhi realized can overcome all error and pretense. The force of truth—*satyagraha*—exposes lies, reveals injustice, and removes the veils of illusion that give temporary advantage to any would-be gossip or saboteur.

A Lesson from Aikido

The nonviolent martial art of aikido gives us a helpful process for dealing with immature people:

1. *Get off the line:* Don't be sucked in by this person's negative energy.
2. *Blend:* Feel compassion for this confused individual. Compassion keeps you from falling into fight or flight. It will not allow polarization to distort your perspective and make you lose your center.
3. *Extend:* Reach out with positive energy. Working with the larger patterns, you can develop an effective strategy to deal with the current challenge.

The *Tao Te Ching* reminds us that energy is all there is. If we stay centered and look to the larger vision, we can redirect any energy, any challenge, into patterns of greater harmony.

Transcending Roles and the Compulsion to Control

The Tao asks us:

> *Can you lead your people*
> *Without seeking to control?*
>
> **(Tao, 10)**

After years of consulting with leaders in California's Silicon Valley, Kichi Iwamoto observes, "Many executives claim that they're into empowerment but still insist on making all the decisions." This behavior, he believes, "is tied to male gender." He recalls many "cases in which traditional men view themselves as weak if they delegate," seeing themselves as "a failure as a man."

As a sociologist, he links this behavior to the traditional stereotype of men as providers, recalling a classmate in graduate school who dropped out of the Ph.D. program because he couldn't stand having his wife work while he pursued his studies. Because his wife earned more than he did, he didn't feel like a man.

Iwamoto says that in corporate decision making many men still cling to the need to control. Falling unconsciously into the old dualism, they see themselves as either "strong providers or a disgrace."

This compulsive controlling behavior afflicts not only men, but women who identify with patriarchal models of power and success.

How do we avoid being trapped by old stereotypes? By taking our cue from the Tao. Leaders who keep growing are more flexible, more accepting of change and diversity. Centered and detached, they transcend ego and aren't threatened by delegation or by excellence in their midst.

Leadership skills in the next century, Iwamoto says, will involve "more traditional female characteristics," focusing on cooperation, rather than competition. A 1990 article in the *Harvard Business Review* called this new approach "transformational" leadership. Unlike those leaders who see work as an exchange of rewards for goods and services, transformational leaders inspire people to see beyond their own self-interests, to work together for the common good. These new leaders are interactive, stressing openness and empowerment, raising people's self-esteem, combining vision with shared decision making.[15] Does all this sound familiar?

The teachings of ancient China and modern research on leadership converge, affirming a dynamic, inclusive, inspirational leadership that will help us deal with the greater diversity, new challenges, rapid change, and uncertainties of life in the twenty-first century.

Some studies have attributed the emergence of this new leadership to the growing number of women in middle and upper management. But progressive *men,* as well, have seen beyond the limits of the old command-and-control model. San Francisco attorney Jeff Capaccio learned from his Italian culture the vision of expanded community that he has affirmed since his college years. As an undergraduate, he was a consultant to Santa Clara University's Faculty Development Program, and his work with the National Italian American Foundation brought him to the Oval Office and a meeting with President Jimmy Carter. Now politically active on many levels, he uses his networking skills in his work to serve existing clients and develop future clients and to support the many causes he believes in, building on the creative synergy of cooperation and community.

British leadership consultant William Peace practices a Taoist paradox, finding strength in vulnerability, which increases a manager's level of trust and credibility among employees. In an article in the *Harvard Business Review,* he explained how he met personally with a group of people his company was laying off—and how this act of courage and vulnerability changed the culture of the company.[16] This is the courage of Tao leaders, who

> *Live with humility*
> *Remaining ahead of their people*
> *By walking behind*

(Tao, 66)

Inspirational leaders have always challenged people to look beyond themselves. In 1960, John F. Kennedy exhorted Americans to take a more active share in realizing our national and global ideals. The words of his inaugural address echoed in the minds and hearts of a generation: "Ask not what your country can do for you; ask what you can do for your country." A nation's youth entered adulthood inspired with a commitment to democratic values. Many entered the Peace Corps, worked for social justice, and campaigned for causes they believed in. Our lives took on greater meaning in a New Frontier that led people to look beyond the narrowness of ego gratification to an expanded sense of self-actualization through public service.

Tao Leaders in Our Midst

Years later, Tao leaders are still in our midst, sometimes going about their work so quietly we fail to notice. But they're everywhere—from the White House to the house next door. Look around and see how many of your neighbors are walking the path of Tao.

My friend and neighbor Emma Kaliterna, who has been in business in Santa Clara for over fifty years, runs a highly effective network, supporting a number of community services from the small beauty shop she owns and operates. Selling raffle tickets from her shop, organizing benefits in her backyard, collecting money to buy gifts for people in need, she has made her hometown more beautiful and humane, raising funds for the art museum, restoring historic buildings, and helping the disadvantaged. All this she does with tremendous vitality and an upbeat attitude that keep her more youthful than people half her age.

While visiting her shop one day, I found a quote on her wall that affirmed for me the power of character, the way of Tao:

> *Pattern your life after the giant bamboo.*
> *The exterior, though smooth and lovely to the touch,*
> *Is tough and resistant to the sword.*
> *Within it is soft and pliable,*
> *With much space for continued growth.*
> *It grows neatly and ordered,*
> *Never cluttered.*
> *Alone, it rises tall and straight,*

Always upward to the sky.
There it spreads its beauty to the sun.
It leans on nothing.
It makes its own way,
Perhaps near others, a part of others,
But very much dependent
On its own strength and force.

So pattern your life.

Leading with the Tao is above all else a matter of character. It is transcending ego, looking beyond ourselves to find lessons all around us. It means living our lives to make a difference, inspired by the strength and resiliency of nature, the ineffable power of Tao.

CHAPTER 12

Creating Harmony

My words are easy to know,
Easy to practice.
Yet few under heaven
Know or practice them.
My words reveal
Eternal principles,
Enduring patterns.
Pathways to harmony.

(Tao, 70)

The Tao leader is a pioneer, a pathfinder, who continually faces the unknown, exploring new territories, dealing with unforeseen challenges. In this complex world of transition, we travel from the known to the unknown with no maps to help us find our destination. Yet we have a compass to guide us and a lamp to light our way. With its enduring principles drawn from nature, the *Tao Te Ching* acts as a compass. The Tao also affirms the power of our intuition, the inner light that dispels the shadows of fear and doubt, revealing to us the hidden possibilities in any situation.

Guided by the principles of Tao and the power of intuition, we can respond successfully to the challenges of our times, creating new patterns of harmony to heal and transform our world.

The Tao reminds us to maintain the vital balance of *yin* and *yang,* action and contemplation, self and other:

> *Hold to this timeless pattern*
> *Throughout the time of your life,*
> *Aware of the eternal cycles,*
> *The essence of Tao.*

(Tao, 14)

Within its timeless pattern, there is dynamic balance: a time to act, a time to pause, a time to reach in, a time to reach out. Over two thousand years ago in another tradition, the Jewish scholar Rabbi Hillel came to a similar realization. His words have inspired many, including Israeli leader Golda Meir. Hillel helped people lead lives of balance and commitment by posing three essential questions:

"If I am not for myself, who will be for me?"
"If I am for myself alone, who am I?"
"If not now, when?"

Addressing these questions and following the principles of Tao, this chapter focuses on the essential task of all Tao leaders: to live more deeply for ourselves while not for ourselves alone. The first section, Tao Leadership in Action: Creating Harmony, shows how some people have applied Taoist principles to today's challenges. The second section, The Leader's Journey: Creating Inner Harmony, describes the inner journey that makes these external transformations possible.

Tao Leadership in Action: Creating Harmony

This section demonstrates how some Tao leaders have created harmony around them by drawing on the timeless principles of the *Tao Te Ching*: (1) honoring the cycles, (2) complementary polarities: *yin* and *yang,* (3) dynamic growth, (4) oneness, (5) respect and community, and (6) conflict resolution.

Honoring the Cycles
The Tao tells us:

> *Ten thousand things move around you.*
> *In detachment, perceive the cycles.*
> *Watch each return to the source.*
> *Returning to the source is harmony*
> *With the way of nature.*
>
> *Knowing the cycles brings wisdom.*
> *Not knowing brings disaster.*
>
> **(Tao, 16)**

Our relationship with the environment dramatically demonstrates this lesson. Shanghai, China's 1,200-year-old port city, seems an appropriate place to study the cycles of Tao. From its origins centuries ago as a small fishing village, Shanghai has always been nourished by the waters surrounding it. Located at the mouth of the Huangpu River, Shanghai's busy harbor is filled with oceangoing vessels; tiny sampans; crowded passenger ferries; and barges carrying coal, produce, and heavy equipment.

But when I visited Shanghai in 1993, I learned that its water supply is so polluted that even local residents cannot drink the water without boiling it first. In recent years, Shanghai has become China's center of trade and industry, producing iron and steel, heavy machinery, and petrochemicals. The result of this rapid technological growth has been widespread pollution. In a tangible form of karma, what people give out comes back to them—in their drinking water.

The lesson is clear: When building up our industrial base, we must not lose sight of our connection with the land; with the natural cycles; and with water, the source of all life. *Shui,* the character for water in Chinese, is the emblem of life in the *Tao Te Ching:* strong, fluid, flowing in endless cycles. To deny this essential element is to deny life itself.

Water pollution afflicts both the East and the West. In 1994, the Environmental Protection Agency declared that 40 percent of American waterways (one-half our lakes and one-third of our rivers) are too polluted to be safe for drinking, fishing, or swimming.

Environmental pollution offers today's leaders a crucial lesson: to work *with* the cycles. Recycling and precycling (the wise use of materials) are effective ways to do so. Using plastic containers works against the cycles. In the United States we use up to 60 billion pounds of plastic a year, only 3 percent of which are ever recycled. Over 20 billion pounds a year find their way into our nation's landfills, which will be filled to 80 percent capacity in the next twenty years.

Glass containers are a better choice because they can be recycled. Aluminum is even better. In the United States 60–70 percent of aluminum cans are recycled annually, and the percentage is continuously increasing. Recycling aluminum is profitable and prevents further damage to the environment from mining aluminum ore. Aluminum can be recycled repeatedly, and its recycling–reuse cycle is highly efficient. The aluminum container you use today can be back on the shelf in three months.[1]

Recently, progressive corporations have begun doing "eco-audits" to see how well corporate policy corresponds to the cycles of nature. When the management at Odwalla, a California health food drink manufacturer, conducted an eco-audit in 1993, they switched vendors, so they could use more recycled paper. Working with the natural cycles can bring a company good corporate karma and save money. The Bank of America saved $2.5 million in energy costs in 1993, after an eco-audit recommended new energy-efficient lighting for its offices.[2]

Working with the natural cycles can create new solutions to old problems. While traveling in Canada in 1993, I learned about Wolfgang Reichmann, a biological engineer who invented a "breathing wall" to purify air in public buildings. The wall is a living ecosystem, made up of lava rocks, tropical plants, moss, orchids, and a small pond. Aided by a ventilation system, it removes pollutants, turning stale air to fresh, while also relieving stress.

A self-contained cycle, the air in the building repeatedly returns to the source, circulating through the moss, water, and flowers to remove impurities; turning carbon dioxide into oxygen; and adding negative ions to the atmosphere. When workers walk by this tropical scene, they take in more than fresh air. The beauty of this tiny ecosystem—the soft sounds of the water, the vision of tropical plants and flowers, the goldfish sparkling in the pond below—refreshes their spirits as well.[3]

Complementary Polarities: *Yin* and *Yang*

The Tao tells us:

> *All life springs*
> *From* yin *and* yang
> *As they blend forever*
> *Into new patterns*
> *Of harmony*

(Tao, 42)

Combining the wisdom of East and West, many progressive ventures are bringing us new insights and new possibilities. Two examples are the East-West Center in Honolulu, Hawaii, and the International Technological University in Santa Clara, California.

Founded by an Act of Congress in 1960 to promote greater understanding among the governments and peoples of Asia, the Pacific, and the United States, the East-West Center is an international university and research and conference center. Each year over two thousand academic researchers, business professionals, journalists, and policymakers from the East and West work with the center's staff on environmental issues, population trends, economics, energy, mineral resources, communications, and international relations. With its seminars, conferences, and research programs, the center not only helps solve complex international problems, but promotes cooperation as a vital leadership skill.

The East-West Center helped analyze China's first census and predicted the rise of Asia as a leader in world trade. Current projects include the implications of Asia as the world's second largest oil consumer, the growing greenhouse gas emissions and environmental depletion in the area, the transfer of Hong Kong from British to Chinese sovereignty in 1997, agricultural development, population trends, family planning, and the status of women in the region. The center's work—very much in keeping with the Tao—is to study emerging patterns—trends and consequences—using the foresight of today to deal with the challenges of tomorrow.[4]

In another innovative educational venture, my friend Dr. Shu-Park Chan realized a lifelong dream as the International Technological University welcomed its first class in fall 1994. After thirty-five years of college teaching, Park retired from his career as professor, department head, and acting dean of the School of Engineering at Santa Clara University to found this new graduate university.

ITU grants master's and Ph.D. degrees in electrical engineering, computer engineering, software engineering, and applied mathematics. It draws students and faculty from the East and West, combining the perspectives of business and the academic world. A number of industrial leaders serve as part-time lecturers to provide a healthy balance between theoretical development and practical applications in all its degree-granting programs. ITU students study with these leaders from industry, as well as with professors from universities in the United States, China, and Russia. Then they complete a year-long internship with a corporation, writing up their findings in a publishable thesis. ITU's combined perspectives should help its graduates create new solutions to today's complex problems and promote the mutual understanding so vital to building world peace.

Shu-Park Chan himself combines the best of East and West in a life that has seen many changes. His father, Chi-Tong Chan, was a Chinese warlord with three wives and eighteen children. A four-star general in the nationalist Chinese army, Park's father was a gifted poet and calligrapher in the tradition of the scholar-warrior. General Chan founded two high schools and two universities in China. Park and his wife, Stella, a teacher and writer, are accomplished painters who have sold hundreds of Chinese watercolors and prints.

Park Chan had originally planned to build a university in China in 1985, when that country began reaching out to establish joint ventures with the West. After extensive negotiations with the Chinese and American governments and pledges of support from major U.S. corporations, Chan obtained a site for the university in Shenzhen, southeastern China, across the harbor from Hong Kong. He took a leave of absence from Santa Clara University and moved to Shenzhen in July 1984, with construction slated to begin in a few weeks. But because of changes in the Chinese government, the project was abruptly canceled.

With the strength of bamboo, which bends but does not break, Chan returned to the United States and modified his plan. Nine years later, he founded the first campus of his international technological graduate school in California's Silicon Valley, with future branches planned for other countries in the Pacific Rim.

Shu-Park Chan comes from a strong family background that upheld the importance of character. He and his two brothers, Shu-Yun Chan and Shu-Gar Chan, coauthored an engineering textbook that they dedicated to their father, who had taught them the traditional Chinese principles of goodness:

> *Set a good goal in mind.*
> *Acquire a good wealth of knowledge.*
> *Exercise good self-discipline.*
> *Perform only good deeds.*

Combining the wisdom of East and West, Dr. Shu-Park Chan is most surely a Tao leader. His International Technological University combines opposing polarities to create greater understanding, and his life upholds a lesson of perseverance and hope.[5]

Dynamic Growth

The Tao tells us:

> *The natural world is like a bellows.*
> *The shape changes, but the essence remains,*
> *Ever moving, ever producing.*

(Tao, 5)

Tao leaders recognize the waves of change and work with them. Recent U.S. defense cutbacks have produced powerful opportunities for this kind of leadership. Turning swords into plowshares, men and women of vision are transforming old military bases into new facilities for peace.

On October 1, 1994, the U.S. Army Presidio of San Francisco was transferred to the National Park Service, becoming Presidio Park, a green retreat for city residents, as well as an international conference center. The 1,480 acres are being converted to many peaceful uses. People can walk beneath the silent pines and look out to the breathtaking waters of San Francisco Bay. The old Letterman Army Hospital will become an educational and research center; the army cavalry stables will house horses for the park police, as well as a riding facility for disabled persons; Crissy Field, which borders the Bay, will become a wetland and a walking and windsurfing area. Some of the Presidio's other buildings and housing have become a global conference center, which has already hosted representatives from Guatemala, helping to support the work for peace in that troubled area.

In an even more ambitious transformation, the U.S. Army has transferred 1,300 acres, 260 buildings, and 1,253 housing units of what was once Fort Ord to the Department of Education to become a new college campus, California State University at Monterey Bay (CSUMB), scheduled to open in fall 1995.

CSUMB will combine the Tao principles of dynamic growth and cooperation to produce a new kind of university. Transforming an old army base from which thousands of troops were once sent to Vietnam into new peacetime uses, the university will work with nearby educational and research centers to create new programs in the environmental sciences, language and culture, the arts, economics, business and trade, education, and technology.

Within its proposed structure are many major innovations. CSUMB will organize its curriculum around interdisciplinary clusters with courses focused on real-world problems. Students will learn academic skills in a pragmatic context, working in teams to develop cooperative skills. CSUMB will share courses, faculty, and facilities with other institutions. In its structure, it will be a living example of interdependence, a model for a global community.

Old facilities will be put to new uses. The Defense Language Institute, which once trained members of the CIA, will now offer college students an in-depth language learning experience. The university will also explore new ways of connecting education with industry. Corporate partnerships with computer firms in California's Silicon Valley will build a state-of-the art technological infrastructure, connecting the campus offices, dormitories, the library, and the conference center, as well as providing global access. Students will participate in organized work-study programs, learning valuable life skills, as well as developing a partnership with the local community. CSUMB will also set up educational exchanges for students and faculty with universities around the Pacific Rim, increasing diversity and expanding its educational mission.

As rising tuition and fees limit access to higher education, CSUMB will reverse this trend, using a sliding-fee scale and innovative financial aid to make a college education possible for all qualified students. By means of the new California Student Service Trust Fund, students will be able to earn tuition credit through community service. An old Chinese proverb says, "If you are planning a year ahead, plant a seed. If you are planning for ten years, plant a tree. If you are planning for a hundred years, educate the people."[6] CSUMB's vision of education is an investment in the future of our society.

Oneness

The Tao tells us:

> In ages past, people followed the One.
> The heavens were bright and clear.
> The earth was in balance.
> The spirits rejoiced.
> The valleys were filled with life.
> The ten thousand things flourished.
> The leaders were wise
> And their people in harmony.
> All this came from oneness.

(Tao, 39)

The Taoist concept of oneness has progressively found its way into medicine, holistic health, and the way we view ourselves. Antonio Demasio, M.D., Ph.D., head of the Department of Neurology at the University of Iowa College of Medicine, has come up with a new hypothesis: that reason and emotion are *not* separate functions, that indeed our feelings are a necessary component of reason. I am reminded of the Chinese character *xin,* which means heart-mind, a unified sensibility that Western philosophy has polarized since Descartes.

In his book, *Descartes' Error,* Demasio cites case studies and describes the still mysterious frontiers of the human brain.[7] He found that within a highly developed area of our frontal lobe, our body awareness and emotions combine to help us make essential self-affirming choices in life.

Demasio's holistic view of cognition has led him to advocate a more holistic study of healing in medical schools, by combining medicine with psychology and the humanities to provide physicians with a deeper and more thorough understanding of human nature.

In another holistic approach to healing, award-winning researcher Michael Lerner founded Commonweal, a health and environmental research center in Bolinas, California. The Cancer Help Program, a week-long residential retreat, offers patients what Lerner calls "complementary" therapies. In addition to supervised care by their own physicians, the patients receive spiritual and emotional support, a low-fat vegetarian diet, light exercise, yoga and meditation, and a creative outlet through the arts. Lerner's program helps participants develop their own approach to healing as they confront the challenge of serious disease, reducing their fear by making them more aware of their choices.

After receiving his Ph.D. at Yale and teaching there for a year, Lerner worked with the Carnegie Council on Children, where he became aware of the profound effect of diet on behavior. He turned his attention to nutrition and healing, founding Commonweal in 1976. In 1982, he began traveling around the world to study different cultures' approaches to cancer treatment. The following year he received a prestigious MacArthur Fellowship. After further study in England, France, Germany, and Japan, he recorded his findings in his book, *Choices in Healing: Integrating the Best of Conventional and Complementary Approaches to Cancer.* With his rare ability to integrate, Lerner has won the respect of the medical community while speaking credibly about alternative approaches, bridging what has too long been a gap between traditional medicine and holistic health.

Other Commonweal programs include the Family Consulting Service and Young Adults Program, which focuses on learning and family relations; the Sustainable Futures Project, which examines the lifestyles, values, knowledge, and technologies necessary to build an environmentally sustainable future; and the Biodynamic/French Intensive teaching garden, a living laboratory for better agricultural methods. Commonweal's approach to personal and planetary healing affirms in many ways the Taoist principle of oneness.[8]

Respect and Community

The Tao tells us that

> *The Tao leader creates harmony*
> *Reaching*
> *From the heart*
> *To build community.*

(Tao, 49)

The wisdom of Tao takes us beyond linear thinking. We learn that we belong to a living ecosystem, that the choices we make each day have major repercussions in the world around us. Extending this vision from the environmental to the political level, we see ourselves as part of a vital global community that begins locally and extends ever outward. As former Speaker of the House Tip O'Neill used to say, "All politics is local." Tao leaders think globally and act locally, reaching out to build a community of respect that can link our world with new bonds of understanding.

One example of this perspective is Pueblo to People, a Houston-based import business established in 1979, which links Third-World cooperatives with American customers in an ongoing exchange of goods, money, friendship, and understanding. Pueblo to People uses world trade to build a community of heart, telling the stories of the people behind the products. On the colorful pages of a recent catalog, I read about Petrona, a Guatemalan woman who has helped obtain more nutritious food for her family and a better education for her children through the Las Artesanas de San Juan weaving project. The faces of Petrona, her husband Gaspar, and their three children smile up at the reader from the catalog, bridging the miles with a personal greeting. Petrona has earned self-respect and a better life for her family as she helps create beautiful clothing for her neighbors to the north. A nonprofit agency, Pueblo to People keeps its overhead low, so that the producers, people like Petrona, get their fair share of the earnings.[9]

Another example of innovative partnership is the one that has been developed between the people of Yoff, Senegal, and Ithaca, New York, unified by their vision of an environmentally sustainable, cooperative community. Yoff, a fishing village nine miles from the capital city of Dakar, Senegal, is a 500-year-old community based on consensus decision making, citizen participation, and care for one another and the environment. The Yoff have always recycled everything, feeding worn-out baskets to goats and building their homes of sand and dirt and their fishing boats from nearby trees. For their thirty thousand people, they have no police force. The community resolves disputes and takes care of its people. It even has a community fishing net, which is lowered into the water and shared with anyone whose own catch is low.

But Western commercial values from nearby Dakar were eroding Yoff's traditional lifestyle. Young people's values were undermined by advertisements and images on their newly acquired television sets. That was until 1992, when Serigne Mbaye Diene, a Yoff student at Cornell University, met Joan Bokaer, a community activist working to establish Ecovillage in Ithaca. The two recognized that what Ithaca's citizens wanted to create, Yoff already had and was in danger of losing. A few months later, Joan Bokaer and five other Ecovillage founders met in Yoff to share ideas.

The New Yorkers gave the people of Yoff positive reinforcement for their traditional values and took away some valuable models. They also helped their neighbors in Yoff come up with ways of introducing Western technology—a new sewage system and housing plans—that were in harmony with the land and one another. Word of the partnership spread. The Canadian Healthy City Network Conference acknowledged Yoff as a model for its own efforts. In December 1995, an international ecocity conference will be held in Yoff, with the president of Senegal presiding.[10]

Conflict Resolution

As was discussed in Chapter 10, Tao leaders work to turn conflict into opportunities for greater understanding, stronger relationships, and better solutions. Instead of fleeing from conflict or fighting with the opposition, people of vision are learning to transform conflict into cooperation.

At Santa Clara University in 1993, writer Sunny Merik's research paper for a graduate course became a call to action for her campus. Her essay, "The Claims We Make Make Claims on Us: An Action Plan for Incorporating Social Justice Within the Employment Practices of Santa Clara University," asked people to apply their mission of education and social justice where they live and work. Sunny focused on "the working poor," low-paid staff members struggling to live in California's expensive Silicon Valley. Many staff members are single mothers who are working full time to support their families. They go without, live in subsidized housing, work extra jobs, shop at flea markets, never take vacations, drive old cars that are falling apart, and worry from one paycheck to the next. She asked some of these people what they needed to improve the quality of their lives, and together they came up with innovative solutions such as group auto insurance, a campus barter system for home repairs, tutoring and child care from college students, free lunches at the student cafeteria, weekend vacations at nearby Catholic retreat centers, airfare for funerals and other family emergencies from frequent-flier miles earned by faculty and administrators, and personal and professional development through free university courses.

Sunny's paper was circulated among faculty, staff, and administrators and discussed at an Ethics Center forum. This led to the formation of the Action Task Force, committed individuals working together to make a difference.

A model for conflict resolution on many levels is the Carter Center in Atlanta, Georgia. Founded as a nonprofit public policy institute in 1982 as part of Jimmy Carter's vision of service after leaving the presidency, the Carter Center combines conflict resolution with prevention in its many innovative programs.

Through its International Negotiation Network, the center monitors global conflicts, offering advice and assistance. It has brought together experts to address conflicts in Angola, Armenia, Azerbaijan, Burma, Cyprus, Haiti, Korea, Liberia, Macedonia, the Sudan, and Zaire. The center has recently begun a long-term program to reduce ethnic tensions in the former Soviet Union.

In an effort to prevent conflict by affirming an open, democratic process, the Carter Center monitors elections in the western hemisphere and Africa. After the elections, the center's staff members work with new governments to uphold human rights and build stronger economic, educational, and health care systems. The center also offers other countries partnership and advice on food production, disease prevention, and environmental protection.

Taking conflict resolution and prevention into our cities, the center's Atlanta Project and its national counterpart, the America Project, work at the community level to support grassroots efforts for positive change. Some results include children's health and immunization projects, the renovation of vacant buildings into affordable housing, antiviolence campaigns, and other community self-help programs.[11]

Committed to helping people find alternatives to violence and despair, Jimmy Carter has worked personally building affordable housing, visiting with neighborhood self-help groups, monitoring elections, and resolving potentially explosive conflicts around the world. He also wrote a book for young people, *Talking Peace: A Vision for the Next Generation,* in an effort to spread the skills of peacemaking and problem solving to our next generation.

The Tao tells us:

> *Compassion triumphs over adversity,*
> *Brings power and protection.*
> *Heaven always arms its leaders*
> *With the strength of compassion.*
>
> **(Tao, 67)**

With compassion and faith guiding his many peacemaking efforts, Jimmy Carter has taken leadership to a new level, becoming a role model for many and a Tao leader of the highest order.

The Leader's Journey: Creating Inner Harmony

As a familiar saying affirms, "As it is within, so it is without." We reach out to create new patterns of harmony by creating harmony within. The quest for inner harmony has been known by many names throughout recorded time. It is the *Odyssey* of Homer, the spiritual journeys of Gautama Siddhartha, Arjuna in the *Bhagavad Gita,* Dante in the *Divine Comedy,* Christian in *Pilgrim's Progress,* and the quests of the Knights of the Round Table. It is as old as the first known epic, as new as *Star Wars,* as intimate as the struggles of our own lives. It is the journey undertaken by courageous individuals and recorded in heroic myths from the dawn of history to the present day.

All too often busy leaders get bogged down by the details of their jobs—the duties, deadlines, budget crises, conflicts, and personnel issues. With our attention splintered, we cannot see the larger patterns of meaning. The *Tao Te Ching* reminds us that like the heroes of myth and legend, we are all on a journey of discovery.[12] This journey, which Joseph Campbell called "the hero's journey," is the leader's journey, our life's journey, filled with significant crossroads, challenges, and rewards. There are decisions we make—crossroads—that irrevocably change our lives. We learn lessons about ourselves and others, often in the most unexpected ways. And the challenges, even day-to-day hassles, are essential spiritual exercises, opportunities to build character and to become stronger, wiser, and more whole.

Seen this way, every external action has an internal consequence, a spiritual equivalent. We are all on the path. The word "Tao" itself means path or journey. The *Tao Te Ching* tells us that a life well lived is the greatest gift we can give to the world—or ourselves:

> *Noble deeds are a rare gift.*
> . . .
> *Therefore, on the inauguration of a great leader,*
> *Or the installation of a high official,*
> *Rather than sending gifts of jade*
> *And fine horses,*
> *Make a gift of living the Tao.*
>
> **(Tao, 62)**

Vocation: The First Stage on the Path

The decision to self-actualize, to become more of what we are, generally begins with a sense of restlessness. The call to leadership comes to us at different times, in different ways. It may be a life-changing event or a subtle longing, a move, a promotion, or an inner need. But the result is inevitable: We cannot stay as we have been. We must move on.

In spiritual traditions, this summons has been known as vocation, the call of the soul. Like the sound of distant trumpets or the vision of a mountain peak, it beckons to us, at first subtly, then more powerfully until its call cannot be ignored. Leaving behind the familiar, the comfortable, the known, we are impelled to move forward in the direction of our dreams.

Crossing the Threshold

As we leave the familiar, we cross the threshold into another world. We enter a new frontier. As a popular science fiction series puts it, we "boldly go where no one has ever gone before."

When we leave the known for the unknown, we inevitably encounter resistance. Resistance can be mental or physical, internal or external. Joseph Campbell tells of Columbus's crew, who were gripped by fear as they left the bounds of civilization to face the Great Unknown. With their emotions and imaginations running wild, they expected to meet some terrifying monster or sail off the edge of the world.[13]

Crossing the threshold often produces external resistance. Chuck Yeager told how his aircraft and instruments began to shake violently as he approached the sound barrier. But when he broke through the barrier, the air was suddenly calm and smooth as glass.

Resistance can come from the people around us. Comfortable with the way we were, our friends and families may resent our emerging self. As we deviate from familiar routines, our actions seem strange and foreign to them. "That's not like you," they'll say, trying to get us to go back to the ways they're comfortable with. Their resistance may make them into what Joseph Campbell called "Threshold Guardians,"[14] individuals who guard the meridian between what was and what will be. Overcoming these guardians, our first test on the journey, helps build our resolve and strength for the trials to come.

At times, resistance may come from deep within us. Our anxieties and fears can be powerful threshold guardians in themselves, creating a chain of worries, what-ifs, and fearful fantasies. We can be haunted by past mistakes and failures, projecting them on the present, fearful that this opportunity, this success, this relationship won't last. But the Tao tells us that we are never limited by what has been. We can always create a new, more positive cycle by centering and blending with the energies within and around us.

Our self-doubt can plague us with a series of negative prophecies, saying that since we've never done something before, we obviously cannot do it, whatever, at this point, "it" happens to be. We can overcome this resistance by becoming centered and detached, by looking at things logically. Common sense will tell us that we've gone through life developing quite a good record of doing things we've never done before: learning to walk, to talk, to read and write, to drive a car, and many other skills we probably now take for granted. At one time, each of them was a new challenge. The Tao tells us that

> *A journey of a thousand miles*
> *Begins with a single step.*

(Tao, 64)

The path of human progress has been cleared, one step at a time, by those who dared to reach out to new possibilities, to do what they'd never done before.

Initiation

As we face the next level of life's journey, leaving behind the familiar, we're initiated into the unfamiliar by means of trials or tests. These tests are spiritual exercises that strengthen and prepare us for our next level of life. In the initiation rituals of Native Americans, a young person would go off on a solitary journey and return to the tribe with a new awareness and a new name. There are times in our lives when we, too, undergo powerful initiations, profound personal changes, *metanoia.*

At such times, everything seems to fall apart, and familiar patterns are no longer there to support us. We must face a new job, a new stage in life, a new challenge, seemingly on our own, like a young Cherokee brave on a vision quest, a solitary Taoist monk on the path, or a Hindu sage in the mountains.

Yet centuries of human history will tell us that we are *not* alone, that men and women of courage have walked that path before us, exploring the unknown, facing the challenge, and returning with a valuable treasure—a gift for themselves and their people. Creative people—artists, scientists, innovators, and leaders—have always walked this path. Twenty-five centuries ago, Lao-tzu wrote in the *Tao Te Ching:*

> *To be alone on the journey*
> *Is what most people fear,*
> *Yet the Tao leader chooses this state.*
>
> **(Tao, 42)**

Facing the Dragon

At some point on the journey, we face the dragon, confronting a challenge that brings us face to face with our own deepest fears, providing a powerful lesson that builds character and prepares us for increased responsibility.[15]

The Tao tells us that

The Tao creates
And Te cultivates,
Nurtures and protects,
Promotes, but does not possess,
Empowers, but does not take credit,
Leads without dominating.

This is the power of character.

(Tao, 51)

Facing the dragon is the ultimate test of character. A powerful archetype in both Eastern and Western literature, the dragon was the symbol of power in ancient China. The emperors were known as "sons of the dragon," believed to have descended from some mythical dragon ancestor. Clothed in robes of golden silk embroidered with dragons, they held court seated on a gold Dragon Throne. Behind the throne loomed a high Dragon Screen, covered with golden dragons. Dragons decorated the eaves of royal buildings, gazing down at the lowly mortals below.

Dragons in the East were associated with ineffable power. Legend has it that when Confucius met Lao-tzu, he was amazed by the power of the Taoist sage because it transcended all that he knew or understood. Lao-tzu's power was like nothing else on earth, he admitted. The Taoist master could ride on the wind, at one with the power of nature. As Confucius said, "He is indeed a dragon."

The more powerful the heights we aspire to, the more powerful the dragons we must face to get there. Some people are attracted to the idea of power but cannot handle the real thing.

The fourth-century Chinese sage Shen Zi told a story about a proud man who was so fond of dragons that he filled his house with dragon paintings, dragon carvings, and dragon tapestries. One day, a real dragon flew down and looked in through the window. Face to face with the dragon, the man convulsed in fear and ran out the door.

This man did not really like dragons at all. He liked the *idea* of dragons, the image and trappings of power. He couldn't handle the real thing when it stared him in the face.

Facing a powerful fire-breathing dragon was, in medieval European literature, the ultimate test for heroic knights. At the end of his life, the Anglo-Saxon hero Beowulf faced a mighty dragon guarding a treasure cave. St. George, patron saint of England, was a renowned dragon slayer. In Renaissance epics and iconography, the dragon gradually became a symbol of the forces of darkness.

Facing the Inner Dragon

In Jungian therapy, the dragon is a symbol of the shadow, the powerful unresolved forces of our unconscious.[16] For every "dragon" or major challenge we face on the outside, there's a corresponding dragon within. The test of the dragon brings up all our unresolved anxieties, our old hurts and fears. Facing the dragon is the ultimate test of confronting ourselves.

The Tao tells us to

> *Know the sunlight*
> *While confronting the shadows,*
> *Becoming a leader to all.*
> *As a Tao leader,*
> *You move with infinite power,*
> *Ever drawing upon the source.*

(Tao, 28)

The Tao calls on us to know ourselves deeply, to face our fears, our dark-shadow side, and come to terms with it. Once we do so, its powerful energies cannot be used against us. When we cast light on a shadow, the shadow disappears. Just so, when we acknowledge our own shadow side, the inner dragon fades away and the outer dragon weakens as well, no longer fueled by the powerful energies of our unconscious.

In medieval legend, knights who successfully faced the dragon returned with a valuable treasure: a magical sword, gold, jewels, or the hand of a fair maiden in marriage. Whenever we face the dragon, we, too, return from this confrontation with a treasure, a valuable insight about ourselves, a deeper awareness and the strengths we'll need to handle the new responsibilities in our next stage in life.

Detachment and Blending

Facing the dragon brings us greater detachment. We don't overreact to challenge and change because we realize that our security lies not in externals but in our ability to stay centered and blend with the energies around us.

Because they transcend themselves, Tao leaders are not limited to their individual strength. As in the legend of Lao-tzu, they draw on the ineffable power of nature. The results seem effortless, paradoxical, defying all logic, as in this passage from the Tao:

> *The best runner leaves no tracks.*
> *The best speaker makes no mistakes.*
> *The best mathematician does problems in his head.*
> *The best door needs nothing to secure it.*
> *The best knot does not bind,*
> *Yet cannot be loosened.*

(Tao, 27)

The Tao leader prevails because he or she transcends ego, recognizing and flowing with the dynamic energies of nature. This is the secret of Tao.

Randori: Taking Chaos

Sometimes we seem to face many dragons at once—coming at us from different directions. The ultimate challenge for people who are accustomed to the illusion of control is when life brings us a *randori*. The word in Japanese means literally "taking chaos," combining *tori* (to take) with *ran* (chaos).[17]

The ultimate test of leadership in this world of rapid transition is how well we can "take chaos," that is, deal with a rush of unexpected forces. At work these forces can be multiple deadlines, conflicts, and crises; in our lives, a combination of powerful challenges coming at us all at once. How do we successfully take chaos?

One answer comes from aikido, the most Taoist of all martial arts. After fending off every possible attack, dealing with different opponents and dozens of complex techniques, including knife attacks, the candidate for an aikido black belt must face the final contest, the *randori*.

Standing at one end of the mat, tired from the previous exertion, breathing heavily and bathed in sweat, the candidate faces a group of fresh opponents, all black belts, who line up at the other end of the mat.

"*Hajime!*"—begin! the head sensei calls out, and the blackbelts rush at the lone contender.

How does one handle a *randori*? By remaining centered, by not getting fixated on any one attacker or overwhelmed by the size of the group. The new black belt stays centered, keeps moving forward, watches for the energy patterns, and deals with the challengers one at a time.

The same principles apply when we face a *randori,* the test of chaos in our lives. A Tao leader doesn't surrender to despair when faced by what seem like overwhelming odds. He or she stays centered, watches for the energy patterns, and deals with challenges one at a time. Getting caught up in any one of them will leave us unprepared for the others. We must stay centered, detached, and flexible, affirming the strength of bamboo, the enduring power of water.

TAO QUESTION
Each of us will answer this Tao question when the time comes: Can you take chaos?

Remember the lesson of *randori*—and the reward that inevitably follows. For when life brings us a *randori* and we pass the test, it also gives us the equivalent of a black belt. Each of us moves forward in life, becoming a master, a Tao leader.

The Leader's Journey: Endings and Beginnings

The lessons of Tao are as old as time and as new as tomorrow. They are guides to the journey of life, a journey of mastery that many are called to follow as we confront the challenge of a new millennium. As the old forms are rapidly replaced by the new, many people are seeking new patterns of leadership to help chart our pathway to the future.

As we have seen from these pages, the answer to the call, the ability to create new harmonies around us, lies deep within us. The *Tao Te Ching* reminds us:

> *With strength of character*
> *Nothing is impossible.*
> *When your heart expands*
> *To embrace the impossible,*
> *You are able to lead with Tao.*
>
> **(Tao, 59)**

The leader's journey is yours and mine. With the wisdom to see beyond ourselves, to flow with the natural patterns, together we can create a new form of leadership to heal and transform our world.

Frontispiece Character: *Tao* (in Chinese); *do* (in Japanese): literally, "the way," "the path," or "the principle." This character is made up of the symbol for "leader," based upon the ancient Chinese ideogram for the human head, together with the symbol for "to walk." The root meaning of this famous character is clearly mindfulness in action, an enduring ideal for today's leaders.

Character: *tama,* literally "jade," the stone that represents infinite beauty and the precious quality of life itself.

Introduction

Character: *haji,* literally, "to begin." The term is comprised of two characters: a young woman and the power of speech.

1. All quotes from the *Tao Te Ching* in this book are from my poetic translation and are cited by chapter numbers to facilitate comparisons with other versions. To comprehend the wisdom of Tao more fully, you will need at least one complete text of the *Tao Te Ching.* A good literal translation is *The Wisdom of Laotse* by

Lin Yutang (New York: Modern Library, 1948). My favorite modern translations are the beautiful *Lao Tsu: Tao Te Ching* by Gia-Fu Feng and Jane English (New York: Random House, 1972), with its photographs and calligraphy echoing the lessons of Tao, and the recent *Tao Te Ching* by Stephen Mitchell (New York: HarperCollins, 1988), which uses both masculine and feminine pronouns to include all the leaders in today's world.

2. For background information on systems theory and family systems, I am grateful to John Berbert, M.A., of Santa Clara University's Counseling Center. For a classic description of systems theory in business, see Douglas McGregor, *The Human Side of Enterprise* (New York: McGraw-Hill, 1960).

Chapter 1 Zanshin

Character: *zanshin,* literally, "the spirit stays or lingers." The term means connection, the ability to extend our energies outward to create new harmonies.

1. Warren Bennis and Burt Nanus, *Leaders: The Strategies for Taking Charge* (New York: Harper & Row, 1985), 13.

2. Carolyn Hennings, director of career services, Santa Clara University, interview, July 15, 1993. Used with permission.

3. Jerald Hage and Charles H. Powers, *Post-Industrial Lives: Roles and Relationships in the 21st Century* (Newbury Park, Calif.: Sage Publications, 1992), 11. For a fuller discussion of the movement from roles to relationships, see 8, 161–93.

4. For a discussion of the convergence of physics and Eastern philosophy, see Fritjof Capra, *The Tao of Physics* (New York: Bantam Books, 1975), passim. For a fuller discussion of *zanshin,* see Mitsugi Saotome, *Aikido and the Harmony of Nature* (Boston: Shambhala, 1993), 175.

5. S. R. Maddi and S. C. Kobasa, *The Hardy Executive: Health Under Stress* (Chicago: Dorsey/Dow Jones-Irwin, 1984), 31–32.

6. Yamamoto Tsunetomo, *Hagakure: The Book of the Samurai,* trans. William Scott Wilson (New York: Kodansha America, 1979), 94.

7. Chungliang Al Huang and Jerry Lynch, *Thinking Body, Dancing Mind: Taosports for Extraordinary Performance in Athletics, Business,*

and Life (New York: Bantam, 1992), 89. Quote and ideas for some of the Tao questions used with permission.

8. Facts about Lincoln are from the excellent biography, *With Malice Toward None: The Life of Abraham Lincoln* by Stephen B. Oates (New York: Harper & Row, 1977). I am grateful to Robert Numan, Ph.D., for sharing this book with me.

9. John Keats, letter to George and Thomas Keats, December 22, 1817. In John Bartlett, *Bartlett's Familiar Quotations,* ed. Justin Kaplan, 16th ed. (Boston: Little, Brown, 1992), 417.

Chapter 2 *Centering, Presence, and Process*

Character: *musubi,* literally, "to bind" or "to connect"; the energy flow that binds us—and all of life—together.

1. For more information on Tohei, see William Reed, *Ki: A Road Anyone Can Walk* (Tokyo: Japan Publications, 1992), 43–48.

2. I have paraphrased Shaw's quotation, "You see things; and you say, 'Why?' But I dream things that never were; and I say, 'Why not?'" from *Back to Methuselah* (1921) Pt. 1, Act 1.

3. Marsha Sinetar, *Ordinary People as Monks and Mystics* (Mahwah, N.J.: Paulist Press, 1986).

4. Ralph Waldo Emerson, *Nature* in *Selections from Ralph Waldo Emerson,* ed. Stephen E. Whicher (Boston: Houghton Mifflin, 1957), 24.

5. John Milton, *Areopagitica* (1644) in *John Milton: Complete Poems and Major Prose,* ed. Merritt Y. Hughes (New York: Odyssey Press, 1957), 733.

6. Thich Nhat Hanh, *Peace Is Every Step: The Path of Mindfulness in Everyday Life* (New York: Bantam, 1991), 10. Used with permission. This is a wonderful guide to the art of mindfulness that applies Buddhist principles to the challenges of modern life.

7. William Blake, "Auguries of Innocence," ll. 1–4, from *The Marriage of Heaven and Hell* (1790–93).

8. Reprinted by permission of Warner Books/New York from Roger von Oech, *A Whack on the Side of the Head* (New York: Warner, 1990), 105. Copyright © 1990 by Roger von Oech.

9. Mitch Saunders, director of programs, California Leadership, interview at Santa Clara University, September 7, 1993. Used with permission.

Chapter 3 Timing

Character: *de-ai,* literally, "to flow together"; timing, interval, the way life's energies flow in cycles or patterns.

1. Interview with Carolyn Hennings, director of career services, Santa Clara University, July 15, 1993. Used with permission.

Chapter 4 Respect

Character: *kyo,* literally, "respectful" or "reverent." Respect for all living things underlies all the Tao leader's decisions and actions.

1. Isabel Briggs Myers with Peter B. Myers, *Gifts Differing* (Palo Alto, Calif.: Consulting Psychologists Press, 1980), 131.
2. Chungliang Al Huang and Jerry Lynch, *Thinking Body, Dancing Mind* (New York: Bantam, 1992), 184.
3. Ibid.
4. James M. Kouzes and Barry Posner, *Credibility* (San Francisco: Jossey-Bass, 1993), 12–13, 131.
5. My thanks to Margaret More and the other members of my class, Tao and the Art of Leadership, at Santa Clara University, May 11–25, 1994.
6. Douglas McGregor, *The Human Side of Enterprise* (New York: McGraw-Hill, 1960), 50.
7. My thanks to Mitch Saunders, director of programs, California Leadership, for information gained during a personal interview in Santa Clara, California, on September 7, 1993. Used with permission.
8. My thanks to Sunny Merik for information gained during a personal interview in Santa Clara, California, on May 23, 1994. Used with permission.
9. My thanks to Rev. Tina Clare, Los Altos, California, for insights and inspiration gained over the years, including this example.
10. My thanks to Sunny Merik for this story (originally told by Leo Rock, S.J.) gained during the interview in Santa Clara cited in note 8.
11. I am grateful to Randal Peoples, M.D., for information and insights gained over the years; in a telephone interview on September 5, 1994; and conversations since then. Material used with permission.

Chapter 5 Yohaku

Character: *Yohaku,* literally, "clearer than a ray of sun"; the empty space, the space of creative potential.

1. For further discussion of the creative process, see George Kneller, *The Art and Science of Creativity* (New York: Holt, Rinehart, & Winston, 1965).

2. Ralph Waldo Emerson, "Self-Reliance," in *Emerson's Essays* (New York: Thomas Y. Crowell, 1926), 35, 38.

3. See Stephen Covey, *Principle-Centered Leadership* (New York: Simon & Schuster, 1991), or phone the Covey Leadership Center (800-255-0777) for further information on conferences, workshops, and time management tools.

4. For drawing my attention to the difference between what is normal and what is natural, I am grateful to my friend Dr. Jerry Lynch.

5. Kazuko Okakura, *The Book of Tea* (New York and Tokyo: Kodansha International, 1989), 57.

6. Ibid., 139.

7. Ibid., 87.

8. Ibid., 82.

9. Quotation and story used by permission of Dr. Shu-Park Chan.

Chapter 6 Joy

Character: *Yoroko,* literally "joy"; to rejoice, to be glad. The rippling energies of laughter and the clarifying energies of joy cleanse and renew our spirits.

1. *The Stress Management Handbook* (Shawnee Mission, Kans.: National Press Publication, 1991), 9.

2. For an extensive explanation of how stress affects the body, see Hans Selye, *The Stress of Life* (New York: Alfred A. Knopf, 1976).

3. James E. Birren and Judy M. Zarit, "Concepts of Health, Behavior, and Aging," in *Cognition, Stress, and Aging,* ed. James E. Birren and Judy Livingston (Englewood Cliffs, N.J.: Prentice-Hall, 1985), 7.

4. Norman Cousins, *Anatomy of an Illness as Perceived by the Patient* (New York: W. W. Norton, 1979), 34–35. © 1979 by W. W. Norton & Company, Inc. Reference here and later in this chapter reprinted by permission of W. W. Norton & Company.

5. I would like to thank Marv Schroth, professor of psychology, and Robert Numan, professor and chair of the Psychology Department, Santa Clara University, for their invaluable assistance with the research in this chapter. For discussions of endorphins and exercise, see Robert E. Franken, *Human Motivation* (Pacific Grove, Calif.: Brooks/Cole, 1994), 42; E. T. Hawley, "The Effect of Different Intensities of Exercise on the Excretion of Epinephrine and Norepinephrine," *Medicine and Science in Sports* 8 (1976): 219–222; Jerry Heckenmueller, "Cognition Control and Endorphins as Mechanisms of Health," in *Cognition, Stress, and Aging,* ed. James E. Birren and Judy M. Livingston (Englewood Cliffs, N.J.: Prentice-Hall, 1985), 90; and R. C. Bolles and M. S. Fanselow, "Endorphins and Behavior," *Annual Review of Psychology* 33 (1982): 87–101.

6. Abraham Maslow, *Toward a Psychology of Being* (Princeton, N.J.: D. Van Nostrand, 1968), 184.

7. Kenneth Pelletier, *Mind as Healer, Mind as Slayer* (New York: Delacorte, 1977), 191–92.

8. A. Kasamatsu and T. Hirai, "Studies of EEG's of Expert Zen Meditators," *Folia Psychiatrica Neurologica Japonica* 28 (1966): 315, cited in ibid., 199.

9. R. K. Wallace and M. D. Garrett, "Decreased Blood Lactate during Transcendental Meditation," *Federation Proceedings* 30 (1971): 376, cited in Pelletier, *Mind as Healer,* 211; and R. K. Wallace, "Physiological Effects of Transcendental Meditation," *Science* 167 (1970): 1751–54, cited in Pelletier, *Mind as Healer,* 197.

10. Pelletier, *Mind as Healer,* 197–201.

11. R. Wallace and H. Benson, "The Physiology of Meditation," *Scientific American* 226 (1972): 84–90; and Joan Borysenko, *Minding the Body, Mending the Mind* (New York: Bantam, 1988), 36.

12. See Hans Selye, *Stress Without Distress* (Philadelphia: J. B. Lippincott, 1974).

13. Franken, *Human Motivation,* 266–67; J. V. Brady, "Emotion and Sensitivity of Psychoendocrine Systems," in *Neuropsychology and Emotion,* ed. D. C. Glass (New York: Rockefeller University Press, 1967); J. W. Mason, "Emotions as Reflected in Patterns of Endocrine Integration," in *Emotions: Their Parameters and Mea-*

surement, ed. L. Levi (New York: Raven Press, 1975); and R. S. Lazarus, "Cognition and Motivation in Emotion," *American Psychologist* 46 (1991): 352–67.

14. C. Peterson, "Explanatory Style as a Risk Factor for Illness," *Cognitive Therapy and Research* 12 (1988): 119–30.

15. Martin E. P. Seligman, *Learned Optimism* (New York: Alfred A. Knopf, 1991). Used with permission. The entire book is an excellent resource on cognition, stress, and mood; the origins of learned helplessness are discussed on pp. 17–53.

16. S. C. Kobasa, S. R. Maddi, and S. Kahn, "Hardiness and Health: A Prospective Study," *Journal of Personality and Social Psychology* 42 (1982): 168–77.

17. C. Peterson, M. Seligman, and G. Vaillant, "Pessimistic Explanatory Style as a Risk Factor for Physical Illness: A Thirty-five Year Longitudinal Study," *Journal of Personality and Social Psychology* 55 (1988): 23–27.

18. Cousins, *Anatomy of an Illness,* 72.

19. For this reference to Thomas Aquinas, I am grateful to Professor James P. Degnan of Santa Clara University's English department.

20. Cousins, *Anatomy of an Illness,* 39–40.

21. R. A. Martin and H. M. Lefcourt, "The Sense of Humor as a Moderator of the Relation between Stressors and Moods," *Journal of Personality and Social Psychology* 45 (1983): 1314, 1323.

22. Franken, *Human Motivation,* 275; and G. Keinan, "Decision Making under Stress: Scanning of Alternatives under Controllable and Uncontrollable Threats," *Journal of Personality and Social Psychology* 52 (1987): 639–44.

23. For a discussion of Lincoln's humor, see Stephen B. Oates, *With Malice Toward None: The Life of Abraham Lincoln* (New York: New American Library, 1985), 98, 249.

24. For a discussion of Kennedy's humor, see Reg Gadney, *Kennedy* (New York: Holt, Rinehart & Winston, 1983), 91.

25. Heckenmueller, "Cognitive Control and Endorphins as Mechanisms of Health," 102–3. Research has shown that people who are loved and supported live better and longer; even an affectionate pet can alleviate the effects of stress and add years to people's lives. See J. M. Siegel, "Stressful Life Events and Use of

Physician Services among the Elderly: The Moderating Role of Pet Ownership," *Journal of Personality and Social Psychology* 58 (1990): 1081–86.

26. J. D. Laird, "Self-attribution of Emotion: The Effects of Expressive Behavior upon the Quality of Emotional Experience," *Journal of Personality and Social Psychology* 29 (1974): 475–86; P. Ekman, R. W. Levenson, and W. V. Friesen, "Autonomic Nervous System Activity Distinguishes among Emotions," *Science* 223 (September 16, 1983), 1208–10; and C. E. Izard, "Facial Expressions and the Regulation of Emotions," *Journal of Personality and Social Psychology* 58 (1990): 487–98.

27. Abraham Maslow, *Toward a Psychology of Being* (Princeton, N.J.: D. Van Nostrand, 1962, 1968), 83. For the character, *yoroko* and much of what it signifies, I am grateful to my aikido sensei, Sunny Skys and Miki Yoneda-Skys of Aiki Zenshin Dojo.

Chapter 7 Building Community

Character: *kyo,* literally, "to be in harmony." The character is made up of the number ten, combined with the character for strength repeated three times. The Tao leader knows that community multiplies our positive power.

1. A Chinese fable from the Zhou Dynasty, third to fourth century B.C.

2. For more on *wa* and the leader's responsibility for group maintenance, see Richard Tanner Pascale and Anthony G. Athos, *The Art of Japanese Management* (New York: Warner Books, 1981), 198–99.

3. Information on North American Tool and Die from James M. Kouzes and Barry Z. Posner, *The Leadership Challenge* (San Francisco: Jossey-Bass, 1987), 4–5, used with permission; and Tom Gustaveson of North American Tool and Die, also used with permission.

4. George J. Church, "Jobs in an Age of Insecurity," *Time,* November 22, 1993, 38. Nadja Aisenberg and Mona Harrington, *Women of Academe: Outsiders in the Sacred Grove* (Amherst: University of Massachusetts Press, 1988), 138.

5. Faith Gabelnick, Ph.D., "Learning in Community: Collabora-

tion for Learning and Leadership Development," workshop held at Santa Clara University, November 2, 1993. Used with permission.

6. *Chuang-Tzu,* trans. Fung Yu-Lan (Beijing: Foreign Languages Press, 1991), 131–32.

7. For a discussion of this ritual in Shakespeare, see C. L. Barber, *Shakespeare's Festive Comedies* (New York: World Books, 1963), 2–15.

8. Douglas McGregor, *Leadership and Motivation* (Cambridge, Mass.: M.I.T. Press, 1966), 60.

9. I am grateful to Mitch Saunders for an interview in Santa Clara, California, on September 7, 1993. Information used with permission.

10. *Toward an Adept California: A Customer Satisfaction State,* preliminary report of the Assembly Democratic Economic Prosperity Team (Sacramento, 1992), 9.

Chapter 8 Vision, Empowerment, and Growth

Character: *sato,* literally, "to be spiritually awakened, to perceive, to comprehend." The verb is the root of the Buddhist term, *satori* (enlightenment). A Tao leader who combines vision, empowerment, and growth practices *sato.*

1. John Vasconcellos, speech to students at the University of California, Berkeley, fall 1984.

2. My thanks to Liahna Babener, Ph.D., head of the English department, Montana State University, for remarks at a conference for English department chairs in Coeur d'Alene, Idaho, July 8, 1994. Used with permission.

3. Warren Bennis, *On Becoming a Leader* (Reading, Mass.: Addison-Wesley, 1990), 22–23.

4. From an interview with Norman Cousins at UCLA, July 1988.

5. Some popular answers are for earth and sky—landscape, listen and speak—communicate, open and closed—door or heart, and water and stone—river. These, however, are not the "right" answers or the only answers. What are yours?

6. From Dr. Roth's talk at the conference on July 8, 1994, cited in note 2. Used with permission.

7. Professor Constantinides's remarks were made on July 7, 1994, at the conference cited in note 2. Used with permission.

8. Rollo May, *The Courage to Create* (New York: W. W. Norton, 1975), 13. © 1975 by Rollo May. Reprinted by permission of W. W. Norton & Company, Inc.

9. For more information on composing your personal mission statement, see Stephen Covey, *Seven Habits of Highly Effective People* (New York: Simon & Schuster, 1989), 106–8. Used with permission of Covey Leadership Center, Inc., 3507 North University Avenue, P.O. Box 19008, Provo, UT 84604-4479; phone (800) 331-7716.

10. Jerry Lynch referred me to Sam Keen's statement in *Fire in the Belly: On Being a Man* (New York: Bantam Books, 1991), 66: "I am lucky to have work that fits skintight over my spirit."

11. I am grateful to Steve Privett, S.J., and Chuck Powers, Ph.D., for interviews at Santa Clara University on August 13, 1993, and November 2, 1993, respectively. Used with permission.

12. Douglas McGregor, *The Human Side of Enterprise* (New York: McGraw-Hill, 1960), 33–45; and Abraham Maslow, *Toward a Psychology of Being* (Princeton, N.J.: D. Van Nostrand, 1962).

13. I am grateful to Mitchell Saunders, director of programs, California Leadership, for an interview in Santa Clara, California, on September 7, 1993. All references to Saunders in this chapter are from this interview and are used with permission.

14. Information on Amanda Fox from the *San Jose Mercury*, Professional Careers Section, Sunday, January 2, 1994, 1; originally printed in the *Chicago Tribune*.

15. I would like to thank my colleague, Professor Chuck Powers, chair, Department of Anthropology and Sociology, for pointing this distinction out to me. For further information, see Jerald Hage and Charles H. Powers, *Post-Industrial Lives* (Newbury Park, CA: Sage Publications, 1992), 69; and Steve Gelber, "A Job You Can't Lose: Work and Hobbies in the Great Depression," *Journal of Social History* 16 (June 1983): 3–22.

16. B. Dumaine, "Who Needs a Boss?" *Fortune*, May 7, 1990, 52–60, cited in James M. Kouzes and Barry Posner, *Credibility* (San Francisco: Jossey-Bass, 1993), 156.

17. Insights from Michael Herzog, chair of the English department, Gonzaga University, on July 7, 1994, from the conference cited in note 2. Used with permission.
18. Information on Tom Chappell from an interview on "Talk of the Nation," National Public Radio, October 21, 1993; information from Dean Hall from the conference cited in note 2, July 7, 1994, and used with permission.
19. Information and quotes about Joe Caldwell and Saturn's team approach from Frances Moore Lappé and Paul Martin Du Bois, *The Quickening of America* (San Francisco: Jossey-Bass, 1994), 4; used with permission. I highly recommend this book, which is filled with examples of the new leadership in action all across the country. For further information on this kind of empowerment, which Lappé and Du Bois call "living democracy," contact them at the Center for Living Democracy, R.R. 1, Black Fox Road, Brattleboro, VT 05301; phone (802) 254-4331, fax (802) 254-1227.
20. Information on Deming from "Deming and Quality," *Toronto Globe and Mail,* December 28, 1993, B10. All references to Deming are from this source.
21. Statistics on IBM from Abby Brown, "Career Development 1986: A Look at Trends and Issues," *Personnel Administrator,* March 1986: 45–109.

Chapter 9 Communication

Characters: *den,* literally "to report, to impart, to transmit," with *tatsu,* literally, "to arrive, to reach, to attain." To communicate clearly is to arrive at a deeper understanding.
1. Jerald Hage and Charles H. Powers, *Post-Industrial Lives* (Newbury Park, Calif.: Sage Publications, 1992), 91–93.
2. Information on Admiral Hopper from "People Shouldn't Be Allergic to Change," *USA Today,* October 3, 1986, A11. Copyright © 1986, *USA Today,* reprinted with permission.
3. Wayne Booth, professor of English, University of Chicago, remarks at a conference for English department chairs in Coeur d'Alene, Idaho, on July 9, 1994. Used with permission.
4. From an interview with Professor Carol Rossi, chair of the

University Diversity Committee and coordinator of Leaders for Tomorrow, Santa Clara University, August 10, 1993. Used with permission.

5. Douglas McGregor, *The Human Side of Enterprise* (New York: McGraw-Hill, 1960), 182.

6. Statistics on listening from Robert W. Rasberry and Laura Lemoine Lindsay, *Effective Managerial Communication* (Belmont, Calif.: Wadsworth, 1994), 223.

7. Information on Deming from "Deming and Quality," *Toronto Globe and Mail,* December 28, 1993, B10. All references to Deming in this chapter are from this source.

8. Interview with Cynthia Brattesani, D.D.S., in San Francisco on August 8, 1993. Used with permission.

9. Hage and Powers, *Post-Industrial Lives,* 166.

10. From an interview with Carolyn Hennings, director of career services, Santa Clara University, July 15, 1993. Used with permission.

11. From an interview with Professor Chuck Powers, chair of the Department of Anthropology and Sociology, Santa Clara University, November 2, 1993. Used with permission.

Chapter 10   Conflict Resolution

Character: *aikido,* literally, "the way of harmony," combining *ai* ("harmony" or "love") with *ki* ("spirit") and *do* ("the way"): resolving conflict without harming the opponent, transforming opposing energies into new patterns of harmony.

1. For this insight, the concept of "conflict partnership," and much of the inspiration on conflict resolution in this chapter, I am indebted to Dudley Weeks, Ph.D., professor of conflict resolution, American University, Washington, D.C. All references to Dudley Weeks, unless otherwise stated, are from an interview in Washington, D.C., on August 3, 1994, and are hereafter cited in the text.

2. Quote from a news broadcast on National Public Radio, January 18, 1993.

3. Information from Angelo Figueroa, "Ends to which people go to file nonsense suits," *San Jose Mercury News,* Sunday, August 7, 1994, B1.

4. Research by Professor Giora Keinan, Department of Psychology, Tel Aviv University, on over 100 undergraduates at the University of Haifa from ages twenty to forty. See G. Keinan, "Decision Making under Stress: Scanning of Alternatives under Controllable and Uncontrollable Threats," *Journal of Personality and Social Psychology* 52 (1987): 639–44.

5. Quote taken from a presentation by Dr. Ken Eisold at a conference for English department chairs in Coeur d'Alene, Idaho, on July 10, 1994. Used with permission.

6. Story and quote from Sunny Skys, aikido sensei, from a demonstration in my class, Tao and the Art of Leadership, Santa Clara University, May 18, 1994. Used with permission.

7. From a conversation with Professor Mary Hegland at Santa Clara University, December 8, 1993. Used with permission.

8. For many insights into Zen Buddhism, I am grateful to Fr. Tennant C. Wright, S.J., of the Religious Studies Department, Santa Clara University.

9. The term "power-with" is from Dudley Weeks, *The Eight Essential Steps to Conflict Resolution* (Los Angeles: Jeremy P. Tarcher 1992), 148. References here and elsewhere are reprinted with permission of the Putnam Publishing Group/Jeremy P. Tarcher, Inc. Copyright © 1992 by Dudley Weeks.

10. For the insights about de Klerk and Mandela, I am grateful to Dudley Weeks in the interview cited in note 1.

11. For ideas on developing a positive atmosphere for conflict resolution, including the term "doables," I am indebted to Weeks, *The Eight Essential Steps to Conflict Resolution,* 71–87.

12. The term "shared needs" is from ibid., 143.

13. Ibid., 146, 224–25.

14. Ibid., 152–53.

15. Ideas for these questions from ibid., 135.

16. The term "conflict partnership" is from ibid., 70.

Chapter 11 Transcending Ego

Character: *makoto,* literally, "sincerity, truth, integrity." The Tao leader transcends ego and self-centeredness. Coming from a deeper center of integrity enables us to inspire trust and promote harmony.

1. Ralph Waldo Emerson, "Spiritual Laws," in *Emerson's Essays* (New York: Thomas Y. Crowell, 1926), 115. By transcending ego, I mean the vital importance of overcoming inflated egos or exaggerated self-importance. Certainly, we all still need to maintain an "ego," as used in developmental psychology to mean a healthy sense of self-identity.

2. Ralph Waldo Emerson, "The American Scholar," in *Selections from Ralph Waldo Emerson,* ed. Stephen E. Whicher (Boston: Houghton Mifflin, 1957), 72; and Charles Peters, *How Washington Really Works,* 3rd ed. (Menlo Park, Calif.: Addison-Wesley, 1992), 157.

3. For the concepts of "power over," "power-with," and "seesaw power," I am grateful to Dudley Weeks for an interview in Washington, D.C., on August 3, 1994; used with permission. For the Quakiutl (Kwakewlth) story, I am grateful to Carol Rossi, coordinator, Leaders for Tomorrow, Santa Clara University, for a conversation on August 10, 1993; used with permission.

4. For this and other insights in this chapter, I am grateful to Kichi Iwamoto, Ph.D., sociologist and leadership consultant, for an interview in his office on August 22, 1994. Used with permission.

5. From the text of his speech intended for delivery at the Dallas Trade Mart, November 22, 1963.

6. See Eknath Easwaren, *Gandhi the Man* (Petaluma, Calif.: Nilgiri Press, 1978), 105.

7. Henry David Thoreau, *The Variorum Walden,* ed. Walter Harding (New York: Washington Square Press, 1962), 68.

8. For this insight about Kennedy, I am grateful to Kichi Iwamoto for information conveyed in the conversation cited in note 4.

9. From *The Autobiography of Eleanor Roosevelt* (New York: Harper & Bros., 1961), 279, by Eleanor Roosevelt. Copyright © 1937, 1949, 1958, 1961, by Anna Eleanor Roosevelt. © 1958 by Curtis Publishing Company. Used with permission of Harper-Collins, Inc.

10. Information taken from Amy E. Schwartz, "Honor Bound," *Washington Post Weekly,* February 21–27, 1994, 29.

11. Research data from James M. Kouzes and Barry Z. Posner, *Credibility* (San Francisco: Jossey-Bass, 1993), 12–15.

12. From Rev. Marcia Pearce, Valley West Church of Religious Science, Campbell, California, who got the expression from the late Dr. Robert Bitzer.

13. For this Taoist insight into the difference between "normal" and "natural," I am grateful to my friend, Jerry Lynch, Ph.D., sports psychologist, teacher, and author.

14. Quote from Steve Privett, S.J., academic vice president, Santa Clara University, August 13, 1993. Used with permission.

15. Information from Judy B. Rosener, "Ways Women Lead," *Harvard Business Review* 68 (November–December 1990): 119–25. I am grateful to Dr. Kichi Iwamoto for pointing this article out to me.

16. Information on Jeff Capaccio, J.D., used with permission. Information on William Peace, formerly an executive with Westinghouse and United Technologies, now director of Doctus Management Consultancy in Chester, England, from "The Hard Work of Being a Soft Manager," *Harvard Business Review* 69 (November–December 1991): 40–47. I am grateful to Dr. Kichi Iwamoto for pointing this article out to me.

Chapter 12 Creating Harmony

Character: *wa,* literally, harmony, peace. Tao leaders create greater harmony around them because they follow the path of greater harmony within.

1. Statistics on recycling from earth preserv fall 1994 catalog, 3. Used with permission from earth preserv, manufacturers of environmentally sustainable bath and personal care products: P.O. Box 142286, Irving, TX 75014; phone (800) 9-earth-9.

2. Information on eco-audits from "Eco-audits can help protect environment—and profits," *San Jose Mercury News,* Sunday, October 2, 1994, 1E, 12E.

3. Story about the Canadian company Genetron Systems, Inc., from Air Canada, *En Route* (December 1993), 15.

4. For information about the East-West Center, I am grateful to John Williams, director of public programs. For further information, contact the East-West Center Office of Public Programs, 1777 East-West Road, Honolulu HI 96848; phone (808) 944-7111.

5. Information about Shu-Park Chan from an interview in Santa Clara, California, in summer 1992. Some of this section appeared in an earlier form in Diane Dreher, "Shu-Park Chan," *Quality Living* (Winter 1993), 25–27. Used by permission of *Quality Living* and Dr. Chan.

6. Information about California State University at Monterey Bay used by permission from Mitch Saunders, director of programs, California Leadership, who is helping to facilitate planning for the new university. For the Chinese proverb, I am indebted to Paul Locatelli, S.J., president of Santa Clara University, who used it in his speech of September 16, 1994.

7. For further information on Demasio's thesis, see *Descartes' Error: Emotion, Reason, and the Human Brain* (New York: G. P. Putnam's Sons, 1994).

8. For information on combined approaches to healing, see Michael Lerner, *Choices in Healing: Integrating the Best of Conventional and Complementary Approaches to Cancer* (Cambridge: M.I.T. Press, 1994). Information on the Cancer Help Program from Michael Castleman, "The New Medicine Man," *San Francisco Focus* (September 1994), 50–53, 104–112, used with permission of the author. For further information about Commonweal and its programs, contact Commonweal, P.O. Box 316, Bolinas, CA 94924; phone (415) 868-0970.

9. For information about Pueblo to People, I am grateful to Joan Stewart, coordinator and producer contact, for a phone interview on October 6, 1994. Material on Petrona reprinted with permission from the Pueblo to People Fall 1994 catalog. For further information or a catalog, contact Pueblo to People, 2105 Silber Road, Suite 101, Houston, TX 77055; phone (800) 843-5257.

10. Information on Yoff and EcoVillage at Ithaca from Anne Zorc, "Trading Dreams: From Senegal to New York and Back," *CO-OP America Quarterly,* no. 35 (Fall 1994), 22, reprinted with permission from CO-OP America. For further information on EcoVillage at Ithaca, contact EcoVillage, Anabel Taylor Hall, Cornell University, Ithaca, NY 14853; phone (607) 255-8276. For further information on CO-OP America, a national non-profit membership organization that educates consumers on

how to use their buying power for people and the planet, contact CO-OP America, 1612 K Street, NW, Suite 600, Washington, DC 20006; phone (202) 872-5307.

11. Information from "The Claims We Make Make Claims on Us," used by permission of Sunny Merik. Information on the Carter Center courtesy of the center's staff. For further information on its programs, contact the Carter Center, One Copenhill, Atlanta, GA 30307; phone (404) 420-5112.

12. Joseph Campbell begins *The Hero of a Thousand Faces* (Princeton, N.J: Princeton University Press, 1968), 3, by referring to "the sonnets of the mystic Lao-tse," the journey implicit in the *Tao Te Ching*. Along with many others, I am grateful to Joseph Campbell for his lifelong study of world myth that so clearly delineates the stages of life's journey of initiation and individuation. Another useful discussion of the hero's journey is Christopher Vogler, *The Writer's Journey: Mythic Structure for Storytellers and Screenwriters* (Studio City, Calif.: Michael Wiese Productions, 1992). I am grateful to Stephen Moore of Redwood Estates, California, for sharing this book with me.

13. Campbell, *The Hero of a Thousand Faces,* 78.

14. Ibid., 82–89. For a contemporary account of threshold guardians, see Vogler, *The Writer's Journey,* 6–7, 63–66.

15. For insights on facing the dragon, I am grateful to Joseph Campbell and Christopher Vogler (loc. cit.) as well as for thirty years of literary study beginning with my professors at the University of California, Riverside, and UCLA and continuing with my colleagues and students at Santa Clara University. I would especially like to thank Dr. Cory Wade, who has done extensive studies of dragon iconography and the hero's quest in Old English literature.

16. For further information on the shadow, see Carl G. Jung et al., *Man and His Symbols* (Garden City, N.Y.: Doubleday, 1964), 165–77.

17. For advice and assistance on Japanese language, I am grateful to my colleague Dr. Maryellen Mori of the Modern Languages Department, Santa Clara University. For insight into the meaning of *randori,* I am grateful to my aikido sensei, Sunny Skys and

Miki Yoneda-Skys, of Aiki Zenshin Dojo, 42307 Osgood Road, Unit J, Fremont, CA 94539; phone (510) 795-8389 or 657-5387.

The author and publisher gratefully acknowledge permission to use selections and information from the following copyrighted materials:

Michael Castleman, "The New Medicine Man," *San Francisco Focus* (September 1994), pp. 50–53, 104–112. © Michael Castleman. Information used by permission of the author.

Norman Cousins, *Anatomy of an Illness as Perceived by the Patient* (New York: Norton, 1979), pp. 35, 39–40, 72. © 1979 W. W. Norton Company, Inc. Reprinted by permission of W.W. Norton & Company.

Stephen R. Covey, *The Seven Habits of Highly Effective People* (New York: Simon & Schuster, 1989), pp. 106–9. © 1989 by Stephen R. Covey. Used with permission of Covey Leadership Center, Inc., 305 North University Avenue. P.O. Box 19008, Provo, UT, 84604-4479; phone (800) 331-7716.

Diane Dreher, "Shu-Park Chan," *Quality Living* (Winter 1993), pp. 25–27. Words and information used by permission of the publisher.

"The Aluminum Solution" and "The Plastic Problem," *earth preserv* Fall 1994 catalog, p. 2. Information used by permission of earth preserv.

Jerald Hage and Charles H. Powers, *Post-Industrial Lives* (Newbury Park, Calif.: Sage Publications, 1992), p. 11. © 1992 by Sage Publications, Inc. Reprinted by permission of Sage Publications, Inc.

Thich Nhat Hanh, *Peace is Every Step* (New York: Bantam Books, 1991), p. 10. © 1991 by Thich Nhat Hanh. Reprinted by permission of Bantam Books.

Chungliang Al Huang and Jerry Lynch, *Thinking Body, Dancing Mind* (New York: Bantam Books, 1992), pp. 89, 184. © 1992 by Chungliang Al Huang and Jerry Lynch. Used by permission of Bantam Books.

James M. Kouzes and Barry Z. Posner, *The Leadership Challenge* (San Francisco: Jossey-Bass, 1987), pp. 4–5. © 1987 by Jossey-Bass, Inc. Used by permission of Jossey-Bass, Inc.

Frances Moore Lappé and Paul Martin DuBois, *The Quickening of America* (San Francisco: Jossey-Bass, 1994), p. 4. © 1994 by Jossey-

Bass, Inc. Reprinted by permission of Jossey-Bass.

Rollo May, *The Courage to Create* (New York: W. W. Norton, Inc., 1975), p. 13. © 1975 by Rollo May. Reprinted by permission of W. W. Norton, Inc.

"People Shouldn't Be Allergic to Change," *USA Today* (October 3, 1986), p. A11. © 1986, *USA Today*. Reprinted with permission of *USA Today*.

The Autobiography of Eleanor Roosevelt (New York: Harper & Bros., 1961), p. 279. © 1937, 1949, © 1958, 1961 by Anna Eleanor Roosevelt. © 1958 by Curtis Publishing Company. Reprinted by permission of HarperCollins Publishers, Inc.

Martin E. P. Seligman, *Learned Optimism* (New York: Alfred A. Knopf, 1991), pp. 17–53. © 1990 by Martin E. P. Seligman. Cited by permission of Alfred A. Knopf, Inc.

Roger van Oech, *A Whack on the Side of the Head* (New York: Warner Books, 1983, 1990), p. 105. © 1990 by Roger van Oech. Reprinted by permission of Warner Books/New York.

Lee Ann Ward and Larry Lack, "Strong Children Come from Strong Families," *Pueblo to People* (Fall 1994), p. 14. Reprinted with permission from the Pueblo to People Fall 1994 catalog.

Dudley Weeks, *The Eight Essential Steps to Conflict Resolution* (Los Angeles: Jeremy Tarcher, 1992). © 1992 by Dudley Weeks. Quotes and ideas from the book reprinted by permission of the Putnam Publishing Group/Jeremy P. Tarcher, Inc.

Anne Zorc, "Trading Dreams: From Senegal to New York and Back," *CO-OP America Quarterly* (Fall 1994), pp. 22–23. Reprinted with permission from *CO-OP America Quarterly* magazine, published by CO-OP America, a national nonprofit membership organization that educates consumers on how to use their buying power for people and the planet.

INDEX

Hall, Dean, 151
Hamlet, 214
Hammarskjöld, Dag, 2
Han Fei Zi, 118
hara, 30, 183
Harrington, Mona, 121
Hartford Courant, 169
Hawaiian Airlines, 170–171
Hegel, Georg Wilhelm, 2
Hegland, Mary, 187
Hennings, Carolyn, 15, 167
hero's journey, 236, 250–251, 259
Herzog, Michael, 149–150
Hillel, Rabbi, 235–236
Hirai, T., 105
Homer, 250
honesty, 21, 52, 56, 74, 78–79, 81,
    148, 164, 203, 219–220,
    222–223, 228
honshin, 64
Hopper, Grace, 157
hubris, 200

IBM, 153
immature people, 226–228
individualism, 129, 158
initiation, 40, 43, 49, 51, 52, 254
integrity, 21, 83, 100, 104, 148, 162,
    164–165, 208, 209, 218–223,
    228
International Technical University,
    94, 239, 240–242
isolation, 216–218, 227, 228
Ithaca, N.Y., 247–248
Iwamoto, Kichi, 207, 216–217,
    229–230
jaku, 103, 104, 107
Japan, 76, 87, 92–93, 100, 118, 130,
    132–133, 138, 141, 153, 168,
    180, 217
Jefferson, Thomas, 135
jen, 64
Johnson, Lyndon B., 201, 217

journey, 6, 36, 76, 81, 140, 209, 236,
    254
joy, 6, 71, 72, 75, 86, 96–114
Jungian therapy, 43, 256

kai-zen, 153
Kaliterna, Emma, 232
Kansas State University, 151
Kasamatsu, A., 105
Keats, John, 26
Keen, Sam, 141
Kekulé, Friedrich August von, 86
Kennedy, John F., 31, 112–113, 135,
    142, 207, 217–218, 231–232
Kennedy, Robert F., 135
ki, 2, 16–17, 88
King, Martin Luther, Jr., 135, 142
King Lear, 206–207
Kobasa, S. C., 17–18
Kouzes, James, 220
kyo, 146

Lao Tzu, 2, 4, 12–13, 67, 91, 92, 128,
    254, 255, 257
leaders, 3, 4, 5, 6–7, 31, 39–40, 44,
    51–52, 55–56, 59, 86, 89–90, 158
  as facilitators, 5, 69–70, 120–127,
    136, 141–145, 151–152,
    167–168, 191, 197–198
  insecure, 150, 203
  as pathfinders, 25, 139–142,
    147–149, 235
  as rescuers, 150, 152–153
  transformational, 230–233
leadership, 3, 5, 26, 29, 43, 50, 54,
    64, 67, 71, 89, 135–155, 158
  cooperative, 5, 39–40, 52–53, 66,
    118–127, 165–168
  hierarchical, 69, 123, 124, 128,
    189, 198
  patriarchal, 144, 167, 230
  as relationship, 114, 118–127,
    161–162, 172–174